Reading & Writing
Informational Text
in the Primary Grades

BY

NELL K. DUKE, ED.D. &
V. SUSAN BENNETT-ARMISTEAD

WITH
ANNE HUXLEY
MARY KAY JOHNSON
DENISE MCLURKIN
EBONY M. ROBERTS
CAROL ROSEN
EMILENE VOGEL

■SCHOLASTIC
Teaching
Resources

NEW YORK • TORONTO • LONDON • AUCKLAND • SYDNEY
MEXICO CITY • NEW DELHI • HONG KONG

DEDICATION

To the many teachers and children who have helped me think about and
envision incorporating informational text in the primary grades. —nkd

For all the children who so wisely asked, "Why?" and didn't expect
the answer to start with "Once upon a time..." —vsb-a

Scholastic Inc. grants teachers permission to photocopy the reproducible pages in this book only for personal
classroom use. No other part of this publication may be reproduced in whole or in part, or stored in a retrieval
system, or transmitted in any form or by any means, electronic, mechanical, photocopying, recording, or otherwise,
without written permission of the publisher. For information regarding permission, write to Permissions
Department, Scholastic Inc., 557 Broadway, New York, NY 10012.

Cover design by James Sarfati
Interior design by LDL Designs
Cover photo by James Levin
Interior photos by Gary Bublitz unless otherwise indicated

ISBN 0-439-53123-3
Copyright © 2003 by Nell K. Duke and V. Susan Bennett-Armistead
All rights reserved. Published by Scholastic Inc.
Printed in the U.S.A.
5 6 7 8 9 10   23 09 08 07 06 05

CREDITS

TABLE OF CONTENTS

Why Include Informational Text in the Primary Classroom?
A Research-Based Rationale

A Framework for Weaving Informational Texts Into the Primary Classroom
The Early Literacy Project

Shared Reading and Read Aloud
Developing Language, World Knowledge, and Comprehension With Informational Text

Guided Reading
Scaffolding Reading Development With Informational Text

Independent Reading
Motivating Children to Read Informational Text in School and at Home

Writing
Teaching Children to Compose Informational Text

ACKNOWLEDGMENTS

We have many people to thank for helping us with this book. First and foremost, we thank our editor, Ray Coutu. Ray and Nell go way back and she continues to feel blessed to know him. He is a truly outstanding editor, educator, and human being; our field is the better for his presence in it.

Next, we thank our many teacher colleagues, some of whom are featured in this book, for helping us think about incorporating informational text in the primary grades and for helping us see ways it can be accomplished. A special thanks to Sharon Taberski who wrote one of the forewords. We also thank the children, whose learning continues to fascinate and inspire us. Their work is represented throughout this book—through examples of their drawing and writing, and descriptions of their reading and discussions—with hope we do justice to the amazing things they do.

The photographs that appear at the start of Chapters 1 to 9 and in the photo essays on pages 196–197 and 216–217 were taken in Jacqulyn Smart's first-grade classroom. Jacqulyn incorporates informational text throughout her space and curriculum. The walls of her class-

Funding Acknowledgment

The Early Literacy Project, which provided some material and much of the impetus for this book, was supported by two funding programs:

The Interagency Education Research Initiative, a joint program of the National Science Foundation, the Institute for Education Sciences (formerly the Office of Educational Research and Improvement), and the National Institute for Child Health and Development (REC 9979864)

The Center for the Improvement of Early Reading Achievement (CIERA), Education Research and Development Centers Program (PR/Award No. R305R70004), as administered by the Institute for Education Sciences (formerly Office of Educational Research and Improvement), U.S. Department of Education

However, the contents of this book do not necessarily represent the positions or policies of these programs, and endorsement by the United States government should not be assumed.

READING & WRITING INFORMATIONAL TEXT IN THE PRIMARY GRADES

room are filled with fascinating texts related to where her students live, the foods they eat, animals in their world, and ecology in their backyard. Her classroom library is rich in quality informational text at a variety of reading levels and on topics of great interest to her students. Classroom activities are saturated with opportunities to learn about the natural and social world. Children are abuzz about what they are learning. We extend a special thanks to Jacqulyn for allowing us into her incredible classroom.

We also thank our many colleagues who have done research on and related to informational text. We are especially grateful to P. David Pearson for his contribution of a foreword. As you will see, we draw heavily on the work of these people and appreciate the many contributions their work makes to our understanding of incorporating informational text in the primary grades. We also thank the research assistants and other personnel who worked with us on the Early Literacy Project for their important contributions to that research.

Finally, we thank our families, who have supported us in many ways while writing this book, and with whom we shared many experiences that led up to it. Our "Daves" (Dave Armistead, Susan's husband, and Dave Ammer, Nell's husband) deserve our deepest love and thanks. And from the time we conceived of this book to the time we completed it, two fantastic little girls—Julia (Nell's daughter) and Violet (Susan's daughter)—entered our lives. We especially thank them for the wonder they leave us with every day. They and Violet's brothers, Tim and Dawson, help us stay focused on the true purpose of our work—sharing the power of literacy with *all* children.

FOREWORD

BY P. DAVID PEARSON, UNIVERSITY OF CALIFORNIA, BERKELEY

I t is common in our culture to talk about an idea whose time has come. And with the publication of *Reading & Writing Informational Text in the Primary Grades,* we certainly have one worth discussing. While not as controversial as other questions in the teaching of reading—such as how and when to teach phonics—the question of how to help students acquire a sense of control, even mastery, over informational text is equally important to answer. Indeed, I would argue that answering that question is likely to pay even greater dividends, in terms of increased student achievement, motivation, and self-efficacy, than answering the more controversial ones.

Informational text provides a medium for helping students acquire the cultural capital that will lead to school success. As described in Chapter 1, informational text:

◆ is key to success in later schooling.

◆ is ubiquitous in society.

◆ is preferred reading material for some children.

◆ often addresses children's interests and questions.

◆ builds knowledge of the natural and social world.

◆ may help build vocabulary and other kinds of literacy knowledge.

Duke, Bennett-Armistead, and colleagues are not the first to champion the cause of informational text in schools. So what makes their effort unique? The answer is as simple as it is compelling: They are the first to take such a definitive stance toward research as the primary standard for shaping and judging the validity of instructional practices related to informational text. The book exudes the ethic of scholarship from every pore. This point is most transparent in the introductory section of each chapter, where they discuss openly not only what the research says, but also what it does not permit us to say. Scholarship is also embedded in the stories of instructional practice they have gathered from classroom teachers, which contain constant reminders of teacher actions that are consistent with the research. Moreover, these stories tell us that the authors work with teachers who embody the principles of scholarly inquiry in shaping practice—using evidence as the basis for including, excluding, or revising instructional routines. The authors are quick to tell us when their recommendations are based on solid cumulative evidence; when they are based on a solid but thin evidentiary base; when they are supported only by inferences from theory; and when, in cases where the research is extremely thin or nonexistent, they are resorting to best practice or even hunches. Above all, they do not, like too many professional writers, comingle research, hunches, and common sense in ways that obscure the evidentiary base for a recommended practice. They have set a standard that all authors should emulate. This book, therefore, will be useful to teachers and administrators who are required by law to point to the research base undergirding their school reading programs.

Another distinguishing feature of the book is the inclusion of teachers' voices. We get to visit a lot of classrooms to learn, up close and personal, how teachers make all of this work. And we don't just get glimpses of exemplary practice. We get a clear picture of what teachers do, how they do it, and why and when they do it. (I find that many accounts of best practice frustrate teachers because they are just that: accounts, without any explanation of how the exemplary teachers made success happen.) To hearken back to a classic piece by Paris, Lipson, and Wixson in the early 1980s, Duke, Bennett-Armistead, and their colleagues provide us with the declarative (the what), procedural (the how), and conditional (the why and when) of instruction.

A third distinctive feature of the book is its marriage of the rich research literature on comprehension strategies and the focus on informational text. We meet some old friends in this book—shared, guided, and independent reading; Reciprocal Teaching; Questioning the Author; semantic webs; and so forth—but we meet them in the context of increasing students' acquaintance with and mastery over informational text genres. Teachers who read this book will understand how to make these important but instructionally vexing strategies a part of their daily classroom life.

Reading & Writing Informational Text in the Primary Grades is as respectful of the wisdom of teachers and their practice as it is of the role that research can and should play in shaping that practice. That is most welcome in a field that sometimes finds itself implementing policies that seem to respect neither. Enjoy this important work. Use it to shape your practice. Help your students build the cultural capital they need to be successful in school, work, community, and everyday life.

FOREWORD

BY SHARON TABERSKI, MANHATTAN NEW SCHOOL

Fiction remains the genre of choice for most primary-grade teachers. And for good reason: Most children love it. They relate naturally to its familiar voice, vocabulary, and structure. When reading aloud, for example, we witness their enchantment with stories—stories that hold them in rapt attention.

One of my students' favorite read alouds is Erica Silverman's *Don't Fidget a Feather.* When listening to it, they can't believe that Gander is going to let himself be eaten by Fox just to win a contest! Or that Duck is going to let him. They cheer when Duck finally comes through for his friend. And because of children's strong response to such stories, we saturate our classrooms with these beloved books.

But when reading about Duck and Gander, my students also ask, "What's a gander?" and, when they find out it's a male goose, they want to know, what is a male duck called? And a mother duck? And the baby? Their questions keep coming because they want to know more and more about the world. So we turn to the nonfiction books in our classroom to learn more. We read May Garelick's *What Makes a Bird a Bird?* and learn that birds are the only creatures on earth with feathers. We read *Ducks Don't Get Wet* by Augusta Goldin and learn how the oil in a duck's feathers makes the water roll right off, and in fact, this very same feature prevents penguins' feathers from freezing in the sub-zero Antarctic.

The information gleaned from reading nonfiction makes my students' world grow larger. So that when our class took a bird-watching trip to New York City's Central Park, Jesse excitedly blurted out: "I never knew there were all these birds! I've been to this park millions of times, and I never knew they were there. I thought there was nothing here, but now I see all kinds of birds. I can't wait to go back this weekend to see more."

The good news is that we don't have to wait until fourth grade to engage children in reading and writing informational text! As Nell K. Duke, V. Susan Bennett-Armistead, and the contributors demonstrate in this volume, young children are perfectly capable of handling well-written informational text and are the better for it. The genre most definitely belongs in primary-grade classrooms.

Reading & Writing Informational Text in the Primary Grades describes research-based practices that can help teachers bring more nonfiction into the classroom from the earliest grades on. Too often we find books filled with research and theory that don't offer much practical advice. Or we find books describing classroom practice without reference to research that would ground our thinking. This book, however, is a perfect blend of research and practice. It describes some of what research indicates should be done, and then, through the examples of actual classroom teachers, suggests how we might do it.

Take, for example, the findings of Isabel Beck, Margaret McKeown, and Linda Kucan (2002) that it may not always be advantageous to introduce new vocabulary words to children before encountering them in text. Their research indicates that during a whole-class reading of a text, it may be better to wait until after the children meet the word in the text before explaining its meaning, since young children need to integrate the meaning of the unfamiliar word with its conceptual framework. Primary-grade children may not have enough background knowledge about the topic to grasp the word's meaning in isolation, nor the memory needed to hold on to its meaning once it's explained.

Another research-based recommendation comes from Linda Gambrell (1996) who states that reading is a social activity and encourages teachers to provide opportunities for children to talk about what they're learning with one another. To implement this, one teacher described in this book has each of her second graders share interesting facts from books on a common topic by recording a fact on a sheet of paper and illustrating it. These pieces are then displayed on a bulletin board, so that all the children can read and discuss them, and then compiled into a class book.

Years ago I never realized the importance of nonfiction for young children. My eyes were closed to the possibilities, and my teaching world was a much smaller place. I'm convinced that this book will open your eyes to help you see, like Jesse, things you never knew were there. You'll become excited as you learn how to incorporate informational text into your primary-grade classroom, and you'll be dying to try some of these ideas out.

INTRODUCTION

If you currently use little or no informational text in your primary-grade classroom, this book is for you. If you already use informational text but want to extend your work in new directions, this book is also for you. If you are an upper-elementary teacher, you might also find the book useful since some of the practices we suggest are adapted from grades 4 to 6.

Research shows that informational text is scarce in primary classrooms, but, by all indications, it should not be. In Chapter 1, we tell you why and provide arguments you can use if you encounter doubters. In Chapter 2, we present a research-based framework for infusing the primary classroom with more informational text. This framework calls for incorporating such text:

◆ onto classroom walls and other surfaces
◆ into the classroom library
◆ into daily activities that involve extended text (i.e., text that is made up of three or more related sentences).

In Chapters 3 through 8, we address in detail how to implement this framework with separate chapters on including informational text in read aloud and shared reading, guided reading, independent reading, writing instruction, content area instruction, and the classroom environment. Each of these chapters provides a portrait of how one or more real teachers incorporates informational text. For example, in Chapter 3, on read aloud and shared reading, we spotlight first-grade teacher Mary Ellen Moffitt by including a transcript from one of her information book read aloud sessions and discussing the ways she promotes higher-order comprehension of informational text. Each chapter also includes specific, research-tested strategies for using informational text. For example, in Chapter 5, on independent reading, we discuss repeated reading, incentive programs, and books on tape as strategies for promoting independent reading of informational text. We provide practical advice, such as the equipment you'll need for making your own information books on tape, as well as brief accounts of the research behind each strategy. These chapters also include other kinds of useful information such as lists of high-quality informational texts, examples of student work, and ideas for lessons and projects.

The final two chapters reach beyond curriculum components. In Chapter 9, we discuss real challenges that primary teachers face as they attempt to incorporate more informational text in their classrooms—and how they meet those challenges. In Chapter 10, the final chapter, we discuss professional development, suggesting ways to use this and other books in a study group or on your own to inform your practice.

The chapters need not be read in order or even in their entirety. We want you to adapt the book to meet your needs and priorities. For example, if you are going to use the book in a study group, you might want to start with the final chapter. If you are particularly interested in improving your writing instruction, you might begin with Chapter 6. Whatever chapters you decide to read, in whatever order, please know that we view incorporating informational text into primary classrooms as a process, not an event that one accomplishes in a day. Therefore if incorporating it into only one area of your teaching is, for now, what you can do, that's fine. We applaud you!

Reading & Writing Informational Text in the Primary Grades was inspired largely by our experiences in the Early Literacy Project, a federally funded research study focusing on the use of informational text in primary classrooms. Nell Duke was Principal Investigator on the project, Susan Bennett-Armistead was Project Manager, and this book's contributors—Anne Huxley, Mary Kay Johnson, Denise McLurkin, Ebony Roberts, Carol Rosen, and Emilene Vogel—were research assistants. (Nell and Susan worked closely with each of these contributors to ensure consistency of content, voice, and format among chapters.)

In the data collection phase of the Early Literacy Project, we worked with a group of first- and second-grade teachers, diversifying the genres that their students read, wrote, and listened to. Since then we have been analyzing the data, measuring the students' achievement and motivation, and learning what happens to children who are fed a healthy diet of informational text. So far, the results have been positive. Some of the teachers featured in this book participated in the Early Literacy Project and some are teachers we have worked with in other projects and capacities. (Inclusion of any individual teacher or student does not necessarily mean that he or she was involved in the Early Literacy Project.) We hope that you will learn as much from these teachers as we have.

CHAPTER 1
Why Include Informational Text In the Primary Classroom?
A Research-Based Rationale

CHAPTER 1: WHY INCLUDE INFORMATIONAL TEXT IN THE PRIMARY CLASSROOM?

15

The fact that you have this book in your hands means you may already believe that informational text should be included in primary classrooms. Perhaps you have had professional or personal experiences that have led you to that belief. Perhaps you have thought of some potential benefits informational text may hold for young learners. We hope this chapter helps bring together much of what you have been thinking. It is designed to extend your thinking and provide access to research and theories that support it.

What's the Difference Between Informational Text and Nonfiction?

Often the terms "informational text" and "nonfiction" are used interchangeably. In our view, however, they are not the same. Informational text is a type of nonfiction—a *very* important type. Nonfiction includes any text that is factual. (Or, by some definitions, any type of *literature* that is factual, which would exclude texts such as menus and street signs.) Informational text differs from other types of nonfiction in purpose, features, and format.

Purpose

The primary purpose of informational text is to convey information about the natural or social world, typically from someone presumed to know that information to someone presumed not to, with particular linguistic features such as headings and technical vocabulary to help accomplish that purpose. By our definition, therefore, biography is nonfiction but is not informational text, because its primary purpose is to convey information about an individual's life. Procedural or how-to text is also nonfiction, but not informational text because its primary purpose is to tell someone how to do something, not convey information about some *thing*. Nonfiction narrative or "true stories" are also nonfiction but not informational text, because their primary purpose is to tell of an event or series of events that have occurred.

This is not to say that biography, procedural text, nonfiction narrative, and other types of nonfiction are not important; they are just not the same as informational text.

Features

It is important to talk about the different types or genres of nonfiction not only because they have different purposes, but because they have different features to achieve those purposes. For example, biographies typically focus on a *single* individual and *specific points in time*. In contrast, informational texts, as we define them, talk about *whole classes of things* and *in a timeless way* (for example, "Sharks live in water."); they therefore have a generalizing quality. Other common features of informational texts include presentation and repetition of a topic or theme; descriptions of attributes and characteristic events; comparative/contrastive and classifactory structures; technical vocabulary; realistic illustrations or photographs; labels and captions; navigational aids such as indexes, page numbers, and headings; and various graphical devices such as diagrams, tables, and charts. Many of these are not found in other types of nonfiction. (See Chapter 6 for more information.)

By our definition, informational text is:

◆ text whose primary purpose is to convey information about the natural and social world.

◆ text that typically has characteristic features such as addressing whole classes of things in a timeless way.

◆ text that comes in many different formats, including books, magazines, handouts, brochures, CD-ROMs, and the Internet.

Informational text is not:

◆ text whose primary purpose is something other than to convey information about the natural and social world, such as telling about an individual's life, an event or series of events, or how to do something.

◆ text that always has particular features; instead, features vary by text.

◆ only books.

What Do We Mean by Research-Based Practice?

Throughout this book, we use the term *research*, so we should say something about what we mean by it. To us, research is the systematic collection and analysis of data for the purpose of addressing a question. For example, to address the question "How much time do primary-grade children spend with informational text in school?" researchers might collect data by observing in classrooms or administering surveys. By applying specific procedures for collecting data, and having specific procedures for analyzing them, those researchers are being systematic. They report conclusions based not just on what they think or guess, but on the data they collect and analyze.

In this book we focus on practices that are *research based*. This means that, whenever possible, the practices we recommend (for example, improving children's reading comprehension) have been tested in one or more research studies and shown to be effective. In some cases they have not been tested themselves through research. In such cases, the practices are very closely related to practices that *have* been tested. For example, sometimes we recommend practices to use with informational text which are modified versions of practices that have been shown to be effective (usually at raising student achievement) using narrative text. We can't guarantee that those practices will be effective with informational text, and indeed we welcome research to find out, but for now they provide the best basis we have.

For each major practice we recommend, we tell you about the research upon which it is based. We hope that you will expect the same from other resources you read on using informational text in the primary grades. Along the way, be sure to draw on your own experiences and judgments, as research alone cannot provide all the answers.

Format

Within informational text, there are several different types of text that might be considered informational text genres or subgenres. For example, there are reference books such as encyclopedias, field guides, and so on. There are "all about" books, such as some of those by Gail Gibbons. There are also books we call process-informational books. These include books about how a particular animal develops from conception to adulthood or about how some substance is created or transformed. And many informational texts are not books at all, but rather magazines or newspapers, posters or pamphlets, Web sites or CD-ROMs, and so on. The format of the text can affect that text and how it is read or written; for example, informational text on Web sites is usually *informational hypertext.* We include many different types of informational text in this book, and you will probably identify many more in your own classroom and experiences.

There are professional books that focus on forms of nonfiction collectively, and these are very useful. (See Appendix B.) However, we believe that informational text is so important, and that there is so much to say about the teaching and learning issues surrounding it, that it deserves a book unto itself. Although many of the principles and practices we discuss—such as teaching comprehension strategies, making reading-writing connections, and attending to the classroom environment—can easily be applied to other types of text, we hope you agree that teaching and learning with informational text is, indeed, important and complex enough to merit its own book.

WHY THINK ABOUT GENRES CHILDREN ENCOUNTER IN THE PRIMARY GRADES?

There are many different dimensions of text that might influence a young child's ability to read that text (Hiebert, 1999; Purcell-Gates & Duke, in press), such as its predictability, decodability, and illustrations. What makes us think that genre is one of the dimensions of text to be concerned about? For the answer, we look to theory and research. Genre theorists believe that differences among texts develop based on the purposes for those texts (e.g.,

Halliday & Hasan, 1985; Miller, 1984). A text written for the purpose of advertising a new car, for example, is fundamentally different from a text written for the purpose of explaining how that car works, which is in turn fundamentally different from a text that chronicles someone's adventures driving that car across the country. These texts have very different purposes, are written for different situations, and have very different characteristics. Genre research indicates that even young children are sensitive to those differences. One of our favorite examples of this comes from a three-year-old girl who scribble-wrote two texts. One had only short scribbles down only the left-hand side of the page. The other had long scribbles that extended across the page. She identified the first as a shopping list and the second as a story! (Harste, Woodward, & Burke, 1984, p. 157) Although not yet writing beyond scribbles, this child already showed awareness of genre features. There are many documented examples of young children producing texts characteristic of particular genres, producing or using genres appropriate to their purposes, talking about differences between genres, and so on. (See Duke & Purcell-Gates, in press, for further discussion.)

WHY INCLUDE MORE INFORMATIONAL TEXT IN PRIMARY CLASSROOMS?

Exposing children to a variety of genres may be wise, but why focus on informational text in particular? There are a number of arguments for doing so. Some of these arguments have a more solid research base than others, and some may be more compelling than others. But based on the research and theories available at this point, we feel children should encounter more informational text in the primary grades for the reasons explained below:

Informational text is key to success in later schooling. We have all heard that from around fourth grade on, "reading to learn" is a major focus in school (Chall, 1983). Students encounter more textbooks and other forms of informational text as they move through the grades. The tests they take contain increasingly more difficult informational texts. College curricula are replete with a variety of informational readings. If we include more informational text in early schooling, we put children in a better position to handle the reading and writing demands of their later schooling. We would like to see a day when children "read to learn" *and* "learn to read" from the earliest days of school and throughout their school careers.

Informational text is ubiquitous in society. Several studies have looked at the kinds of things people write *outside of* school—what children and adults read and write in their workplaces, homes, and communities. Again and again these studies have shown that adults read a great deal of nonfiction, including informational text (e.g., Venezky, 1982, Smith, 2000). This is not likely to change and, in fact, in our increasingly information-based economy, it may only increase. According to one study (Kamil & Lane, 1998), 96 percent of the text on the World Wide Web is expository. If we are going to prepare children for this world, we need to be serious about teaching them to read and write informational text. It may not be difficult to convince children of the need for this, as we draw their attention to the informational text that surrounds them in their world.

Informational text is preferred reading material for some children. When researchers investigate the kinds of texts children like to read, they've found something that isn't surprising: Different children have different reading preferences. Some children seem to prefer informational text, some seem to prefer narrative text, many don't seem to have preferences for any particular genre. For those children who prefer informational text—children Ron Jobe and Mary Dayton-Sakari (2002) call "Info-Kids"—including more informational text in classrooms may improve attitudes toward reading and even serve as a catalyst for overall literacy development (Caswell & Duke, 1998).

Informational text often addresses children's interests and questions. Regardless of a child's text preference, when the text's topic is of particular interest to that child, his or her reading is likely to improve (Schiefele, Krapp, & Winteler, 1992). Not surprisingly, then, approaches that emphasize reading for the purpose of addressing real questions children have about their world tend to lead to higher achievement and motivation (e.g., Guthrie, Van Meter, McCann, Wigfield, Bennett, Poundstone, et al., 1996). Including more informational text in classrooms may help us address the interests and questions of more of our students.

Informational text builds knowledge of the natural and social world. By definition, informational text conveys information about the natural and social world (Duke, 2000a). Reading and listening to informational text therefore can develop children's knowledge of that world (e.g., Anderson & Guthrie, 1999; Duke & Kays, 1998). This in turn can pro-

mote children's comprehension of subsequent texts they read (e.g., Wilson & Anderson, 1986), because it can build background knowledge. And the more background knowledge children have, the stronger their comprehension is likely to be. Including more informational text in classrooms may help us develop more knowledgeable and skilled readers.

Informational text may help build vocabulary and other kinds of literacy knowledge. Studies show that parents and teachers attend more to vocabulary and concepts when reading aloud informational text (Mason, Peterman, Powell, & Kerr, 1989; Pellegrini, Perlmutter, Galda, & Brody, 1990) than when reading narrative text. Because of this

How Much Informational Text Is in Primary Classrooms?

A few years ago, Nell conducted a study in twenty first-grade classrooms in the Greater Boston Metropolitan Area. She observed each classroom for four full days over the course of a school year and noted the genre of text used during each minute of instruction. She found that classes spent an average of 3.6 minutes per day with informational text, and classrooms in low-socioeconomic status (SES) districts spent even less than this (1.4 minutes per day) (Duke, 2000a). She also found relatively little informational text on classroom walls and other surfaces and in the classroom libraries, and again the amount was especially low in the low-SES districts. She is not alone in finding a scarcity of informational text in primary-grade classrooms. Other observational studies (Kamberelis, 1998), teacher surveys (Pressley, Rankin, & Yokoi, 1996; Yopp & Yopp, 2000), and analyses of basal readers (Hoffman, McCarthey, Abbott, Christian, Corman, Curry, et al., 1994; Moss & Newton, 1998) also find little informational text in primary grade classrooms and curriculum materials. Of course, there are exceptions (e.g., Duthie, 1996; Kamil & Lane, 1997; Taberski, 2000), and perhaps your classroom is among them. But generally, informational text does not currently have a major role in primary classrooms.

presence of technical vocabulary, and the attention that parents and teachers seem to pay to it, informational text may be particularly well suited to building children's word knowledge (Dreher, 2000; Duke, Bennett-Armistead, & Roberts, 2002; 2003). Further, learning to read the graphical devices that informational text often includes, such as diagrams and tables, may support children's overall visual literacy development.

There may be additional reasons why informational text is beneficial to primary students, but these are some key ones. The next section examines something of a counterargument: the reasons why some people feel that young children cannot handle informational text.

WHAT ARE SOME MAJOR RESERVATIONS ABOUT USING INFORMATIONAL TEXT?

So what has been standing in the way of incorporating more informational text in primary classrooms? There are probably many answers to that question, but this section addresses three reservations that we have encountered time and time again in writings and conversations.

Reservation #1:
"Young children can't handle informational text."

Most of the research on informational text and young children has been aimed at establishing that young children really can handle such text, that it is in fact developmentally appropriate for them. This research is inspired by both the practical fact that there is little informational text included in primary classrooms and curricula—and there must be some reason for this— as well as by theoretical work arguing that narrative is the best and, perhaps, the only way that young children can make sense of the world around them (e.g., Britton, Burgess, Martin, McLeod, & Rosen, 1975; Egan, 1986, 1993; Moffett, 1968; Sawyer & Watson, 1987).

The research is clear. Young children *can* interact successfully with informational text. (See Dreher, 2000; Duke, 2003; and Duke, Bennett-Armistead, & Roberts, 2002; 2003, for reviews of research on this point.) You will find references to studies supporting this point throughout this book. For example, in Chapter 3, we discuss studies showing that kindergarten children can develop knowledge of information-book language and content from information-book read alouds and shared readings. Chapters 4 and 5, on guided and independent reading, reveal evidence that primary-grade students can comprehend informational text that they read themselves. In Chapter 6, you will learn about research indicating that young children can also write informational text. So you needn't worry that informational text is inherently "over the heads" of your students, and you should be able to respond with confidence to colleagues who have doubts.

Reservation #2:
"There isn't enough informational text appropriate for young learners."

Another argument is that there isn't enough quality informational text available for young learners. We disagree, and hope that the many informational texts cited throughout this book will support our position. Although there is undoubtedly room in publishing for improvement, there *are* a large number of informational texts containing language and content that is appropriate for even our youngest learners. And while quality is subjective, many informational texts appropriate for primary-grade students have received prestigious awards for their excellence and contributions to learning. (See Appendix A.) We do not believe that a supposed lack of appropriate texts is adequate justification for inattention to informational text in the primary grades.

Reservation #3:
"This is something brand new and, therefore, risky."

It may be reassuring to you—as it has been to us—that we are not trying something completely new here. Consider history: There have been points in time when published readers for children included a lot of informational text. Some, in fact, were made up primarily of informational text. (See discussion and references in Duke, Bennett-Armistead, & Roberts, 2002;

2003.) However, because there were no research studies on the use of informational text when those readers were being used, we don't know the impact they had on children. Researchers have begun only recently to examine the impact of informational text in the primary grades.

SO WHAT HAPPENS WHEN WE INCLUDE MORE INFORMATIONAL TEXT IN PRIMARY CLASSROOMS?

We have been conducting a research study called the Early Literacy Project to address this question. The study is designed to tell us what happens when first and second graders read, write, and listen to a variety of genres. Here, we provide a description of the study and some results thus far.

The study compares the achievement and motivation of three groups of students from thirty schools in Michigan:

◆ The first group of students, made up of ten classes, had first- and second-grade teachers who were given funding and support to diversify the genres children read, wrote, and listened to, in particular to include more informational text. We called this the experimental group.

◆ The second group of students, made up of another ten classes, had first- and second-grade teachers who were given the same amount of funding and support as the experimental group to increase children's exposure to text, but were not directed to increase exposure to informational text in particular (and didn't know that the study had to do with genre). We called this the hawthorne control group.

◆ The third group of students, made up of another ten classes, had first- and second-grade teachers who did not receive any funding or support from us during the year they had the students (but did receive some after that year) and were not asked to change anything about their practice. We called this the traditional control group.

Each class we studied was randomly assigned to one of the three groups. We studied only one class per school. We made sure that there was at least one classroom from each of the three groups in every school district, so we could make comparisons between the classes within districts. We did a lot of other things, too, to try to ensure that we were carrying out a good and unbiased study, but unfortunately don't have the space to go into more detail about them here.

Results Thus Far of the "Early Literacy Project" Study

We're finding that including more informational text benefits first graders (Duke, Martineau, Frank, & Bennett-Armistead, 2003). Specifically, children in the experimental group had the same levels of overall reading and writing achievement (as measured by a norm-referenced standardized test of decoding and reading comprehension, and by prompted writing samples scored for spelling, punctuation, and capitalization) as children in the other groups. Moreover, classes in the experimental group with relatively low initial literacy knowledge (as measured by a letter identification and sound-letter association task) did better in their reading comprehension and writing achievement than comparable classes in the other groups did. Including more informational text seemed to "level the playing field" a bit for these classes.

With respect to genre-specific achievement—that is, achievement in reading and writing of informational and narrative text in particular—we found that children in the experimental group were better informational writers (as measured by holistic scoring of prompted informational writing) and were equally good narrative writers (as measured by holistic scoring of prompted narrative writing). We observed no differences in genre-specific reading (ability to read narrative versus informational text) by the end of grade one, though we acknowledge some limitations of our measure for that.

Our findings related to motivation also favor the experimental group. Children in this group did not show the decline in attitudes toward recreational reading that children in the other groups showed; their attitudes toward academic reading, however, were no different from those of the other groups (both measured by the Elementary Reading Attitudes or 'Garfield' Survey, McKenna & Kear, 1990). There were no differences between groups in their attitudes toward particular kinds of text. For example, children in the experimental group were no less interested in narrative texts than those in the other groups.

A Letter to Inform and Involve Parents

Given the scarcity of informational text in primary classrooms, some parents may be surprised to see their children reading a lot of it in school. Here's an example of a letter you might send home at the beginning of the school year to let parents know that you will be including a lot of informational text, why, and how they can help.

Dear Parents:

This year you will notice us using many different kinds of reading materials in our classroom. Of course, your child will be reading, writing, and listening to many stories, but you may be surprised to hear that he or she will also encounter many information books, magazines, newspapers, and other kinds of nonfiction texts. Research shows that even young children can have successful experiences with these kinds of texts if given the opportunity. I will give your child lots of opportunities and support to read, write, and listen to informational texts. By the end of the year, I expect that your child will be comfortable reading, writing, and listening to informational text, which will help him or her throughout life.

You can support your child's learning from and about information books in many ways. For example, a couple of times a week, ask your child if he or she learned anything interesting from a book at school. When you go to the library or bookstore, encourage your child to look at many different kinds of books and other materials, including information books. When buying presents for your child, consider not only storybooks but also other kinds of texts. For example, many children would appreciate a subscription to a magazine that focuses on news, sports, or history. (Please contact me if you'd like suggestions.)

Both my own experiences and the research in this area suggest that young children benefit from exposure to informational texts. Thank you for your support.

Sincerely,

Of course, this is just one study, with results so far only for first grade. (For results from the second-grade study, contact Nell Duke at nkduke@msu.edu.) We need much more research in this area. Notably, we have some individual cases in which teachers have reported positive effects of including substantial informational text in their classrooms (e.g., Duthie, 1996; Kamil & Lane, 1997; Taberski, 2000). But we don't know if there is a selection bias here; perhaps other teachers have tried incorporating more informational text and found no positive effects, but have not written about their experience.

Concluding Thoughts

There are a number of arguments for exposing primary students to more informational text. Although we do not have much research yet to indicate what happens when we do this, the research we do have, along with teacher testimonials, suggests that the effects are positive. It suggests that we should, indeed, expose primary students to more informational text. In the next chapter, we explain a framework—the one used in the Early Literacy Project—for doing just that.

CHAPTER 2

A Framework for Weaving Informational Texts Into the Primary Classroom

The Early Literacy Project

"Is it storytime or read aloud time?" "Are they storybooks or picture books?" "Is it the next story or the next selection?" "Are the children's writings called stories or texts?" It is amazing how much not only narrative text dominates primary classrooms, but how the *terminology* of narrative text does, too. In this chapter, we present a framework for changing that—a framework for including a greater variety of texts, including more informational texts, in primary-grade classrooms. We call this framework the genre-diversification framework. The first-grade teachers in the Early Literacy Project who used this framework had students with higher achievement and motivation in key areas than teachers in other classrooms. We are in the process of analyzing data about what happens to second graders whose teachers also use this framework.

Three is a key number in the genre-diversification framework. Teachers diversify the genres in three areas of the classroom: in print on the walls and other surfaces; among books and other materials in the library; and within daily activities that involve print. They use three categories of text within these areas: narrative texts, informational texts, and other kinds of texts such as poetry and biography. In other words, in each of the three classroom areas, the teachers aim for about one-third narrative genres, one-third informational genres, and one-third other genres. They do this only for activities and displays involving extended text (text that is composed of three or more related sentences). So they do not apply the genre-diversification framework to displays such as alphabet friezes or word walls, or to activities that require students to work solely at the letter, word, or sentence level. Here are examples of extended text by children that you might find in their classrooms:

The Genre-Diversification Framework

We use:

◆ one-third narrative genres
◆ one-third informational genres
◆ one-third other genres such as poetry and biography

We incorporate these genres into:

◆ classroom walls and other surfaces
◆ the classroom library
◆ daily activities that involve print

Narrative: "I went to the park with my sister. She fell down and hurt her knee. Mom put a bandage on it."

Informational: "Whales are mammals. Dogs are mammals. Spiders are not mammals."

Other: "Roses are red. Violets are blue. My mommy loves me and I love her too."

That, in a nutshell, is the genre-diversification framework. Next, we provide details about the three classroom areas and three text categories.

AREAS OF THE CLASSROOM

Classroom Walls and Other Surfaces

Many educators call for "print-rich" classroom environments, which means having a great deal of print—posters, children's writing, webs and maps, book jackets, and so forth—on classroom walls and other surfaces. Research suggests that some genres, particularly informational genres, are not well represented (Duke, 2000a). The genre-diversification framework seeks to change this by working toward balancing extended text genres found on walls and other surfaces, such as the sides of bookcases and the fronts of desks. So if there are thirty extended texts on the classroom walls and other surfaces, ten should be narrative, ten should be informational, and ten should be of other genres. Many examples of extended texts for classroom walls and other surfaces are presented in Chapter 8.

The Classroom Library

The books and other materials found in their classroom library can make a difference in children's literacy development. (See discussion in Chapter 8.) But again, research indicates that certain genres, especially informational genres, are underrepresented (Duke, 2000a). Using the genre-diversification framework, teachers work to strike a balance of narrative, informational, and other genres in their classroom libraries. They achieve this balance not only with books and other materials on library shelves, but also with materials on display in the classroom library and around the room. Research suggests that children gravitate toward texts that are displayed (Martinez & Teale, 1989 cited in Fractor, Woodruff, Martinez, & Teale, 1993) so it may be especially important for a variety of genres to be represented.

Daily Activities That Involve Print

Perhaps even more important than diversifying the text genres found in the classroom environment is diversifying them for activities involving written language—not only for language

---

Why We Don't Use the Categories "Fiction" and "Nonfiction"

Many people feel that text should be categorized as fiction or nonfiction—or as "true" or "not true." While we think that "truth value" (Kamil & Lane, 1997) is one important distinction among texts, we do not think that it is necessarily the most important distinction, particularly for young learners. Rather, we believe that the purpose of the text, the way it is generally read, its typical organization, and other key features constitute more important distinctions. (See Figure 2.1, page 35.) For example, we believe that a true story about Ibis the whale (nonfiction) and a made-up but realistic story about some other whale (fiction) have much more in common than any story about a whale and an "all about whales" book.

Moreover, different kinds of nonfiction texts are very different from one another. Compare, for example, the purpose, ways of reading, organization, and other features of a biography to a how-to text or an encyclopedia. We generally don't find it useful to lump such texts together.

In this book, then, we focus on one very important category of nonfiction text: informational text. Even within informational text, as you will see, there are many variations, but they generally have much more in common with each another than they do with other types of text. (For further discussion of some different types of nonfiction and how they differ, see Duke & Tower, in press.)

---

arts activities, but also for science, social studies, and mathematics activities. In the genre-diversification framework, teachers attempt to balance the genres used in each print activity. For example, if a teacher reads aloud each day, she might choose a fairy tale, an article on space exploration, and a poem by Bobbi Katz. She would not necessarily read aloud texts from all three categories in the same day, but she would choose a range of genres over several days. The teacher applies the same thinking to other activities such as guided reading, writing, content area instruction, and so on.

Why We Don't Advocate "Genre of the Month"

Some teachers have thought about diversifying genres by focusing on a single genre for a period of time, then moving to another genre, then another, and so on. For example, a teacher might spend a month on fairy tales, then a month on concept books, and so on. Think twice about this approach. One thing we know about learning is that we generally need to revisit things many times as we grow and change. To spend a month on fairy tales in September and then not encounter them again for a year probably will result in less learning for students than if they encounter fairy tales throughout the year, as they are also developing in other areas. Moreover, when focusing on a single genre, there is an increased danger that other genres might not be considered for a purpose for which they are appropriate. For example, while it is true that procedural texts are normally what children would use to find out how to conduct a particular investigation in science, in some cases a biography detailing how a particular scientist conducted that investigation could be equally or more useful. Such texts should not be ignored simply because they are not of the genre of the month. On the contrary, children should be expected to draw appropriately upon many different genres of text in the work that they do.

Teachers using the framework also attempt to diversify within domain or content area. For example, rather than including only narrative texts in language arts and only informational texts in science, they include both narrative and informational texts in both language arts and science.

Language arts time is when teachers are most likely to provide instruction in reading skills and strategies—hopefully for both informational and narrative text. Therefore it is important to diversify genres during language arts time. At the same time, during content area instruction it is important that children are exposed to a variety of genres because disciplines themselves involve many different genres. Consider science, for example. When recounting what they observed in an experiment or reading the "true story" of the discovery of electricity, children are engaged with narrative genres. When reading about how to do an experiment or writing a biography of a famous inventor, children are engaged with other genres (in this case procedural and biographical text, respectively). Just as adults encounter a variety of genres in any given field, children working within this framework experience a range of texts in each content area and domain.

THE GENRE CATEGORIES

There are many different kinds of text in our world—texts with very different purposes, for very different situations, and with very different characteristics. If you look around now, you probably see examples of them. Labeling and categorizing texts is not easy. But to implement the genre-diversification framework, you have to be able to think about the categories in which texts belong. This can be a messy process, but we hope that messiness doesn't have to be overwhelming. Providing children with exposure to and experience with a *variety* of different genres of text, including genres you think are especially important or challenging, is much more important than being definitive or exact in categorizing texts. In these next two sections we explain how there is diversity both *within* and *across* genre categories, and why we need to diversify in both ways.

Diversity Across Categories

For the genre-diversification framework, we use three very broad categories for text: narrative, informational, and other. As shown in Figure 2.1, within these categories are texts that are very different from one another in many respects.

	Narrative Genres	Informational Genres	Other Genres
Primary Purpose	To entertain or convey an experience	To convey information about the natural or social world	Varies by genre
Examples	fairy tales, mysteries, fables, true stories, personal narratives, historical fiction	all-about books, question-and-answer books, most reference books	poetry, biography, menus, instructions, rules
Typical Organization	Temporally for all or nearly all of the text	Topically for all or nearly all of the text	Varies by genre
Some Other Key Features	Includes characters; is goal-based in some way	Uses timeless verbs; uses generic nouns*	Vary by genre
How They're Typically Read	Linearly, as a whole	Linearly or nonlinearly, in parts	Varies by genre

Figure 2.1: Distinctions among the three text categories in the genre-diversification framework

* For more information about key features of informational text, see Chapter 6.

And some texts are not easily placed even into these broad categories. For example, we have encountered a number of what we call narrative-informational texts, such as The Magic School Bus books (e.g., Cole, 1990). These texts have some purposes and characteristics associated with fictional narrative texts and some purposes and characteristics associated with all-about or process-informational texts. So it is not clear whether these texts are best placed in our narrative genres category or our informational genres category. (For our analyses in the Early Literacy Project, we count them as being half in one and half in the other.) Similarly, we have encountered texts we call informational-poetic, such as *Beast Feast* by Douglas Florian (1994). An example from that book is a poem called "The Ants":

The Ants

Ants are scantily
Half an inch long
But for their size
They're very strong.
Ants tote leaves
Five times their weight
Back to their nest
At a speedy rate.
They walk on tree limbs
Upside down
A hundred feet
Above the ground,
While down below
Beneath a mount
They're building tunnels
Underground.
And so it's been—
And it will be—
Since greatest
Ant antiquity.

Informational-poetic texts have purposes and characteristics of both all-about informational texts and poetry. (For the Early Literacy Project, we made an arbitrary decision to place them in the informational category, but we acknowledge that it is not a perfect fit.)

Why We Incorporate "One-Third Narrative, One-Third Informational, One-Third Other"

You might wonder where we came up with the one-third, one-third, one-third guideline. Why not one-half, one-quarter, one-quarter or some other breakdown? To be honest, because there has not been any research to suggest that a particular distribution of genres is most efficacious for young learners, we did not have much to go on when setting our targets. Aiming to balance equally these three important categories seemed like a good starting place. Analyses of the data from the Early Literacy Project might end up suggesting another configuration, but we doubt there will be enough consistency across areas of the classroom (environmental print, classroom library, and print activities), across outcome measures (reading, writing, motivation, overall and genre-specific), and across grades (first and second), to come up with any one definitive distribution of genres. For now, we suggest thinking of one-third, one-third, one-third as a starting guideline, and making adjustments as it seems appropriate given your particular context and any future research on this question.

Diversity Within Categories

Theoretically, you could spend an entire year exposing children to nothing but one-third mysteries, one-third encyclopedias, and one-third biographies. This certainly represents equally each of the three categories in the genre-diversification framework (narrative, informational, and other, respectively), however, you would not meet the spirit of the framework. Diversity *within* as well as across categories is important. We do not specify which particular genres within the categories are most important, or in what proportion they should be represented, but we do expect that many genres within each category will be represented.

Further, there is an issue Dr. P. David Pearson calls the "zero-sum game problem." That is, if we aim for one-third, one-third, one-third, doesn't increasing exposure in one category necessarily mean decreasing exposure in another? In some cases it probably does. If a teacher can only read aloud for twenty minutes each day, and she has been reading aloud only storybooks in the past, under the genre-diversification framework, she would have to sacrifice storybooks to some degree to read aloud informational and other genres. However, it might also be possible that the teacher could find a way to squeeze in a bit more read aloud time each day, so that perhaps storybook reading isn't decreased so much as read aloud in general is increased. Similarly, diversifying texts on classroom walls and other surfaces and in classroom libraries might be more a matter of adding underrepresented categories of text than of taking away some of the texts already present. Since the Early Literacy Project as well as many other studies indicate that more print exposure and experience is generally better, this model of adding rather than subtracting texts is preferable.

Criteria for Selecting Informational Text

A few years ago, choices for informational text were very limited. Today, because there is a wide range of texts that are appropriate for young readers, it can sometimes be overwhelming to separate the wheat from the chaff. Recognizing that text selection is and should be a subjective process, we offer these guidelines. The guidelines work together—please don't consider one without considering the others as well. For example, Carl Sagan was a well-known author on space who received many awards for his *accurate* work, but we would never consider his work *accessible* for the beginning reader.

GUIDING PRINCIPLE	CONSIDER
Accuracy	As information changes and is updated, accuracy becomes slippery. Does the text reflect current trends in research? If there is reason to think that there have been changes in the knowledge in this area, is the copyright date recent? Does the author admit that some things are not known, and that new and revised information is gathered all the time?
Accessibility	Is this text at the reading level of the students for whom it is intended? Does it mostly use language in ways that they can understand? Does the amount of specialized vocabulary seem overwhelming (technicality, amount, frequency)? Does the level of accessibility fit with your purpose for the book? For example, a more challenging text is fine for a teacher read aloud but not appropriate for independent reading. The level of support you expect to give can help determine whether or not the text is right for your students.

GUIDING PRINCIPLE	CONSIDER
Appropriateness	Is the text appropriate for your teaching purposes, not only in terms of accessibility but also in terms of content, functions, and features? For example, if your goal is to teach particular science content, does the text address that? If your goal is to teach a summarization strategy, does the text lend itself to summarization? If you want students to learn to navigate text, are features such as an index and headings available to help them do so?
Appeal	Will your students like the layout, the topic, the cover? Even if the topic is not one you usually use for whole-class work, is it one that will match the interests of a child in your class whom you have been trying to reach?
Text type	Is the format in which the text is presented—a book, a pamphlet, a poster, for example—the most appropriate for the topic and purpose? Would a Web site provide more current information? Would a poster make the information more accessible? (See Chapter 8 for a discussion of non-book information text.) Considering the text format can maximize the match of the text and context to the child. Some children read magazine articles more happily and successfully than other types of text; some children are comfortable working independently on the Web while others will need considerable scaffolding from you.
Recommendations	Was this text suggested to you by a colleague? Do your colleague's students seem similar to yours? Did the text win an award or receive positive reviews in a journal you respect? Did a child bring this book to your attention? What do online reviews of the text say (for example, reader comments on Amazon.com)? And do the reviewers have purposes and standards of accuracy similar to your own? Can you tell?
Your Students	Finally and most important, keep in mind that you know your students and your purposes better than anyone. That knowledge is your best tool for selecting materials. We hope these guidelines help you think about that knowledge in useful ways.

Please note: These suggestions were informed by Sudol and King (1996). A checklist for choosing nonfiction trade books. *The Reading Teacher, 49*, 422-424. For a list of resources locating and selecting information books, see Appendix A.

CONCLUDING THOUGHTS

This chapter presented a framework for diversifying the genres used in primary classrooms. The number three is prominent in this framework—diversification happens in three areas of the classroom, using three categories of text. We explained *why* we focus on these three areas of the classroom and these three categories of text. In the remainder of the book, we focus on the *what* and the *how*: What do classrooms using this framework look like, especially with respect to use of informational text? How do we include more informational text in classrooms?

CHAPTER 3
Shared Reading and Read Aloud
Developing Language, World Knowledge, and Comprehension With Informational Text

Why do we sneeze? Why does gelatin wobble? How do airships fly? Are all mushrooms fungi? Children have so many questions about the world around them, and reading information books to and with them can provide answers. Of all instructional contexts in which informational text is used, we believe that read aloud and shared reading may be the most important for children's learning and enjoyment. In this chapter we:

◆ Briefly discuss research on informational text read aloud.

◆ Describe read aloud and shared reading as used by one teacher.

◆ Give some tips for selecting informational text for read aloud and shared reading.

◆ Identify three research-based instructional strategies for use in read aloud and shared reading.

◆ Suggest some great information books for read aloud and shared reading.

By the end of the chapter, we hope that you will have many ideas about ways to include informational text in your read aloud and shared reading times.

What Is the Difference Between Read Aloud and Shared Reading?

We view read aloud as an activity in which one person, usually the teacher, reads while others, usually the students, listen and—ideally—discuss and question the text before, during, and after the reading.

Shared reading involves multiple people, usually teachers and students, reading aloud together, as in choral reading, or one person reading aloud while others read along subvocally or silently. Shared reading usually requires a text large enough for all readers to see, often in the form of a Big Book or overhead transparency, unless a predictable or memorized text is used. Reading informational text may be shared even when children aren't likely to be able to read the words, because much of the "reading" is of photos, diagrams, charts, and other graphical features.

Read Aloud and Informational Text in the Primary Grades: What the Research Says

What happens when informational text is read aloud in the primary grades? Researchers have found that children learn both the language and content of informational text, which suggests that they are capable of understanding and generating it themselves. In the following sections, we present an overview of important studies.

Children Learn *Language* from Information Book Read Alouds

In one study, researcher Christine Pappas (1991a, 1991b) read three information books aloud to kindergarten children three times each. After each reading, she asked the children to "pretend to read" or read in "their own way" the same information book. Pappas found that children's pretend readings increasingly reflected language features of information books. (See page 150 in Chapter 6 for a list of some of those features.) The children appeared to be internalizing the language of these books.

In another study, Nell and teacher-researcher Jane Kays studied kindergarten children's ability to pretend to read an information book that they had never seen before (Duke & Kays, 1998). They first asked children to pretend to read the book early in their kindergarten year, in September, and then asked them to pretend to read it again approximately three months later, in

(See page 150 in Chapter 6 for a list of some of those features.)

> ## FOR YOUR INFORMATION...
>
> ### Try Reading a Text More than Once
>
> Just as children benefit from hearing the same storybooks read aloud again and again over time, they may also benefit from hearing some informational texts read to them repeatedly. So select some information books, or portions of information books, to read more than once. You might also ask students if there's a book or passage they would like to hear again.

December. In the meantime, Jane read aloud information books as well as storybooks to children every day. Nell and Jane found that the kindergartners' pretend readings in December showed a greater knowledge of information book language and purposes. For example, one child's pretend reading in September began:

> Tree... house... car... bell... that's the fire when the house burnt up... there he got to squirt the house because... or it's going to burn up... and that's the operator... for the house don't burn up...

She was primarily labeling and describing each picture in the text. In contrast, in December this child's pretend reading began:

> First people call... the firefighters... and then... the firefighters come... and then sometimes... operators help the firefighters... and firefighters have to learn how.... to do this stuff.

The child did less labeling and picture describing. Instead, she said more about what firefighters do, in a general and timeless way. This child, and others in the class, appeared to have learned language of information books from hearing them read aloud.

FOR YOUR INFORMATION...

Listen for Book Language

One way you might gauge children's developing knowledge of information book language is to listen to them as they pretend to read, or begin to write, informational texts. Do their productions sound like information books? What aspects of information book language do you hear? What don't you hear? (For a list containing some language features of informational text, see page 150 in Chapter 6).

Children Learn *Content* from Information Book Read Alouds

Research suggests that children not only learn language from information book read alouds, but learn content as well. In the study described above, Nell and Jane found evidence of this in children's journals. For example, after hearing the book *Potato* (Watts, 1988) read aloud, one child drew a picture of a potato plant sprouting and was able to describe the process with some detail. (See Figure 3.1.) Another child showed an understanding of the segmented structure of earthworms' bodies through a drawing in his journal; he had recently heard the book *Earthworm* (Soutter-Perrot, 1993). In another study (Moss, 1997), first-grade students were asked to retell an information book that had been read to them (Selsam, 1973). In general, these retellings were good, also suggesting that the children had acquired content knowledge from the read aloud. These studies indicate that children can learn about the world around them from listening to information books read aloud.

Figure 3.1: This kindergartner shows knowledge of how potatoes grow, after listening to the information book *Potato* (Watts, 1988).

READ ALOUD AND SHARED READING OF INFORMATIONAL TEXT: ONE TEACHER'S APPROACH

When we visited Mary Ellen Moffitt, she was in her third year of teaching and working toward a master's degree in education. Her first-grade class was made up of 25 students from a variety of ethnic backgrounds. Some were English language learners. Most were of low-socioeconomic status.

Mary Ellen does read aloud or shared reading once or twice every day in a carpeted area of the room, using one to two texts per session. Late afternoon is her favorite time to carry out this activity, because it engages students at a point in the day when they often have trouble focusing. She chooses materials based on a variety of goals: to connect to a particular theme or unit in the class, to teach a particular strategy or concept, or to capitalize on children's interests. In some cases, she meets multiple purposes with a single text. For example, when the class was studying insects, she noticed a fascination with spiders among many students. So she selected an information book on spiders for read aloud, and also used the book to do some work she had been planning on the *sp-* blend.

The most notable characteristic of Mary Ellen's read aloud and shared reading—of both informational texts and other genres—is a great deal of talk about the text. As Mary Ellen reads, she regularly stops to ask questions, make comments, and lead discussion related to the text. Following her lead, children also frequently ask questions, offer comments, and engage in discussion during read aloud and shared reading. Consider this excerpt from Mary Ellen's shared reading of the informational Big Book *From Sand to Glass* (Ellis, 1995a), a reading which is based on eight pages, containing only seven sentences and eight photos. We call this a shared reading because the children could see the text and many of them read along silently or subvocally. Some even chimed in with their ideas about what the text says. Moreover, because the book is a photo-essay, according to the author, much of the content is conveyed through images that the children can "read."

MARY ELLEN: [Reads the text:] "As the glassmaker works, the glass may get wider and wider..."

STUDENT: ...until it's flat

MARY ELLEN: [Continues reading the text:] "...or narrower at one end!" [Says to the students:] Or it may get narrower and narrower. What does *narrower* mean?

STUDENTS: [Several respond. The most audible one says:] It means getting smaller on top. [From there, many talk at once about the photograph of a bowl with a narrow top.]

MARY ELLEN: [Continues to read the text:] "Different sizes and shapes. Glass can be just about anything you want. It can be a bowl or slim flower vase gleaming in the light of the glassmaker's furnace."...What's a furnace? Think about it. You've got a furnace at home.

STUDENTS: I know, I know!

STUDENT: An oven!

STUDENT: A big metal thing and when you turn it on heat comes out of it and it keeps you warm.

MARY ELLEN: That's right. A furnace is what heats up your house and a glassmaker's furnace heats up glass....[Continues reading the text:] "It can be a stained-glass window..." What do you think that is? [Points to a picture in the book.]

STUDENTS: A church.

MARY ELLEN: [Continues reading the text:] "...or a pair of eyeglasses to help you see."
[Pauses.] Shelby has eyeglasses. I have eyeglasses. Autumn has sunglasses.

STUDENT: My dad and sister have eyeglasses.

MARY ELLEN: [Notices much movement and discussion among the students.] Shhh!

MARY ELLEN: [Continues reading the text:] "It can even be piled up, crushed, and melted
down—to use all over again." How many of you have a recycling bin at home?

STUDENTS: [Many raise their hands.]

MARY ELLEN: What are some things that we recycle? Paper, plastic, glass. [Students offer suggestions as well.] That's because if you take the glass back to a glassmaking factory...

STUDENT: How come they want to recycle it?

MARY ELLEN: So they won't have to go out and get all that sand again.

STUDENT: That would be a big pile of glass.

MARY ELLEN: That's right, and do you want a big pile of glass sitting around?

STUDENTS: Nooooo!

STUDENT: You wouldn't want to jump in it.

MARY ELLEN: It's better if you recycle.

STUDENT: It would be better if it were a pile of sand to jump in, but not glass.

MARY ELLEN: So recycling saves our natural resources and glass is one of those things that
can be recycled.

STUDENT: What if we took all of the sand and you won't have anymore?

MARY ELLEN: There is a lot of sand around. [Pauses and turns to the final page, which contains the words "It's glass!" and a photograph of a piece of glass being shaped.] What do
you all think this is going to be?

STUDENT: Glass.

STUDENT: A bowl.

MARY ELLEN: It looks like it could be a bowl.

STUDENT: Or a bell.

STUDENTS: [Many talk at once, apparently about what they think the glass piece might be
and why.]

MARY ELLEN: I like the way Keisha is raising her hand. Keisha…

KEISHA: [Offers an inaudible response, perhaps about a personal experience connected to glass.]

MARY ELLEN: [Closes the book.] Think about things you need to make glass.

STUDENTS: [Many raise their hands.]

MARY ELLEN: Maria.

MARIA: Sand.

MARY ELLEN: Right. What are some things we have to do to the sand?

STUDENTS: [Many talk at once. The most audible student says:] Melt.

MARY ELLEN: And you need a furnace or something hot and you need someone who knows how to do it. How many of you want to grow up and make glass?

STUDENTS: [Many call out.] Me!

MARY ELLEN: All right, are you ready? Let's think of some things around us that are glass. Sheila.

SHEILA: Window.

MARY ELLEN: Good. What else? Michael?

MICHAEL: TV.

MARY ELLEN: Right, not the whole TV, just the screen. Good. On my desk I have some glass. I have glass jars.

STUDENTS: [Many respond.] I know, I know.

STUDENT: I know, the camera lens.

MARY ELLEN: What else?

STUDENT: Our door.

MARY ELLEN: Good. Our door has a window in it. What else?

STUDENT: A magnifying glass.

MARY ELLEN: Good. What do magnifying glasses help us do?

STUDENT: They help us see little things.

STUDENT: The goldfish bowl.

STUDENT: No, that's plastic.

MARY ELLEN: That's right. I was going to show you that the goldfish bowl is plastic because you can kind-of bend it. Does glass bend?

STUDENT: No or else you will break it.

STUDENTS: [Many talk at once, some about similarities between glass and plastic, and others about breaking glass.]

MARY ELLEN: Right. They are kind-of alike. You can see through them.

STUDENT: You can put things in it. [Student repeats that statement multiple times.]

MARY ELLEN: So glass and plastic have some parts that are similar. One other thing, when we go back to our seats I want you to write in your journals about glass.

What We Can Learn from Mary Ellen's Approach to Read Alouds and Shared Readings

Mary Ellen's read alouds and shared readings reflect many strengths, such as those described below.

The interactive nature of the reading. There is a great deal of interaction between the teacher and students about the text, and among the students themselves, too. Interactive read alouds of informational text have been conducted by excellent classroom teachers (e.g., Oyler & Barry, 1996) and recommended by researchers because they are thought to increase comprehension and promote active reading (e.g., Smolkin & Donovan, 2002).

The inclusion of lower- and higher-level questions. Mary Ellen takes care to ask a number of questions for which the answer is not simple or obvious in the text (and in some cases, for which there is no one right answer). In the excerpt above, some questions for which the answer is not necessarily "right there" in the text include:

◆ What does narrower mean?

◆ What's a furnace?

◆ What are some things that we recycle?

◆ All right, are you ready? Let's think of some things around us that are glass.

◆ Does glass bend?

Teacher questioning in general has been shown to improve children's comprehension; asking many higher-level questions such as those above encourages children to process text at a higher level. (See Duke & Pearson, 2002 for a review.) Teachers who are particularly successful developing low-SES children's literacy ask more higher-level questions than teachers who are less successful (Taylor, Pearson, Peterson, & Rodriguez, 2002).

The emphasis on making connections. Mary Ellen tries to help her students make many connections. To use Debbie Miller's terminology (as reported in Ellin Oliver Keene and Susan Zimmerman's [1997] book *Mosaic of Thought*), these include text-to-text connections, text-to-self connections, and text-to-world connections.

◆ **Text-to-text connections:** Children make connections between the text they are reading or hearing and other texts they have read or heard in the past. For example, when reading *From Sand to Glass,* they might make text-to-text connections with books of a similar structure (e.g., Berger's [1993] *Make Mine Ice Cream),* with books from the same author (e.g., Ellis's [1995b] *From Tree to Paper),* or books with related content.

◆ **Text-to-self connections:** Children make connections between the text and their own experiences. For example, in the *From Sand to Glass* reading Mary Ellen encouraged text-to-self connections when inquiring about children's familiarity with recycling, and when highlighting one student's report that she had actually seen the glassmaking process (earlier in the reading; not transcribed here).

◆ **Text-to-world connections:** Children make connections between the text and the world around them, such as when Mary Ellen suggests to them, "Let's think of some things that are glass."

As will become clearer in the next section of this chapter, research supports helping children make connections during reading, because this is what readers do when they read and because it is often necessary for comprehension.

The attention to challenging aspects of informational text. Mary Ellen's read alouds and shared readings include considerable discussion of technical vocabulary, an aspect of informational text that can be particularly challenging. In the *From Sand to Glass* discussion, for example, the class explored the words *furnace* and *narrower.* Mary Ellen also uses read alouds and shared readings as occasions to encourage application of informational text strategies (such as by ending readings with a discussion regarding the question "What did you learn?") and of features (such as an index or headings).

Mary Ellen provides and promotes a range of valuable talk during her read alouds and shared readings. And the interactive and informative nature of these readings capture and hold her students' attention much of the time. Indeed, Mary Ellen's classroom provides strong testimony for the value of information-book read aloud.

TIPS FOR SELECTING INFORMATIONAL TEXT FOR READ ALOUD AND SHARED READING

General factors to consider when selecting informational texts can be found in Chapter 2. Below, we offer suggestions for selecting informational texts for read aloud and shared reading in particular.

Choose texts that are a bit too challenging for students to read independently. As with any type of text for read aloud or shared reading, it is important to read informational material that is too difficult for children to read by themselves. Select books with language, concepts, and other features that are a bit challenging (though, of course, not overly challenging). As a rule of thumb, introduce texts that children will handle on their own sometime in the not-too-near, but not-too-distant future. For shared reading in particular, be sure to invite children to read along and chime in at points.

Choose only sections of texts sometimes. It is important to remember that informational texts need not be read in their entirety. You can select bits and pieces that are of particular interest and/or of particular relevance to a current topic of study. Be sure to show students how you located the particular excerpt you read. This can provide a context to explain features (such as the index and headings) and strategies (such as skimming and scanning) for navigating informational text. See Figure 3.2 for an example of a text you might use.

For shared reading, choose texts large enough for all students to see. Ensuring that all children can see the illustrations, photographs, and other graphics can be a challenge. Big Books are very helpful, resulting in less competition among children to sit closest to you and allowing more students to read along with you. Mary Ellen found a big difference in shared reading when she read Big Book texts. There are now a few informational Big Books available online

Figure 3.2: *Going to School* by Philip Steele has many different intermingled pieces of text and illustrations. It is wise to enlarge texts like these for discussion.

and at some bookstores. Several educational publishers also offer Big Book versions of certain information books. (See list of publishers' Web sites on pages 83–84 in Chapter 4.) Some teachers put portions of text on overhead transparencies, which may be particularly helpful for texts with a high density of illustrations and text on a page.

Choose all kinds of texts. Books are not the only source of informational text appropriate for read aloud and shared reading. Magazines and newspapers for adults and children, Web material, pamphlets, and other forms of text may also be valuable. (See Chapter 8 for more about non-book informational texts.)

Letting students know why you selected a particular text may increase their engagement with the text and teach them about the process of book selection. Good reasons might include:

◆ The text was recommended to you by someone.

◆ The text has won an award or honor.

◆ The text relates to the current topic of study.

◆ The text is on a topic of interest to a particular student or group of students in the class.

◆ The text addresses a question that came up recently in class.

◆ The text is by a favorite author, a favorite series, or on a topic that you or your students like.

◆ You think the text interesting!

FOR YOUR INFORMATION...

Invite in Guest Readers

Guest readers of information books provide a good change of pace. Invite readers who are experts on the topic, such as a firefighter to read *Fire Fighters* (Maass, 1989), a postal worker to read *The Post Office Book: Mail and How It Moves* (Gibbons, 1982), or a local artist to read *Portraits* (Delafosse, 1993). That way, the guest readers can also tell students about their own experiences and answer questions.

THREE INSTRUCTIONAL STRATEGIES FOR READ ALOUD AND SHARED READING

This section presents three research-tested instructional strategies that can be used with informational-text read aloud or shared reading. The first two—Experience-Text-Relationship and Instructional Conversations—are ways to structure discussions before, after, and, to some extent, during informational-text read aloud and shared reading. The third, Think Aloud, is a way to make internal processes visible during the reading.

Experience–Text–Relationship

Discussion is an important instructional part of informational-text read aloud and shared reading. In many cases, as in Mary Ellen's, the discussion is not guided by any predetermined structure, but rather by the teacher's judgment, the students' contributions, and the features and content of the text itself. In other cases, however, it may be helpful to have a predetermined structure. One structure that is useful is the E - T - R, or Experience-Text-Relationship, approach (Tharp, 1982). In this approach, the teacher first leads children in a discussion of their experiences related to the text to be read. Next, the teacher focuses children on the *text* by reading it aloud and questioning or commenting on portions of it related to experiences discussed. Finally, the teacher leads children to discuss relationships between the text and their experiences.

> ### Sample Questions for an E - T - R Lesson Based on *The Mystery of Magnets* (Berger, 1995)
>
> **Experience:** How many of you have ever played with a magnet, like on your refrigerator door? What did you notice about magnets?
>
> **Text:** What are some of the things the book has said so far about magnets? What are some of the different kinds of magnets in the book?
>
> **Relationship:** Which things that you noticed about magnets were also talked about in the book? What are some uses of magnets that we didn't think of?

This approach is consistent with research on the value of activating relevant background knowledge when reading. (See Duke & Pearson 2002 for a review.) To our knowledge the E-T-R structure has been used mainly with narrative texts; however, we believe it can be effective with informational texts as well. With informational text, the approach might be especially useful when children are led to relate hands-on experiences, such as the one described in the box below, with text experiences.

Sample E-T-R Lesson Based on *Rain and Hail* (Branley, 1983)

Experience: Children are asked to leave equal amounts of water in uncovered trays of various sizes on a table over the weekend. On Monday, they find that there is much less water, in some cases no water, left in the trays, depending on the tray size. They discuss and record their findings. The teacher encourages students to think of any similar things that might have happened to them in the past, such as with backyard baby pools, laundry on clotheslines, or water left boiling too long.

Text: The teacher reads *Rain and Hail,* using questions and comments to emphasize the section of text dealing with evaporation.

Relationship: The teacher leads a discussion of ways in which the concept of evaporation may help explain what happened with the trays of water and other experiences the children raised. During the discussion the children realize that the specific question of why different amounts of water evaporated from different-sized trays is not really addressed in the book, so they seek out other resources for explaining that phenomenon.

Instructional Conversations

A group of southern California researchers and elementary-school teachers developed a set of guidelines for text discussions called "Instructional Conversations" (Goldenberg, 1992/1993). Instructional Conversations, or ICs, are discussion-based lessons intended to encourage higher-level thinking and learning. They are designed to develop language and concept knowledge. Guidelines for ICs are as follows:

1. **Choose a theme.** Select a theme or idea to serve as a starting point for focusing the discussion and have a general plan for how the theme will unfold, including how to "chunk" the text to permit optimal exploration of the theme.

2. **Activate the use of background knowledge and relevant schemata.** Either "hook into" or provide students with pertinent background knowledge and relevant schemata necessary for understanding a text. Then weave background knowledge and schemata into the discussion that follows.

3. **Use direct teaching.** When necessary, provide direct teaching of a skill or concept.

4. **Promote more complex language and expression.** Elicit extended student contributions by using a variety of elicitation techniques: invitations to expand ("Tell me more about that."), questions ("What do you mean?"), restatements ("In other words…"), and pauses.

5. **Elicit bases for statements or positions.** Promote students' use of text, pictures, and reasoning to support an argument or position. Without overwhelming students, probe for the bases of students' statements (for example, "How do you know?" "What makes you think that?" "Show us where it says…")

6. **Use fewer "known-answer" questions.** Much of the discussion should center on questions and answers for which there might be more than one correct answer.

7. **Be responsive to student contributions.** Have an initial plan and maintain the focus and coherence of the discussion, but be responsive to students' statements and the opportunities these provide.

8. **Encourage connected discourse.** The discussion should be characterized by multiple, interactive, connected turns; succeeding utterances should build upon and extend previous ones.

9. **Create a challenging but nonthreatening atmosphere.** Create a "zone of proximal development," and balance a challenging atmosphere with a positive affective climate. Act more as a collaborator than an evaluator to create an atmosphere that challenges students and allows them to negotiate and construct meaning from text.

10. **Promote general participation, including self-selected turns.** Encourage general participation among students. Do not hold the exclusive right to determine who talks, but encourage students to volunteer or otherwise influence the selection of speaking turns.

Carrying out ICs may be difficult at first, but it gets easier with practice. And, when it comes to student learning, the payoff is grand. To become more comfortable with the strategy, some teachers in Los Angeles met weekly to discuss, plan, and evaluate one another's ICs. They even watched videotapes of themselves leading ICs and evaluated their quality.

Researchers have found that fourth- and fifth-grade students—both those with limited English proficiency as well as those fluent in English—who engaged in Instructional Conversations as part of a literature unit developed better factual and interpretive comprehension skills than those who did not (Saunders & Goldenberg, 1999). Although there have been no formal studies of earlier grades, we have good reason to believe that ICs using informational text are also beneficial to younger children.

Planning an Instructional Conversation: An Example Based on *On the Go* (Morris, 1990)

◆ **Select a Text.** We knew a rich conversation would be more likely to occur if we chose a rich text, so we began by looking for a high-quality informational text using guidelines including those listed in Chapter 2. We also considered the context of the classroom in which we would be working. We wanted to select a book that would not be too challenging for the students, who had very little previous experience with informational texts in school, and that would connect to their upcoming social studies unit. After some thought, we decided to use the book *On the Go* by Ann Morris (Morris, 1990).

◆ **Choose and Articulate a Theme.** We chose and made ourselves articulate a theme on which to focus the Instructional Conversation, at least in the beginning. We chose a theme about cultural universals: "Some things are the same for all different groups of people around the world. One thing that is the same is that people all over the world have ways to move from place to place."

◆ **Anticipate Difficulties.** We read and looked through the book carefully thinking about things that might be difficult for the students. We found places where they could possibly bring to bear their background knowledge, such as on a page showing a bicycle. We also looked for places where we might need to help build relevant background knowledge, such as where

Think Aloud

Think Aloud essentially involves saying aloud or articulating some of your thoughts as you read. Doing this gives children a window into otherwise invisible processes. Children get to hear what they cannot see: what goes on in the mind of a good reader when she or he reads.

Think Aloud is a part of many approaches to comprehension instruction that have been shown to be effective, such as transactional strategies instruction discussed in Chapter 4. (See Duke & Pearson, 2002, for a review of research.) When students are water-based modes of moving from place to place are pictured. We also thought about how to get the conversation started, which is often the most difficult part of an IC. We decided that two questions—"What are some ways people move around from place to place?" and "What do you think the author is trying to tell us in this book?"—would be good conversation starters.

◆ **Anticipate Conversation Content.** We thought about the kinds of things students might say during the discussion, and things we might say to help move the conversation along. For example, we anticipated that the children might want to discuss other activities, beyond those related to transportation, that people all over the world do. This would lead in nicely to some follow-up work.

◆ **Follow Up.** We thought about different ways we might follow up the IC, especially about activities that would help us find out what children took away from it. One possibility was bringing in several more books by Ann Morris and other authors about other cultural universals and having children listen to and discuss them in small groups. This would both further the children's learning and, we hoped, make it more manageable for us to examine each child's contributions and understandings. Another possibility we considered was suggesting that children write their own books in the style of *On the Go*. What children incorporated into their own writings (for example, if they focused on things that are the same across many cultures) would be very telling.

urged to think aloud to themselves, their comprehension improves. (See Kucan & Beck, 1997, for a review of research.) The strategy has been used with many genres, including informational texts, but most published examples are with narratives and with older children. (See Jeffrey Wilhelm's *Improving Comprehension With Think-Aloud Strategies,* 2001.) Below is an example of one teacher's Think Aloud which might occur with third graders gathered on the rug, mainly listening rather than contributing. However, Think Aloud is a flexible technique that can be used in any primary grade, with any size group, and with varying degrees of student interaction.

What Good Readers Do When They Read

Researchers have used Think Aloud as a way of studying what good readers do when they read (Pressley & Afflerbach, 1995). They have found that good readers:

◆ have clear purposes for their reading and constantly evaluate whether they are achieving those purposes.

◆ often read selectively, continually making decisions about their reading—what to read carefully, what to read quickly, what not to read, what to reread, and so on—based on their goals.

◆ use their prior knowledge to construct meaning from/with the text.

◆ think ahead to what might come next in the text.

◆ monitor their understanding of the text, making adjustments in their reading or thinking as needed.

◆ try to fill in gaps or inconsistencies in a text so that the text makes sense. If they encounter unfamiliar words or concepts, they try to figure them out.

◆ ask themselves questions as they read.

◆ think about the authors of the text—their perspective, agenda, qualifications, and so on.

◆ respond to text in many different ways, both intellectually and emotionally.

◆ read different kinds of text differently.

◆ think about the text not only before and during reading, but also after reading. Often, good readers apply what they learned from the text in appropriate situations later on.

◆ draw inferences.

When reading informational text, good readers also:

◆ construct summaries of what they are reading.

◆ pay attention to the organization or structure of the text, both overall and for particular sections and concepts.

Adapted from Duke & Pearson, 2002

Thinking Aloud About an Article

Following is a transcript of Nell Duke's Think Aloud, which was based on the article "Put on a Happy Face!" in the "Health Beat" section of *National Geographic for Kids*. (See Figure 3.3.) The article discusses a study suggesting that thinking positive thoughts may help people live longer.

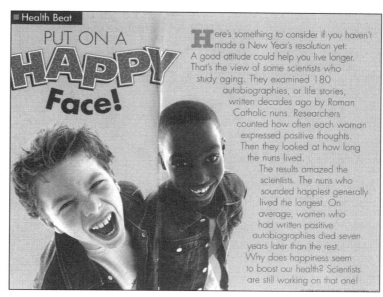

■ Health Beat

PUT ON A HAPPY Face!

Here's something to consider if you haven't made a New Year's resolution yet: A good attitude could help you live longer. That's the view of some scientists who study aging. They examined 180 autobiographies, or life stories, written decades ago by Roman Catholic nuns. Researchers counted how often each woman expressed positive thoughts. Then they looked at how long the nuns lived.

The results amazed the scientists. The nuns who sounded happiest generally lived the longest. On average, women who had written positive autobiographies died seven years later than the rest. Why does happiness seem to boost our health? Scientists are still working on that one!

Figure 3.3: The short article Nell used for her Think Aloud.

NELL: [Opens the magazine and shows the article.] I only have a minute.... This piece down here is short and it looks interesting. The title—"Put on a Happy Face!"—and the two smiling kids makes me think that it has something to do with smiling. But the section it's in is called "Health Beat." What does smiling have to do with health? Maybe smiling is good for your health or something like that. [With that, she begins reading the text aloud.]

TEXT: "Here's something to consider if you haven't made a New Year's resolution yet."

NELL: A resolution... I know that's something you promise yourself you're going to do in the new year, like exercise more or eat less junk food. Actually I really haven't made one this year. I haven't made one for a few years. I guess they're going to suggest one.

TEXT: "A good attitude could help you live longer."

NELL: I wonder what they mean by a good attitude?

TEXT: "That's the view of some scientists who study aging. They examined 180 autobiographies, or life stories, written decades ago..."

NELL: I need to do some quick translating... a decade is ten years so decades ago would be like twenty or thirty or more years ago.

TEXT: "…by Roman Catholic nuns. Researchers counted how often each woman expressed positive thoughts."

NELL: So I guess they think a positive attitude is just having positive thoughts. I think that would probably be thoughts like, "It's a nice day outside" or "I enjoyed that."

TEXT: "Then they looked at how long the nuns lived."

NELL: I figure they were seeing if the ones who had more positive thoughts lived longer than the other ones.

TEXT: "The results amazed the scientists. The nuns who sounded happiest generally lived the longest."

NELL: Being happy is good for your health! I wonder how much longer the more positive nuns lived.

TEXT: "On average, women who had written positive autobiographies died seven years later than the rest."

NELL: This time the text answered my question right away. Seven years—that's a lot! So nuns who had more positive thoughts lived an average of seven years longer that the others!

TEXT: "Why does happiness seem to boost our health? Scientists are still working on that one!"

NELL: Huh, I guess there are scientists whose job is to study why being happy makes you more healthy. That's an unusual job! I have some ideas of my own. Maybe when you are happy your heart doesn't have to work as hard, so it can last longer. I know a lot of people have heart problems. Maybe we need to work on being happier!

Nell didn't focus on only one reading strategy but instead incorporated several strategies and moves into her Think Aloud, such as asking oneself questions as one reads and drawing inferences.

Thinking Aloud About a Graph

In the next example, Nell's Think Aloud focuses on a somewhat narrower set of strategies, having to do with reading graphs. She bases her Think Aloud on "Pumpkin Powerhouses" in *National Geographic for Kids*.

NELL: I'm going to take a look at this month's "Geo Graph". (See Figure 3.4.) I love the "Geo Graph" section of the magazine. I try never to miss it. I see it's a pumpkin. That's neat, it fits with Halloween.

NELL: [Points to the graph's title.] Let's see, the title is "Pumpkin Powerhouses/Which states grow the most pumpkins?" That tells me the graph is going to show which states grow the most pumpkins. So the names of the states listed on the graph must be the ones that grow the most pumpkins: Illinois, California, New York, Pennsylvania, Michigan. I notice they're mostly northern states. I'm surprised I don't see Florida, Georgia, and other warmer states. I guess pumpkins need it to be cold part of the year.

Figure 3.4: The graph Nell used for her Think Aloud.

NELL: Okay, now how many pumpkins do these states grow?… Well, I can tell that this is a bar graph, even though instead of regular bars it has pumpkin teeth for bars! Each state name goes with one tooth or bar and there's a number on each tooth. The number must tell how many pumpkins. So Illinois has 364 pumpkins, California has 180 pumpkins…. Wait a minute! That doesn't really make sense. I'm sure they would grow more than 180 pumpkins in the whole state of California! Plus, even all together this isn't that many pumpkins when we would need millions of pumpkins for all the families that want one to have one!…

NELL: [Pauses and scans the graph.] Oh, look at the bottom of the graph, the label is "millions of pounds" so it's not just 364 pumpkins, it's 364 million pumpkins… no, 364 million *pounds* of pumpkins. But I don't know how many pounds most pumpkins weigh. So to really understand how many pumpkins, I'd have to find that out and then do the math to figure out how many pumpkins that comes out to. I don't think that's worth it. This graph isn't telling me exactly what I wanted to know.

NELL: [Pauses and studies each bar.] I guess the graph does tell me who has the most pumpkins anyway… Illinois. It has the highest bar and of course the highest number too. Illinois could be called The Pumpkin State!

NELL: [Points to the source.] Before I finish I'd better check my source since I'm always telling you to check your sources! It says, "The U.S. Department of Agriculture provided these figures for 2000." That makes sense… Agriculture has to do with things that farmers grow and pumpkins are one thing farmers grow, and the U.S. government can collect information from all the different states. The figures are from 2000, already one year old, but I guess they wouldn't have them for 2001 yet. Okay, I checked my source, now I'm done.

Ultimately, the number and range of strategies and other components of your Think Aloud will depend on your goals for teaching comprehension and comprehension strategies— what you want to communicate and reinforce. Although Think Alouds are certainly not a replacement for explicit teaching of comprehension strategies, they are a good complement to that. (See Chapter 4 for a discussion of explicit teaching of comprehension strategies.) You can be confident that Think Aloud is part of the repertoire of many successful comprehension teachers.

Some Prompts for Think Aloud

Monitoring and adjusting comprehension
- That does/doesn't make sense to me because…
- I didn't understand that last part, I'd better go back…
- I still don't understand what that means, I'm going to try…

Activating relevant prior knowledge
- I know some things about…
- That reminds me of…
- That's fits/doesn't fit with what I know about…

Generating questions and responses
- I wonder…
- I notice…
- It's interesting/frustrating/exciting/etc. that…

Attending to and uncovering text structure
- I think this is organized by…
- This section talked all about… so I think this next section will talk about…
- Looking at these headings/titles/graphics/etc., I see that…

Summarizing
- So far I've read that…
- I think the main points of this are…
- This was about…

Eight Great Information Books for Read Aloud and Shared Reading

Wonderful Worms by **Linda Glaser.** Especially appropriate for kindergarten and first grade, this book describes earthworms and their behavior, including how they contribute to soil. The end of the book includes two pages for adults with questions young children might ask about earthworms and answers to these questions. The book was selected by the National Science Teachers Association (NSTA) and the Children's Book Council as an outstanding science trade book for children. It can be read in one sitting.

The Spice Alphabet Book: Herbs, Spices, and Other Natural Flavors by **Jerry Pallotta.** Especially appropriate for second and third grade, this book gives interesting facts about a range of different spices—one for each letter of the alphabet. The illustrations are especially wonderful and artist's notes for each are included. Pallotta is well known for his numerous informational alphabet books. This, like many of them, is probably best read in pieces rather than in one sitting. For example, a class might encounter a "spice a day" through the book and taste tests.

Why I Sneeze, Shiver, Hiccup, and Yawn by **Melvin Berger.** We have yet to encounter a child of any age who is not interested in the answer to these questions, though Berger's explanations would probably work best with children in grade one or higher, and in a unit on the human body. The book is rich in material to examine authors' craft. For example, there is the use of scenario-setting to create interest and context ("You are playing hide-and-seek. You've found a good hiding place [in what appears from the illustration in the book to be a dusty old attic]. You want to be as quiet as you can. All of a sudden—*ka-choo!* You sneeze. Everyone knows where you are.") Berger himself has written hundreds of children's informational texts and therefore might be a good subject of an author study. (See Chapter 6 for other ideas of authors for author studies.)

Let's Find Out About Ice Cream by **Mary Ebeltoft Reid.** The process of making ice cream—from ingredients to mixing to packaging to delivery—is explained simply in this book, which is probably most appropriate for kindergarten or first grade. The photographs, mostly taken at the Ben and Jerry's® factory in Waterbury, Vermont, are quite illustrative and many features of informational text that tells about a process are well represented. This book probably won't link meaningfully to a content area, but it will certainly connect to children's interests!

Plants that Never Ever Bloom by **Ruth Heller.** Ruth Heller is another good subject for an author study. As with several of her books, this one is informational-poetic ("A MUSH-ROOM doesn't ever bloom. It grows on trees and leaves and things…or in the grass in fairy rings.") The book can be understood at many levels and therefore is, in our view, appropriate for read aloud from kindergarten to third grade. We especially like to point out to students one of Heller's acknowledgments in the front material for the book, in which she thanks an expert, noting his degree and positions, presumably for some contribution to the content and accuracy of the book.

Why Are Pineapples Prickly? Questions Children Ask About Food by **Christopher Maynard.** The content in this book is "all over the place" in terms of topic, so it would probably not lend itself to a particular unit in science or even health. Reading parts of it could work for some units, though, such as reading the section "Why is fruit good for me?" for a unit on health and nutrition. For general interest, the book is surely worth reading in its entirety. Explanations are brief but pack a punch, and raise questions or spark interest for further investigation. The question-and-answer information-book format is one many children like to use in their own writing.

The Life and Times of the Honeybee by **Charles Micucci.** Chosen as the NSTA-CBC Outstanding Science Trade Book for Children in 1996, this book is a real treasure in the arena of children's information books. It is probably not one to read all at once, but rather in pieces like a chapter book. (In fact, why not take a break from reading chapter books aloud and spend a couple of weeks on this one instead?) It fits very nicely in a unit on life cycles, in some interdisciplinary units, or as general interest reading (though it would be challenging for early primary-grade students).

Everyday Mysteries **by Jerome Wexler.** The photographs in this book are nothing short of dazzling and the text—if you can tear yourself away from the photographs to read it—is also fascinating. The basic idea is that when we view things up close, we see them differently. So the photographs depict everyday objects, such as a sponge or a strawberry, up very close, and the text explains both the overall idea (that when we view things up close, we see them differently) and specific concepts such as cross section and silhouette. The book links nicely to topics in art or science, and is probably most appropriate for grade two and above.

CONCLUDING THOUGHTS

Research suggests that young children learn language and content from hearing information books read aloud to them. Talk during informational read aloud and shared reading is especially important. Talk can be guided solely by the text, teacher, and student contributions, or it can have particular structures, including E - T - R, Instructional Conversations, or Think Aloud. There are many excellent information books for reading aloud to even young children. Of course, as children grow, they begin to be able to read books themselves. In the next chapter, we show you ways to guide children's reading of informational text.

CHAPTER 4
Guided Reading
Scaffolding Reading Development With Informational Text

BY CAROL ROSEN

"**T**his is awesome!" "Oh, I know, I know!!" "Oh, cool…!!!" Believe it or not, these are not the words of children playing on the playground, watching a movie, or enjoying a field trip. They are words we've heard from first graders engaged with informational text during guided reading sessions. Using informational text in guided reading gives primary-grade students opportunities to learn about their natural and social worlds. It also provides opportunities for them to explore worlds beyond their own. Indeed, through guided reading of informational texts, children can learn about people, places, and things they may never have an opportunity to experience firsthand. It also provides a platform for building word-level and comprehension skills. In this chapter, we:

◆ briefly discuss research on informational text guided reading.

◆ describe how one teacher carried out guided reading with informational text.

◆ give some ideas for grouping children for guided reading of informational text.

◆ identify three research-based instructional strategies for use in guided reading of informational text.

By the end of the chapter, we hope that you will feel confident about implementing informational text guided reading in your classroom or, if you already practice it, that you will discover ways to enhance your program.

GUIDED READING OF INFORMATIONAL TEXT IN THE PRIMARY GRADES: WHAT THE RESEARCH SAYS

The term "guided reading" has been used a great deal in recent years, and not always in the same way. We define it as a context in which the child is the primary reader and the teacher is the coach or supporter of the reading. It occurs most frequently in small groups, but sometimes takes place one-on-one or as a whole class. The child may read aloud (often called "guided oral reading") or subvocally or silently. The teacher is nearby, guiding the reading by talking with the child before, after, and—in some cases—during the reading.

Studies indicate that especially effective teachers of reading provide a great deal of coaching, as well as direct instruction, often in small-group contexts (Taylor, Pearson, Clark, & Walpole, 2000; Pressley, Wharton-McDonald, Allington, Block, Morrow, Tracey, et al., 2001). This suggests that guided reading is an important component of primary-grade literacy instruction. Guided reading is an effective context for teaching comprehension strategies. Guided oral reading in particular helps children to apply their developing phonics and word recognition knowledge, and has been shown to improve reading fluency (National Reading Panel, 2000).

Unfortunately, few researchers have examined guided reading of informational texts specifically, and those who have haven't investigated its use in primary-grade contexts. We do not have studies, for example, on how young children's reading development is affected by opportunities (or a lack of opportunities) to engage in guided reading of informational texts. We have little documented evidence about which strategies for guided reading of informational text are most effective with young children.

That said, in the final section of this chapter, we describe three instructional strategies that are based on research: Reciprocal Teaching, which has been studied with children as young as first grade; Collaborative Strategic Reading, which has been studied in middle elementary school and beyond; and Idea Circles, which have been studied in grades 3 through 5. All three approaches use informational text primarily, although not exclusively.

GUIDED READING OF INFORMATIONAL TEXT: ONE TEACHER'S APPROACH

Research on reading has repeatedly supported the importance of teaching comprehension strategies (e.g., Dole, Duffy, Roehler, & Pearson, 1991). Strategy instruction is especially beneficial to students with learning problems, who often do not work on tasks systematically (Lipson & Wixson, 1997). It may begin in the primary grades (Pearson & Duke, 2002) and continue throughout a child's education. This section introduces you to one teacher, Carrie Preuninger, who includes considerable strategy instruction in her guided-reading program using all kinds of text.

Carrie is a veteran teacher, with over 25 years of experience, yet she has eagerly taken up the challenge of incorporating more informational text into her teaching. Her first-grade class is made up of thirty students from a variety of ethnic backgrounds. Many of the students are of low socioeconomic status. Carrie has a teaching assistant who is available to help out in the classroom while Carrie conducts guided reading.

Carrie's Daily Schedule

Carrie's daily schedule is like that of many first-grade teachers. She starts the day around eight o'clock with early-morning activities, a welcome, attendance taking, lunch count, and any necessary school business. Her day then progresses with the activities described below.

Journal Writing. Fifteen minutes of journal writing follow the morning's housekeeping tasks. Early in the school year, journal writing consists of writing to fill-in-the-blank prompts—sometimes called "cloze prompts"—for stories, poems, and informational text. For example, a prompt for informational text might be, *"A frog can _____. A frog can _____. A frog can _____ and _____ but, a frog cannot _____."* Carrie asks her students to copy the sentences and, as a class, give her some examples of words to put in the blanks. She lists these on the board and allows students to choose words from the list to complete their sentences, or to come up with their own. As the year moves on, journal prompts become more open-ended, but remain focused on stories some days, poetry other days, informational text other days, and so on. Throughout the year, Carrie stresses the importance of writing journal entries that make sense.

Social Studies. Carrie then moves on to approximately one hour of social studies instruction, usually with the whole class. She uses a great deal of read aloud, shared reading, individual shared writing, and discussion. She also assigns related activities, such as role plays and art projects. Whenever possible, she connects social studies work to other parts of the school day.

Reading. Reading instruction begins at 9:30 and lasts for approximately 90 minutes. On Mondays, Carrie introduces a theme for the week, which she reinforces through reading, writing, and other activities. (In that sense, this block is about more than reading; it's about *literacy*.) Usually the selected theme is based on a selection from the class's basal reader or on a science or social studies unit they are studying. Themes have included "Turkeys" for Thanksgiving, "People We Care About" for Sweetest Day (a holiday to honor loved ones celebrated in October), and "The Desert," inspired by the story *Listen to the Desert/Oye al desierto* (Mora, 2001).

During reading instruction on Tuesdays through Thursdays, Carrie works with guided reading groups of four to six students, while the other children engage in a variety of other reading and writing activities. The texts she chooses for guided reading sometimes relate to the week's theme, but not always.

On Fridays, which are known as "Theme Day," children participate in a variety of whole- and small-group activities related to the week's theme—not only during the reading block but throughout the day. Often these activities involve art, music, drama, cooking, or other literacy-related domains.

Other Subject Areas. Carrie devotes Monday through Thursday afternoons to writers' workshop, math, science, phonics, and spelling. Children also go to one "special" per day.

Carrie's Guided Reading Sessions

As noted earlier, Carrie's guided reading sessions include considerable strategy instruction, including comprehension strategy instruction. To highlight this point, below you will find transcripts from some of her sessions in late spring. In the left-hand margin, we identify particular strategies she is emphasizing. Of course, these are by no means the only strategies that Carrie addresses in her teaching, and, indeed, research indicates that others are also helpful for students. (See discussion later in this chapter.) However, the transcripts offer a glimpse into the strategy-focused nature of her teaching.

Checking Reading Logs

The first item of business in Carrie's guided reading sessions is checking students' reading logs, which they use to keep track of reading and vocabulary work they do at home. Each day, Carrie sends students home with personalized zip-closed bags containing their log, a list of vocabulary words, and two books used in guided reading that day (whenever possible, one narrative and one informational). She also encloses a note to parents encouraging them to review the list, read the books with their child, and write what they accomplished in the log. Since the books are familiar to children from the day's guided reading, they are much more likely be able to read them successfully, with minimal help. Carrie encourages children and their parents to take the home reading and vocabulary work seriously; by checking students' logs at the start of each guided reading session, she holds them accountable.

Previewing the Texts

Once she checks the reading logs of all children in the small group, Carrie previews the books to be read that day. Early in the year, she takes the lead. But as the year progresses, she gradually hands over responsibility for previews to the children.

A "picture walk" is one approach to previewing. When a child takes a picture walk, he or she looks through all or most of the pictures in the book to begin learning about the book—what it's about, what the child knows in relation to it, its parts, and so on. By this point in the year (spring), most of Carrie's students can do picture walks on their own. They seem to have internalized this strategy through Carrie's repeated modeling and guiding of it throughout the year. In the example below, a student takes a picture walk through two books:

STRATEGY: Previewing the text

CARRIE: What are you looking at?

STUDENT: The pictures.

CARRIE: That's good; you are doing a picture walk.

What are you seeing?…

Among the things children should observe when doing a picture walk or otherwise previewing a text is the type of text it is:

CARRIE: Now that your picture walk is done, put your two books in front of you. What kind of reading are we going to do today?

STUDENT: [Points to one book and then the other.] This one is expository and this one is narrative.

CARRIE: Give me some reasons why. You have to back that up.

STUDENT: This explains [points to the informational text] and this one is narrative [points to the narrative text].

CARRIE: Okay, what do you mean "explains"? What do you think the main idea is going to be about? What is the title?

WHOLE GROUP: *How Many?* (Nayer, 1996)

CARRIE: If it is *How Many?* what do you think the book is going to be about?

WHOLE GROUP: Numbers.

STRATEGY: Thinking about the text type and purpose

The children think about the kind of text they are going to be reading. We believe her students are able to do this successfully at this point because, from the beginning of the year, Carrie has both used a variety of texts and encouraged students to attend to text type. She has done this not only during guided reading, but throughout the school day.

Reading the Texts

After previewing the text, the group reads it. Sometimes children read collectively by taking turns or engaging in choral reading. Other times they read more independently, with Carrie alternately listening to each of them individually and coaching as needed. As a general rule, children read more independently as the year progresses. In the following example, the group is reading a book together called *Where Are the Eggs?* (Parkes, 1999):

KNOWLEDGE/ SKILL: The title page, which is important for book identification and previewing

CARRIE: Go to the title page and read it.

STUDENTS: *Where Are the Eggs?*

CARRIE: [Looks around and notices that not all children are actually on the title page.] You are on the title page. You are not, and you are not. [Directs children to the title page.] There, now you are all on the title page. What did the author do when [s]he wrote *Where Are the Eggs?* Look at the words.

STUDENT: Question.

STRATEGY: Noticing the author's craft

CARRIE: [S]he got your attention by asking a question. Put your finger on the question mark. What kind of eggs are they?

STUDENT: I know, I know!

CARRIE: (Calls on student.)

STUDENT: Robin eggs [determined from the photograph].

CARRIE: Very good. Let's read together.

KNOWLEDGE/
SKILL:
Concept of
plural, which is
related to a
feature of
informational
text—generic
nouns. (See
Chapter 6
for more
information).

WHOLE GROUP: "Some animals lay eggs. They lay eggs in many different
places."

CARRIE: [Stops the reading.] Look at me. Go to the words you just read and
find a word that means more than one.

STUDENT: "Different."

CARRIE: If I want to know if a word means more than one, what is going to be
on the end of that word?

STUDENT: I know!

STUDENT: Oh, I know. I know.

STUDENT: "Eggs."

STUDENT: "Places."

STUDENT: "Animals."

As the reading progresses, students discuss when they have seen nests, with or
without eggs. Students seem free to discuss the text, and when that discussion
reflects a comprehension strategy, Carrie sometimes comments. For example:

STRATEGY:
Activating
relevant
background
knowledge

CARRIE: Do you know what you did just now? You asked questions while you
were reading. That is good. You *should* ask questions as you read.

With Carrie's encouragement, the children also make predictions about
where each animal described will lay its eggs.

STRATEGIES:
Asking
questions
while reading;
making
predictions

STUDENT: "Where will this alligator lay her eggs?"

STUDENT: I know!

STUDENT: Oo, oo!

STUDENT: I know, I think.

STUDENT: Grass?

STUDENT: Sometimes, like (when) I lived down in Mississippi.

CARRIE: Let's read and find out if you are right. Keep it in your brain. [Students go on to scan the book silently for information on where alligators lay their eggs.]

WHOLE GROUP: Here they are. They are in a hole in the sand.

CARRIE: Were you right?

STUDENTS: [Respond individually.]

Carrie works with students on decoding as well as comprehension strategies. In this segment, she helps the whole group as it struggles with the word *does*:

CARRIE: Let's try using a strategy here. If we don't know the word let's skip it and go to the next word. Then, let's reread the sentence and try a word to see if it makes sense.

WHOLE group: "What _____ a spider look like?"

STUDENT: "What do a spider look like?"

CARRIE: Let's look at the whole word. What letters are in the word?

STUDENT: "*e, s.*"

CARRIE: Let's try that word.

WHOLE group: "What *does* a spider look like?"

CARRIE: Very good!

After this, students continue to read silently. When one student has difficulty with the word "hairy," she works through it by looking at the picture. Of course, chunking and other decoding strategies are also taught.

Responding to the Text

After students read the text, Carrie leads them in some form of response. Sometimes she facilitates a group discussion, sometimes she assigns a follow-up activity for later in the school day or at home, and at other times she asks students to write a response. She may also combine activities. In the example that follows, Carrie uses writing and discussion around the book *Day and Night* (Anton, 1999).

CARRIE: This last page is interesting… Now I want everyone to write one fact. [Passes out paper and pencils, and gives students time to write a fact. When they are finished, each student reads aloud the fact they wrote.]

STUDENT: "You do not see the sun at night."

Keep Other Students Engaged

Ensuring that other students are working independently and productively while you are
with a guided reading group is often a challenge. Giving children busy work isn't a desirable solution, but providing meaningful tasks which don't require direct teacher involvement can be difficult. Many of the activities in this book don't require direct teacher
involvement, such as Reciprocal Teaching (described later in this chapter), partner reading (described in Chapter 5), and various writing activities (described in Chapter 6).

Regardless of the activity, excellent organization and management is also key. (See
Fountas and Pinnell's *Guided Reading: Good First Teaching for All Children* and Taberski's
On Solid Ground: Strategies for Teaching Reading, K–3, for more information.) Excellent
organization and management is supported by research on exemplary teachers. For example, Michael Pressley and colleagues (2001) found that in the classrooms of the most
effective literacy teachers, 90 percent of the students were engaged over 90 percent of the
time! In Carrie's classroom, establishing classroom rules and getting students settled into a
routine is a priority from the first day of school. To let students know what they need to
do while she works with guided reading groups, Carrie draws a chart on the blackboard
with three sections showing three different tasks, such as journal writing or map work.
Carrie makes certain that students understand what each task requires and she is careful
not to introduce too many new tasks at any one time. She matches tasks to students
appropriately, ensuring that the task is neither overly difficult nor overly easy. As the year
goes on she increases the amount of time children are expected to work independently—
expectations grow as the children do. She consistently emphasizes that students should use
quiet voices and remain focused on the task. Finally, whenever she "catches 'em being
good," she praises students. For example, she might say, "You look like marshmallows.
Marshmallows can't talk and they move very quietly. I like the way Takira is working.
Good job, Jovani and Phillip. I am so proud, Danesha. You all did a nice job."

STUDENT: "When the sun rises you wake up."

STUDENT: "The stars help you know when it is night."

STUDENT: "The full moon is in the sky every night."

CARRIE: Is the full moon in the sky every night?

STUDENT: No.

CARRIE: How can we make that sentence true? You like compound words. What compound word can you put in there that will make the sentence true? Put "sometimes" in there. [Student inserts a carat symbol (^) with the word "sometimes" above it into the sentence.]

STUDENT: [A different student, prior to reading his sentence:] I got it wrong.

CARRIE: Let's see what you did right.

STUDENT: I learned that you see more and more of the moon every day.

CARRIE: That's fine. You're not wrong. That's true.

STUDENT: "Every night it gets bigger."

CARRIE: What gets bigger?

STUDENT: The moon.

CARRIE: Okay, put that in.

KNOWLEDGE/ SKILLS: Qualifiers such as *sometimes, often, many, some,* and *all* are common in informational text; as they write, students get practice using informational text language. (See Chapter 6 for more information.)

As the year goes on, discussions and writing in response to text become more elaborate and student-directed. As we stated in Chapter 3, great discussions involve complex instructional and conversational elements, including considerable student-to-student interaction.

Preparing for Later Reading

Carrie ends her guided reading sessions by putting new books and vocabulary words into children's zip-closed bags and entering them into the reading log—a simple sheet with one column for "Name of book" and another for "Date." She may also remind students of one or more strategies they have worked on and the need to apply those strategies when reading.

Ideas for Grouping for Guided Reading of Informational Text

Guided reading is normally conducted in a small-group format, and with good reason. Research suggests that more effective teachers work with small groups more often than less effective teachers do (Taylor, Pearson, Clark, & Walpole, 2000). Deciding how to group students for guided reading can be difficult. Most educators agree that grouping should be flexible (Opitz, 1998). That is, rather than placing children in the same groups for the entire year, their placement will shift depending on each child's progress, needs, strengths, and other factors. However, research has not identified any one approach to flexible grouping that is most effective. Below we describe six types of groupings that may be useful with informational text in primary classrooms. You may want to try one or more of these options or create your own.

Interest-based grouping. Children are grouped according to a common interest. For example, children interested in a particular world culture might meet to discuss informational and other texts related to that culture, those interested in a particular sport or hobby might meet to read texts related to that sport or hobby, and so on. In some cases, all children read the same text, with varying degrees of scaffolding or support from you or their classmates. In other cases it may be more effective for children to read different texts, ones that are topically related but of varying degrees of reading difficulty.

Needs-based grouping. Children are grouped by a common need, such as applying a particular comprehension strategy, learning a particular set of sound-letter relationships, acquiring vocabulary and concept knowledge related to an upcoming unit, and so on. Use ongoing assessment to determine children's needs and select texts based on their appropriateness for teaching or reinforcing the particular skill or strategy.

Level-based grouping. Grouping children at similar reading levels is perhaps the most common approach for guided reading with narrative text. This approach can also be used with informational text, although at least one caution is in order: There is reason to think, based on theory and research, that a child's reading level for informational text is more variable than for narrative texts. A child may have several different reading levels for informational text depending on how much background knowledge he or she has on the text's topic, and on his or her knowledge of the text structures and other devices (such as diagrams) in the text. For example, suppose a child knows a lot about dinosaurs, is really interested in dinosaurs, and has read several books in a series of books about dinosaurs. When trying to read a new book in that series, the child is likely to read it better than he or she can read a book on a topic that he or she doesn't know as much about, isn't interested in, and that isn't part of a familiar series. So the child's level for one book may be very different than for another. Because of this, it may be difficult to form groups that remain constant from text to text. On the bright side, this forces us to keep the groupings flexible rather than static.

FOR YOUR INFORMATION...

Think Beyond the Book

Topic-based grouping requires lots of texts on related topics, at different reading levels. Issues of access to text are discussed at length in Chapter 8, but here we want to underscore that the text for guided reading need not be a book. You can use parts of a book, a magazine or newspaper article, pamphlets, text from the Internet, text on CD-ROM, and more. From many of these sources, obtaining multiple copies of the same text may be as simple as clicking "print" on your computer screen—and they are likely to cost less than multiple-copy book sets.

Topic-based grouping. Students are grouped according to content-area topics related to in-depth study they will carry out. For example, if the class is studying mammals, each group might read about and discuss a different habitat. Children's Press publishes a series (Forman, 1997; G. Davis, 1997; Berquist & Berquist, 1997; and W. Davis, 1997) that works well for such a study. The series consists of four information books, each one about a different mammal habitat, with beautiful photographs, running text containing small information boxes, and a section at the end of each book that summarizes the habitat. (For more on topic-based grouping, see the discussion of Idea Circles on pages 96–98.)

Author's craft grouping. Groups can be formed to examine particular aspects of the author's craft. For example, a group could focus on reading and constructing diagrams using texts that contain models, such as *What's Inside? Planes* (Dorling Kindersley, 1992). A group could read information books organized in a question-and-answer format, such as *Why Are Pineapples Prickly? Questions Children Ask About Food* (Maynard, 1997). Or groups could read different books by the same author and talk about techniques the author uses across books, as well as those the author uses in single titles only. Jane Goodall, for example, has written a set of eight books that could be used for this purpose: *Elephant Family, Giraffe Family, Lion Family, Hyena Family, Wildebeest Family, Chimpanzee Family, Baboon Family,* and *Zebra Family* (Goodall, all 1991). (For ideas for authors for author studies, see Chapter 6.)

Random grouping. In some cases, the best choice is grouping students randomly with no criteria in mind. Random grouping sometimes yields pleasant surprises. For example, children who we never thought would work well together do, children with common backgrounds or interests discover one another, and so on. Try putting children's names in a basket and pulling them out one at a time. The first children chosen get put in the first group, the next batch goes into the second group, and so on. To build anticipation, wrap each set of books a group can choose from in brown paper and string, and let groups select from the stack of packages, unwrap the books, and start reading. (For each set, be sure to choose engaging books at a range of reading levels). After guided reading, each group can present what it learned to the rest of the class.

"Little Books" Series for Guided Reading

Here are some series to consider for guided reading. Although there are many nonfiction books included in this list, they may not necessarily all be information books as we define them. Nonetheless, this list provides a good starting point.

◆ *Early Childhood Connection Nonfiction,* Benchmark Education (www.benchmarkeducation.com)

◆ *Pebble Books,* Capstone Press (www.capstone-press.com)

◆ *Little Celebrations Nonfiction,* Celebration Press (www.pearsonlearning.com)

◆ *iOpeners,* Celebration Press/D. K. (www.pearsonlearning.com)

◆ *Think About Science, Think About Social Studies,* and *Think About Math,* Curriculum Associates (www.curriculumassociates.com)

◆ *Factivity,* Dominie Press (www.dominie.com)

◆ *Little Readers for Guided Reading,* Houghton Mifflin (www.houghtonmifflin.com)

◆ *Ready Readers,* Modern Curriculum Press (www.pearsonlearning.com)

◆ *BookShop* (certain theme and genre packs), Mondo Publishing (www.mondopub.com)

◆ *Windows on Literacy,* National Geographic (www.nationalgeographic.com)

◆ *Discovery Links Science* and *Discovery Links Social Studies,* Newbridge (www.newbridgeonline.com)

continued on next page

- *Discovery World* and *PM Nonfiction*, Rigby (www.rigby.com)

- *Content Area Readers*, Sadlier-Oxford (www.sadlier-oxford.com)

- *Science Emergent Readers* and *Social Studies Emergent Readers* and *Guided Reading Program Blue (Nonfiction) Edition*, Scholastic (www.scholastic.com)

- *Storyteller Nonfiction*, Shortland Publications (www.wrightgroup.com)

- *Pair-It Books*, Steck-Vaughn (www.steck-vaughn.com)

- *Little Green Readers*, Sundance (www. sundancepub.com)

- *Twig Books Nonfiction* and *Wonder World*, The Wright Group (www.wrightgroup.com)

This list is not intended to be exhaustive. A series' inclusion or exclusion is not intended to reflect our judgment of the series' quality.

It is important to remember that not all texts for guided reading must come from series. There are many high-quality information trade books that can be used, even for our most emergent readers. We have cited some throughout this book. See the box entitled "Have Students Read Board Books to Little Ones" on page 112 in Chapter 5.

THREE INSTRUCTIONAL STRATEGIES FOR GUIDED READING

This section focuses on three research-tested strategies that are especially appropriate for guided reading of informational texts: explicit teaching of individual comprehension strategies, explicit teaching of groups of comprehension strategies, and Idea Circles. Of course, you'll find many others elsewhere in this book and in other resources, but we've found these three strategies to be especially effective.

Explicit Teaching of Individual Comprehension Strategies

Research indicates that explicitly teaching children to apply comprehension strategies when they read improves their comprehension (Duke & Pearson, 2002; National Reading Panel, 2000). Although most of the studies have been conducted with children in third grade and above, research suggests that the same holds true for K–2 students as well (Pearson & Duke, 2002). The strategies include:

◆ monitoring comprehension and adjusting as needed.

◆ activating and applying relevant prior knowledge (including making predictions).

◆ generating questions and/or thinking aloud.

◆ attending to and uncovering text structure.

◆ drawing inferences.

◆ constructing visual representations.

◆ summarizing.

It is beyond the scope of this book to discuss each of these strategies and the approaches to teaching them in depth. We recommend looking to other books and articles for that information. (See box, next page.) Generally, when teaching a comprehension strategy explicitly, it's important to tell *what* the strategy is, *when* and *how* it is used, and *why* its use will be beneficial. Some teachers find that talking about strategies in terms of "what good readers do when they read" is helpful. They might say, for example, "Good readers ask themselves questions as they read." Although it's not a substitute for explicit teaching, modeling application of a strategy by thinking aloud is also an effective approach. (See Chapter 3 for discussions of Think Aloud and the qualities of good readers.)

Resources on
Effective Comprehension Instruction

This list is by no means exhaustive, but it is a place to start if you're interested in learning more about research on and teaching of comprehension strategies.

Reviews of research on comprehension

◆ "Comprehension" by the National Reading Panel, in *Teaching Children to Read: An Evidence-Based Assessment of the Scientific Research Literature on Reading and Its Implications for Reading Instruction: Reports of the Subgroups.* National Institute of Child Health and Development.

◆ *Comprehension Instruction: Research-Based Best Practices* by Cathy Collins Block and Michael Pressley (editors). Guilford Press. Note: This book includes a chapter by Pearson and Duke on comprehension instruction in the primary grades.

◆ "Effective Practices for Developing Reading Comprehension" by Nell K. Duke and P. David Pearson, in *What Research Has to Say About Reading Instruction, Third Edition,* by Alan E. Farstrup and S. Jay Samuels (editors). International Reading Association.

◆ "Metacognition and Self-Regulated Comprehension" by Michael Pressley, in *What Research Has to Say About Reading Instruction, Third Edition,* by Alan E. Farstrup and S. Jay Samuels (editors). International Reading Association.

◆ "Metacognitive Strategies: Research Bases" by Shirley V. Dickson, Vicki L. Collins, Deborah C. Simmons, and Edward J. Kameenui, in *What Reading Research Tells Us About Children With Diverse Learning Needs: Bases and Basics* by Deborah C. Simmons and Edward J. Kameenui (editors). Lawrence Erlbaum Associates.

◆ *Rethinking Reading Comprehension* by Anne Polselli Sweet and Catherine E. Snow (editors). Guilford Press.

◆ "What Should Comprehension Instruction Be the Instruction of?" by Michael Pressley, in *Handbook of Reading Research, Volume 3,* by Michael L. Kamil, Peter B. Mosenthal, P. David Pearson, and Rebecca Barr (editors). Lawrence Erlbaum Associates.

Books on teaching comprehension:

◆ *Improving Comprehension Instruction: Rethinking Research, Theory, and Classroom Practice* by Cathy Collins Block, Linda B. Gambrell, and Michael Pressley (editors). Jossey-Bass.

◆ *Improving Comprehension With Think-Aloud Strategies: Modeling What Good Readers Do* by Jeffrey D. Wilhelm. Scholastic.

◆ *Improving Reading Comprehension: Research-Based Principles and Practices* by Joanne F. Carlisle and Melinda S. Rice. York Press. Note: This book focuses primarily on children who are struggling with comprehension.

◆ *Mosaic of Thought: Teaching Comprehension in a Readers' Workshop* by Ellin Oliver Keene and Susan Zimmerman. Heinemann.

◆ *Reading Comprehension: Strategies for Independent Learners* by Camille Blachowicz and Donna Ogle. Guilford Press.

◆ *Reading With Meaning: Teaching Comprehension in the Primary Grades* by Debbie Miller. Stenhouse.

◆ *Strategies That Work: Teaching Comprehension to Enhance Understanding* by Stephanie Harvey and Anne Goudvis. Stenhouse.

◆ *Teaching for Comprehension in Reading, Grades K–2: Strategies for Helping Students Read with Ease, Confidence, and Understanding* by Gay Su Pinnell and Patricia L. Scharer. Scholastic.

Teachers are often overwhelmed by the number and range of comprehension strategies to choose from. But teaching even just one of these strategies will lead to some improvement, according to research (Pearson, Roehler, Dole, & Duffy, 1992). That said, teaching of multiple strategies, which we address in the next section, seems to lead to greater gains among students.

Explicit Teaching of Groups of Comprehension Strategies

There are a number of research-tested approaches to teaching groups of comprehension strategies. This section focuses on two: Reciprocal Teaching and a variation on it known as Collaborative Strategic Reading. We write briefly about Transactional Strategies Instruction (TSI) approaches as well.

Reciprocal Teaching

Reciprocal Teaching, which was developed several years ago by Annemarie Palincsar and Ann Brown (Palincsar, 1982; Palincsar, 1986; Palincsar & Brown, 1984; Palincsar & Brown, 1986), has been examined in a number of research studies with a variety of grade levels and populations (Rosenshine & Meister, 1994). One study found that first graders could successfully engage in Reciprocal Teaching, suggesting that this technique can indeed be used fruitfully in the primary grades (Palincsar, Brown, & Campione, 1993). Reciprocal Teaching provides guided practice in applying four concrete strategies for understanding text:

1) *Asking questions* about the text
2) *Summarizing* the gist of what has been read and discussed
3) *Clarifying* to help restore meaning of the text when a concept, word, or phrase has been misunderstood or is unfamiliar
4) *Making predictions* regarding upcoming events or content in the text

Reciprocal Teaching sessions are normally conducted in groups of four children, with or without the teacher, using informational text. Children read short sections of text, applying the four comprehension strategies listed above. At first, the teacher explains, models, and leads application of the strategies. Over time, however, the children apply the strategies independently. They begin to take turns acting as teacher and leading the group, with the teacher providing support and feedback as needed. Eventually, with sufficient preparation, children run

Reciprocal Teaching sessions without the participation of the teacher—who is then free to work with other groups.

Below is a brief excerpt of a session with first graders, which was part of a unit on animal survival. The children discuss when baby rabbits are born and how their mother keeps them safe. Notice how a student, Kam, leads the discussion while the teacher provides feedback and modeling:

KAM: When [were] the babies born?

TEACHER: That's a good question to ask. Call on someone to answer that question.

KAM: Robby? Milly?

MILLY: Summer.

TEACHER: What would happen if the babies were born in the winter? Let's think.

[Students offer a number of responses, including "The baby would be very cold." "They would need food." "They don't have no fur when they are born."]

KAM: I have another question. How does she get the babies safe?

KRIS: She hides them.

KAM: That's right. But something else…

TEACHER: There is something very unusual about how she hides them that surprised me. I didn't know this.

TRAVIS: They are all in a different place.

(Palinscar, Brown, & Campione, 1993, pp. 47–48)

Kam, the dialogue leader, goes on to summarize, clarify, and predict, and then the next child takes his or her turn applying these strategies with the next section of text. Throughout the session, understanding the text and using strategies to aid that understanding are the focus.

Collaborative Strategic Reading

Collaborative Strategic Reading (CSR) is a variation of Reciprocal Teaching which emphasizes cooperative learning (Klingner & Vaughn, 1999; Vaughn & Klingner, 1999). Like Reciprocal Teaching, CSR has been found to be effective at improving children's comprehension. (See Vaughn, Klingner, & Bryant, 2001, for a review of the research.) Although studies have involved children in grades four and up, there is good reason to believe that CSR is also effective with younger learners. Figures 4.1 and 4.3 include versions of materials that we've modified for primary-grade children.

Carrying Out CSR

CSR involves four strategy phases: *preview, click and clunk, getting the gist,* and *wrapping up.* Start by modeling each phase for the whole class and then move students into small groups to try it on their own.

Preview. In the preview phase, children brainstorm aloud what they know about the text's topic and what the text might be about before they start reading. As with Reciprocal Teaching, after reading each section one or more children predict what will come in subsequent sections. Encourage children to look at the title and headings, and think about what they might learn. Have them write their ideas in learning logs (described below) and discuss them in the group as well.

Click and clunk. Click and clunk helps children to monitor their understanding of what they are reading. When children are reading along and understanding what they are reading, it's "click, click, click." But when they encounter a word they do not know or realize they are not understanding something, then they have hit a "clunk." Teach children to recognize when they have hit a clunk and how to apply strategies for "fixing up" the situation, such as rereading difficult sentences or breaking unfamiliar words into smaller parts.

Getting the gist. In the next phase of CSR, children work on summarizing what they have read. Some of the questions they are taught to ask themselves or one another when working to get the gist include: "What is the most important idea to be gained from the text?" and "What are the specific parts of the text that are important to know?"

Wrapping up. In this phase, students:

◆ Ask questions about the content of what they read.

◆ Write the questions in their learning logs.

◆ Ask their best questions of group members.

◆ Write as much as they can about what they have learned in their learning logs.

◆ Listen to the encourager (see "Group Roles" below) as he or she tells the group what it did well.

◆ Discuss how the group could improve its performance the next time it meets.

Issues to Consider When Carrying Out CSR

The instructional context. Because CSR is carried out primarily in small groups, it is a natural fit for guided reading. However, before breaking children into groups, it's important to explain CSR to the whole class so that children get the big picture. Emphasize that they will learn four strategies that will help them understand what they read. Also emphasize the value of working in groups, reminding students of any previous cooperative group work they've done. Then, on subsequent days, provide explicit instruction in each phase of CSR.

Group roles. In CSR, members of the group are given different roles to help manage the discussion. The most important role, perhaps, is group leader. The leader is responsible for running the session, using a cue card that provides structure and language. See Figure 4.1 for a sample Group Leader Cue Card (adapted from Klingner and Vaughn, 1999, but illustrated and modified for primary-grade students). See reproducible, page 92.

In addition to group leader, other roles include these:

◆ **The Clunk Expert** helps group members problem-solve when they encounter clunks. Like the group leader, the clunk expert uses cue cards for assistance. See Figure 4.2 and reproducible, page 93.

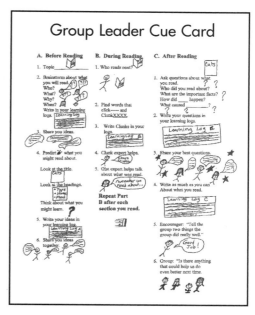

Figure 4.1: This cue card reminds children what to do before, during, and after reading. Teachers can add illustrations as cues for younger children.

Clunk Expert Cue Cards	
Clunk Card 1: Reread the sentence with the clunk and look for key ideas to help you figure out the unknown word. Think about what makes sense.	**Clunk Card 2:** Reread the sentences before and after the clunk, looking for clues.
Clunk Card 3: Look for a prefix or suffix in the word that might help.	**Clunk Card 4:** Break the word apart and look for smaller words you know.

Figure 4.2: These cue card suggest strategies for dealing with "clunks." From Klingner & Vaughn, 1999.

Group Leader Cue Card

A. Before Reading

1. Topic _____

2. Brainstorm about what you will read.
   Who?
   What?
   Why?
   When?
   Write in your learning logs.

3. Share your ideas.

4. Predict what you might read about.

   Look at the title and headings.

   Look at the pictures.

   Think about what you might learn.

5. Write your ideas in your learning logs.

6. Share your ideas together.

B. During Reading

1. Who reads next?

2. Is this clicking? Any clunks?

3. Write clunks in your logs.

4. Clunk expert helps.

5. Gist expert helps talk about what was read.

Repeat Part B after each section you read.

C. After Reading

1. Ask questions about what you read.
   Who did you read about?
   What are the important facts?
   How did _____ happen?
   What caused _____?

2. Write your questions in your learning logs.

3. Share your best questions.

4. Write as much as you can about what you learned.

5. Encourager: Tell the group two things the group did really well.

6. Group: Is there anything that could help us do even better next time?

Adapted from Klingner & Vaughn (1999)

Clunk Expert Cue Cards

From Klingner & Vaughn (1999)

CLUNK CARD 1:

Reread the sentence with the clunk and look for key ideas to help you figure out the unknown word. Think about what makes sense.

CLUNK CARD 2:

Reread the sentences before and after the clunk, looking for clues.

CLUNK CARD 3:

Look for a prefix or suffix in the word that might help.

CLUNK CARD 4:

Break the word apart and look for smaller words you know.

- **The Gist Expert** helps the group remain focused on the most important aspects of the text. With the gist expert's help, members can concentrate on the big picture without getting bogged down in little details.

- **The Announcer** calls on group members to read, making sure that everyone gets a chance. He or she is also in charge of making sure that only one person speaks at a time.

- **The Encourager** provides positive feedback to group members when necessary and appropriate.

Over time, rotate roles within CSR groups and make sure that each child has the opportunity to take on all roles.

Learning logs. In CSR, children complete learning logs related to their reading. Each learning log has three sections: before reading, during reading, and after reading:

- In the before reading section, children write what they already know about the topic and what they predict they will learn.

- In the during reading section, children write about any clunks they encountered while reading.

- In the after reading section, children write questions about important ideas in the passage and comments about what they learned.

See Figure 4.3 and reproducible, page 95, for a sample learning log adapted slightly from Klingner and Vaughn, 1999, for the primary grades.

CSR Learning Log

Today's topic _Starfish_   Date _March 9_

A. Before reading: preview
   1. What I already know about the topic.
   Starfish are alive. They live in the ocean. They are star shapes. They are ruff.

   2. What I predict I will learn.
   What they eat. What kinds there are. How many there are.

B. During reading
   1. Clunk words.
   oysters, underside "It's tiny mouth is on its underside."

   Remember: Repeat parts A and B until you finish the entire reading assignment.

C. After reading: wrap-up
   1. Questions about the important ideas in the passage.
   Why doesn't it hurt them to lose a ray? How many different kinds of starfish are there?

   2. What I learned from the text.
   There are many different kinds of starfish. Different kinds look different and do different things. None of them have legs. They move on tiny tubes.

Figure 4.3: This log helps children focus on what they are learning from text.

Gradual Release of Responsibility

As with Reciprocal Teaching, CSR requires a gradual release of responsibility (Pearson & Gallagher, 1983) from the teacher to the students. We have found that with appropriate preparation, children will become increasingly independent in their application of CSR strategies.

CSR Learning Log

Today's topic _____ Date _____

A. Before reading: preview

1. What I already know about the topic.

_____

_____

_____

2. What I predict I will learn.

_____

_____

_____

B. During reading

1. Clunk words.

_____

_____

Remember: Repeat parts A and B until you finish the entire reading assignment.

C. After reading: wrap-up

1. Questions about the important ideas in the passage.

_____

_____

_____

2. What I learned from the text.

_____

_____

_____

Adapted from Klingner & Vaughn (1999)

Transactional Strategies Instruction

Another way to teach multiple comprehension strategies is through Transactional Strategies Instruction (TSI) (Pressley, Almasi, Schuder, Bergman, Hite, El-Dinary, et al., 1994; Pressley, El-Dinary, Gaskins, Schuder, Bergman, Almasi, et. al., 1992). With TSI, children learn to apply a large number of comprehension strategies flexibly, along with interpretive strategies such as reading for multiple meanings. Children learn these strategies over an extended period of time—usually across an entire school year, but sometimes from one year to the next. TSI involves explicit teaching, guided practice, independent practice, and a great deal of teacher and student Think Aloud.

Because it is a complex approach and few professional resources are available to help teachers master it, TSI can be a challenge. But when implemented well, there is a substantial payoff in student achievement. One TSI approach, SAIL (Students Achievement Independent Learning), has been proven highly effective with second-grade students (Brown, Pressley, Van Meter, & Schuder, 1996). We hope the future brings widespread implementation of TSI in primary classrooms with dissemination of materials necessary to support it.

Idea Circles

Idea Circles are another way to teach comprehension in small groups (Guthrie & McCann, 1996). They were developed as part of Concept-Oriented Reading Instruction (CORI), an approach to teaching reading comprehension mainly for content area materials (Guthrie & McCann, 1997). In CORI, reading strategies are taught and practiced not in isolation, but in support of learning science concepts. For example, during a unit on animal survival in which groups of children are assigned different habitats to investigate, children might work on summarizing for the purpose of explaining their findings succinctly to other groups. (For more information about CORI, see Swan, 2003.) Although the effectiveness of Idea Circles specifically has not been researched, the effectiveness of CORI has been. Researchers found that it had a positive impact on the comprehension and engagement of third- and fifth-grade students (Guthrie, Van Meter, McCann, Wigfield, Bennett, Poundstone, et al., 1996).

Idea Circles are similar to Literature Circles in a few ways. Groups of three to six children meet for in-depth discussion of a text or texts. Circles are usually peer-led, except for early in the year, when the teacher demonstrates procedures by modeling for groups and the whole class. Throughout the process, peer collaboration is central.

In Idea Circles, students usually read many different texts—most or all of them informational texts—as opposed to reading a single narrative text, as they might in Literature Circles. Their focus is on higher-order understanding of a particular concept or set of related concepts.

Literature Circles Usually...	Idea Circles Usually...
Use a single text read by all students	Use a variety of texts read by different students
Focus on the text	Focus on a concept (addressed in the texts)
Involve narrative texts	Involve informational texts

Researchers Guthrie and McCann found that it takes four to six weeks for Idea Circle groups to build cohesion. Some keys to success, as children in their study noted, include participants' ability to "listen to each other," "speak one at a time," "let everyone have a turn," and "listen to the leader" (Guthrie & McCann, 1996).

There are multiple ways to structure Idea Circles. One of them is called the jigsaw (Aronson, 1978). Jigsaw is a flexible grouping strategy in which students build knowledge about a topic together by gathering and sharing information incrementally within rotating groups. For example, consider a second-grade class that is studying continents in social studies. The teacher may first split the class into groups, each of which focuses on a different feature of continents, such as mountains, rivers, or climates. Each group would learn about its feature for *all* continents of the world. Then the teacher would regroup students so that there is at least one person with knowledge of each feature in each new group. The new groups would each focus on an individual continent and discuss each feature—mountains, rivers, climates—for that continent. Each group might then give a description of its continent to the rest of the class. By the time the process is complete, each student has in-depth knowledge of one feature and continent, as well as broader knowledge of other features and continents. When expertise is distributed in this way, more information is likely to be offered by individuals, checked by other individuals, and discussed more deeply (Guthrie & McCann, 1996). In essence, that is the goal of Idea Circles: Students learn and help each other to learn.

Each Idea Circle should have open-ended, self-determined goals that are clear to all members. For example, a goal might be to learn about different pond organisms and write a brochure to display at a local nature center. If students are permitted to choose how they learn about a concept, how they assemble their ideas, and how they express their understanding of those ideas, they become more motivated. The emphasis is not on which student can write the best report or make the best presentation, but on how group members can help one another reach a common goal (Guthrie & McCann, 1996).

Closing Thoughts

Guided reading is an important component of primary-grade instruction—and efforts should be made to incorporate informational text into it. We hope that this chapter has provided new ideas. As you have seen, there are many research-tested approaches to helping students comprehend informational text in guided reading and other small-group activities. Doing this is exciting but also, perhaps, a bit daunting. Keep in mind that implementing even one of these approaches can have a significant impact on children's learning (Pearson, Roehler, Dole, & Duffy, 1992).

Having laid a foundation of quality direct instruction, we now turn to what might be considered the fruits of our labor: situations in which children read informational text independently.

CHAPTER 5

Independent Reading

Motivating Children to Read Informational Text in School and at Home

BY ANNE HUXLEY

I magine walking into a classroom where children are scattered all over in a variety of positions—some alone, some with partners, and some in small groups. They are quietly reading books or other materials, occasionally pointing to pictures or murmuring comments. The teacher looks up from his desk where he is reading as well, smiles, and returns to his book. Everyone is engaged… everyone is on task… *everyone is reading.*

This scene would be a dream come true for many teachers. Most of us struggle to find

What Exactly Do We Mean by Independent Reading?

To us, independent reading is time in the school day when students read without direct assistance from the teacher. It includes reading alone, reading with partners, and reading along to books on tape. We do not use the term *silent reading* because we believe that the reading needn't be silent. It may be helpful to some students to subvocalize (read under their breaths) or read aloud. We also do not use the term *self-selected reading* because we believe that independent reading can occur without children choosing the texts. That said, research shows that giving children some choice over the texts they read is beneficial in many respects. For example, Linda Gambrell (1996) found that children were more motivated to read when they were able to select books based on their own interests. As a rule of thumb, allow students to have some choice in their reading material unless you have a compelling reason to choose it for them—such as when you want a group of students to discuss the same book together later.

Independent reading is not the time to coach or instruct students directly. (We consider that guided reading. See Chapter 4.). Nor is it a time for students to read along with you or listen to you read. (We consider those shared reading and read aloud, respectively. See Chapter 3.) It is possible, however, to conduct guided reading, shared reading, or read aloud with some children while other children are reading independently. That is, independent reading time does not have to be independent for all children at the same time.

ways of motivating students to read for pleasure at home and at school. And when we do find ways, finding the time to implement them can be an even bigger challenge. Given its appeal to students, we believe that including more informational text in the classroom may actually encourage more independent reading at home and at school. In this chapter we:

◆ briefly discuss research on independent reading and informational text.

◆ describe how one teacher encouraged independent reading of informational text.

◆ identify three research-based practices for independent reading.

◆ explain ways to assess how deeply students are processing text during independent reading.

We hope that this chapter will provide many ideas for promoting and enhancing independent reading of informational text at home and at school.

INDEPENDENT READING IN THE PRIMARY GRADES: WHAT THE RESEARCH SAYS

Most teachers are committed to the notion that extensive, self-selected reading is a highly desirable, even necessary component of an effective reading program. For many years, researchers and educators have recommended daily independent reading, when children read on their own with little or no coaching (Anderson, Wilson, & Fielding, 1988). It provides time for children to practice their reading skills, establish good reading habits, and learn to enjoy reading. Although it may go by different names such as Sustained Silent Reading (SSR) or Drop Everything and Read (DEAR), independent reading is in place in many schools across the country.

In recent years, however, some theorists and researchers have questioned independent reading's effectiveness in improving literacy achievement (Armbruster, Lehr, & Osborn, 2001; Carver & Liebert, 1995; National Reading Panel, 2000). In 2000, the National Reading Panel released a report arguing that there is insufficient research evidence to support daily independent reading in school, concluding that "It is not that studies have proven that this cannot work, only that it is yet unproven…. In fact, the handful of experimental studies in which this idea has been tried raise serious questions about the efficacy of some of these procedures" (National Reading Panel, 2000, pp. 3–27). Indeed, there have not been many experimental studies—studies that have compared the achievement of children who engage in independent reading periods in school to the achievement of those who don't. The body of experimental studies the panel reviewed did not clearly support independent reading and, in fact, several studies found no positive effects of independent reading.

However, some educators argue that research evidence *does* support daily independent reading in school. For example, Steven Krashen (2001) critiques the panel's conclusion by identifying problems with the studies it reviewed. Specifically, the studies did not consider:

◆ the ability level of the readers participating.
◆ the type of independent practice provided.
◆ the duration of the studies.

Krashen elaborates on these problems as follows:

Ability level. Two studies showed no differences between groups that did and did not have independent reading periods, but the participants were high-performing readers. Krashen argues that reading practice is more likely to result in demonstrable benefits for low to moderate readers, who have not yet developed a healthy appetite for books and have more room to grow. Higher-achieving readers are more likely to be near their maximal potential.

Type of practice. In another study the panel considered, Krashen questions the researchers' definition of independent reading. Rather than reading under relatively natural circumstances, children in this study read in two-hour blocks and then took tests. Rather than self-selecting any text, they could only choose from a list of 135 books (Carver & Liebert, 1995). According to Krashen, marathon reading, testing sessions, and limited choice are not in harmony with the typical goals of independent reading: encouraging children to read for pleasure and increasing reading achievement.

Duration of the studies. Krashen notes that many studies the panel considered were too short. If the researchers had looked at independent reading over longer periods of time, they might have seen more positive results.

Krashen and others who have argued that research *does* support daily independent reading tend to cite a broader range of studies, including those that show correlations between how much time children spend on their own reading each day and their reading achievement (Anderson, Wilson, & Fielding, 1988; Krashen, 2001; Watkins & Edwards, 1992). But we have to be careful when interpreting these results: Just because better readers engage in more independent reading does not necessarily mean that engaging in more independent reading *makes* children better readers. We must consider the possibility that better readers read more because they are better at it or enjoy it more. However, research also shows that fluent readers are more likely to be found in classrooms that offer time to read self-selected books every day. In one study, for example, three times as many least-fluent readers than most-fluent readers indicated that that they had free-reading time "never or once or twice a month." (Pinnell, Pikulski, Wixson, Campbell, Gough, & Beatty, 1995). But, again, we cannot conclude from this that increased time for self-selected reading *causes* improved reading performance. Other characteristics of these classrooms could explain the relationship. In any case, it is clear that children who have more opportunities to read independently, and in fact do so, perform with higher levels of proficiency.

So What's a Teacher to Do?

In light of these mixed messages from the research community, and until more definitive data is available, we recommend making your own decisions based on the following considerations:

The activity your independent-reading time is supplanting. Ideally, the time you choose for independent reading should not crowd out other worthwhile literacy activities. For example, if independent reading replaces children sitting alone at their seats completing worksheets or coloring, it is worth implementing. But if it replaces daily instruction on sound-letter relationships or comprehension strategies, it may not be.

The texts students are reading. Reading hastily-chosen texts (or what we've come to call D.E.A.F.W.—Drop Everything and Find Waldo) is not likely to be as beneficial as reading texts that are carefully chosen for each child's literacy development. As you have probably noticed, some children choose texts that are far too difficult for them (Fresch, 1995) and need assistance in selecting appealing materials of an appropriate level.

The structure of the independent reading time. Another important consideration is what children are doing during independent reading time. Some students do not perform well when given unstructured activities; they tend to mill about and never settle down to read. At best, they flip through books quickly and discard them after a few seconds (Fielding & Roller, 1992). For these students, independent reading may have to be continually modified or even eliminated. We have found that teachers who have more structured independent reading—those who have established clear procedures for independent reading, introduce reading time gradually, and hold students accountable for their reading—have more productive independent reading periods.

Your role during independent reading. It is tempting to use independent reading time to do paperwork or other forms of housekeeping, but this probably lessens the value of independent reading. Many teachers we know work with children individually and in small groups during this time, coaching them as they read or providing other forms of instruction. Some teachers use the time to model independent reading of their own books, though we believe a little of that goes a long way.

Which children are given the opportunity to engage in independent reading. Very often, teachers allow time for independent reading only when children are done with their work. This makes sense in terms of management. But the children who are most in need of extra reading practice are typically those who struggle to finish their other work. If the same children are always still at their desks working when the majority of the class is reading independently, these children are effectively being deprived of the experience. If independent reading time is going to happen, it must be available for all children who would benefit.

The potential of the home as a place for students to engage in independent reading. Reading at home does not compete with instructional time, and it can be a valuable tool in increasing interest in reading, providing extra time for practicing what has been learned in school, and so on. As noted earlier, correlational studies such as Anderson, Wilson, and Fielding (1988) suggest that children who read more at home are better readers. For example, one study found that fourth graders who had higher levels of fluency reported engaging in significantly more out-of-school (as well as in-school) reading (Pinnell, Pikulski, Wixson, Campbell, Gough, & Beatty, 1995). Of the children who read most fluently, only 7 percent indicated that they had read no books outside of school during the previous month. In contrast, of the children who read least fluently, four times as many reported no book reading outside of school. Research indicates that children who are provided with stand-alone books and books with audiotapes to read at home realize benefits in their reading development, including ESL speakers (e.g., Koskinen, Blum, Bisson, Phillips, Creamer, & Baker, 2000). This suggests that more reading at home can actually *cause* greater reading achievement.

What the Research Says About Independent Reading of Informational Text in the Primary Grades

Although there has been a fair amount of research related to independent reading in general, there has been little on independent reading with informational text in particular. For example, we know of no published studies that have examined how children's achievement or motivation to read is impacted by encouraging more informational text in independent reading time. (This is just one of many parts of the Early Literacy Project framework, so we can't isolate its effects.) That said, some studies provide reason to believe that including informational text in independent reading is good for children. For example, recall from Chapter 1 that some children seem to prefer to read informational text, that informational text addresses topics and questions of strong interest to many children, and that exposure to informational text appears to improve informational reading and writing.

As far as we know, there is also no published research on the impact of sending informational text home to read. However, again based on research in other areas, we believe this could be helpful to children. For example, research indicates that parent-child storybook reading provides an environment that enhances familiarity with print and book awareness as well as narrative knowledge (Heath, 1982; Teale & Sulzby, 1986; Snow & Ninio, 1986). Perhaps, then, similar learning would occur in parent-child information book reading. Interestingly, some research suggests that some parents interact differently with their children around informational texts than they do with narrative texts, focusing more on text concepts and vocabulary (Lennox, 1995; Pellegrini, Perlmutter, Galda, & Brody, 1990). The opportunities for parent-child interaction around informational texts seem rich. That said, home reading doesn't always have to involve parents. In our experience, children in kindergarten—and those even younger—can take home books to read and look at on their own.

INDEPENDENT READING OF INFORMATIONAL TEXT: ONE TEACHER'S APPROACH

Ann Marie Stevens, a teacher with over 25 years of experience, has been working with first graders for much of her career. In her school, she is known as a teacher who has a special way with needy students. As a result, her classroom is typically filled with children who might be considered "at risk." With class sizes approaching thirty students, she has found ways to build interest in a wide variety of topics and create structures that allow each child to be successful.

Ann Marie works hard to incorporate informational text throughout her classroom and curriculum. By integrating informational text into all aspects of her program, she found that her students—especially those needing a little extra help—surpassed the achievement of her students from previous years and were more excited about interacting with books. Her independent reading program is a particularly successful one.

Reading Books Aloud to Build Interest

Imagine entering Ann Marie's classroom just before read aloud time. The students are at their desks, which are arranged in fairly traditional rows. Ann Marie, who has always done read alouds, brings out one of the children's favorite books: *Fighters* (Stonehouse, 2000), which is part of a series on interesting animal traits. Many of the children lean on their desks, craning their necks to see. Ann Marie reminds the children that one reason this book is so good is because it contains lots of interesting information—and they will learn lots of neat things about all different kinds of fighting animals. As she flips through the book to find a new page to read (on each spread, there's a picture of a "fighter" on the left-hand page and text on the facing page), she briefly displays some of the animals they have already explored. The children begin to squirm in their seats and raise their hands. Some of the more eager ones are practically standing—but all of this is acceptable, because, what matters is that the children are focused on the book. The children release a quick barrage of facts about animals such as sticklebacks (a fish) and poison dart frogs.

Ann Marie begins to read about timber wolves. Again, the children seem transfixed, mouths open, occasionally glancing and smiling at each other as if to say "cool." As she continues to read, the children become very quiet, offering only an occasional "Oooh" or "Wooaa." As Ann Marie reads, individual students relate what they have learned about timber wolves to other animals and to their own personal experience. Ann Marie tells the children that the book will be available on the back browsing shelf, where she has chosen to display the books that she has recently read. She also reminds the children that they also have other fascinating books to explore—books on bats, weather, dinosaurs, and other topics. The children remain quiet while the teacher is talking, but look at their friends and indicate with nods and gestures which books they will attempt to get. Then, to avoid overcrowding, Ann Marie selects small groups of children to choose their independent reading books.

Independent but Interactive Reading

The first children asked to make their independent reading selections walk quickly to get the "best" books. *Fighters* is snapped up almost immediately, along with the many other books Ann Marie has read aloud. As the supply of recently read books dwindles, children explore other areas of the room, where Ann Marie has placed books and magazines. On this day, she has chosen to let the children wander a bit.

Small groups begin to form around children who were lucky enough to procure one of the highly desirable books. Nathan, a child who has been experiencing some problems interacting appropriately with classmates, is getting lots of positive attention because he got *Fighters*. In fact, he is the most popular child in the room at the moment. He sits on the floor with three other boys who point at and discuss the pictures and the text. They work together to figure out some of the words, since the book is a little beyond their level, but maintain a high degree of focus on the material.

Other children also form groups. They talk quietly about the texts they are looking at, pointing at and rereading sections to clarify disputed facts. The children routinely walk up to Ann Marie—and to any volunteers and visitors who may be in the classroom—to show pictures, ask for help with a word, or relay information they have just learned. When this happens, other children often voluntarily join the discussion. Children wander and explore, but this isn't a problem. For the most part, they are well behaved and focused on the text. They talk with one another about the books, holding them so everyone in the group can see.

In another section of the room, two children listen to a tape Ann Marie made of one of their read aloud books, a Rookie Read-About Science book entitled *Horses, Horses, Horses* (Fowler, 1994). Because they don't have headphones, they sit closely together to listen, with a bit of initial disagreement over who gets control of the volume. With the book between them and the tape playing, the children take turns pointing to the words on each page as they read along. This seems to be negotiated almost seamlessly, after one child nudges the other to start pointing.

Ann Marie spends a bit of time reading a book that she has brought to school, occasionally stopping and sharing a fact or interesting picture with a nearby child. Children frequently come up to her, often in pairs, to share something they have found or to ask about something they are reading.

This independent reading period invites a lot of choice. Ann Marie does not require children to sit at their desks silently, reading assigned texts. Instead, she allows them to choose what they read, where they read, with whom they read (if anyone), as well as the amount of support they receive while reading.

Despite the success of this independent-reading period, there are times when Ann Marie wants to be sure that children are reading books at their independent and instructional reading level. She also wants to make sure they are reading a variety of books, and books that are readily available, especially for periods when there isn't time for children to self-select. To address these goals, Ann Marie instituted "silent reading bags."

Silent Reading Bags

To ensure that children have access to a range of materials, Ann Marie has children keep three types of books in personalized freezer bags, which are large enough to hold books of all sizes and durable enough to last the year. The bags include:

◆ one book at the child's independent reading level (often a "little book" from a guided-reading set)

◆ one information book

◆ one book or other type of text that has been used in that week's direct instruction, from a variety of genres, but usually narrative or descriptive.

Once a week, children are allowed to exchange books from the first two categories with others from their classroom library. (Books in the last category are exchanged by Ann Marie when a new text from direct instruction is introduced.)

Children keep their silent reading bags in their desks so that they are readily available for when windows of time open up for reading. Ann Marie may direct children to read any book in their bag or a specific book—their "easy," "information," or "reading" book. This is another way Ann Marie provides choice in reading, yet maintains some level of control over what is read.

What We Can Learn from Ann Marie's Approach to Independent Reading

Independent reading in Ann Marie's classroom works well. Based on her work, as well as the work of other teachers and researchers, we offer these strategies for encouraging independent reading of informational text:

Read informational text aloud. Research indicates that children are more likely to choose books that they have heard read aloud (Martinez, Roser, Worthy, Strecker, & Gough, 1997). One study found that when teachers read informational text aloud and placed it in the classroom library, students were more likely to select it for independent reading (Dreher & Dromsky, 2000). In Ann Marie's classroom, children are unquestionably influenced by read alouds in determining books to read.

Make it available. When Linda Gambrell (1996) asked children to talk about books they had enjoyed reading, she found that 80 percent of them chose books from their classroom libraries. Classroom libraries are a primary source of print for many children, especially those in poorer areas, where public library access may be limited by lack of transportation, restricted hours, or other factors. Ann Marie fills her classroom library with informational and other texts. (See Chapter 8 for more on classroom libraries.)

Display it. Common sense tells us that we're more likely to choose things that are right in front of us. That's why store managers put the merchandise they want to move at eye level (Copple, 2002). Indeed, as we noted in Chapter 2, some research suggests that children gravitate toward books that are displayed (Martinez & Teale, 1989, cited in Fractor, Woodruff, Martinez, & Teale, 1993). Prominently displaying recently read books greatly assists Ann Marie's students in selecting texts and stresses the value she places on the books.

Rave about it. Create enthusiasm for informational text by commenting on the exciting things that students will learn by reading it. Ann Marie frequently identifies books that she finds particularly fascinating. As she reads, she stops to comment on facts that are new to her. She deliberately ties reading to learning, and shares her enthusiasm for this with her students in highly visible ways.

Model reading it. Gambrell (1996) found that teachers who explicitly model reading are more likely to create a motivating context for reading. She suggests that we actively share aspects of books we find particularly interesting or meaningful. For instance, if you are reading about a new hobby or a fascinating scientific breakthrough, share it with your students.

Encourage students to talk about texts and share their learning. Interacting socially around reading is one of children's favorite book-related activities (Gambrell, 1996). Some children recommend titles to their friends. Some enjoy reading the same book separately at the same time and then coming together to discuss it. Reading with a partner is another

READING & WRITING INFORMATIONAL TEXT IN THE PRIMARY GRADES

pleasurable activity for many children, and it can also promote fluency (Kuhn & Stahl, 2000).

Another way to encourage discussion is to ask children to find interesting facts in their books and then share them, either orally or in writing. One teacher we know has her second graders read from books on the same topic and create fact sheets. Each child writes an interesting fact they learned—for example, "Americans eat 12 pounds of chocolate a year!" (inspired by Conover, 2001)—and illustrates it. The fact sheets are displayed on the wall and then, after all children have had the opportunity to read them, the class makes a book of fascinating facts on the topic. These books become popular additions to the classroom library.

Rely on recommendations. Children are great sources of information on informational text. In Ann Marie's classroom, children form groups around texts that one or more of them identify as worth reading. Allowing children to write reviews of texts encourages them to think more deeply about qualities of that text—both qualities they like and those they do not like. It also requires them to think about their audience, since classmates will depend on their recommendations. Reviews can be posted on a classroom wall or even on a Web page. (See pages 124–125 for more about writing reviews.) Of course, book recommendations can come from sources other than children. Appendix A contains resources for finding information books that are likely to appeal to your students.

Link specific texts to specific children. Perhaps one of the most powerful ways you can promote children's independent reading of informational text is to help them find texts that match their own interests and preferences for particular authors, styles, and other criteria. Moreover, when you are aware of a child's interest in a topic, you can assign that child the role of class expert on that topic. Identifying a child as expert on a topic establishes a more authentic purpose for reading—that child is recognized for contributing something unique.

It is amazing how much effort many children will exert to learn about something that interests them. Children who read material of their choice tend to work harder at processing the information (Schiefele, 1991). Ann Marie recognizes this and always tries to link children to topics, and to a range of texts on those topics.

Hold students accountable. It's important to have a system for holding students accountable for what they read during independent reading. However, this does not necessarily mean giving a test. There are other ways: Students might keep reading logs, complete an oral retelling for you or the class, write a review of the book, make an audiotape of the book, or become enough of an expert on the book to help another student read it.

Send it home. Children get very excited about the prospect of taking books home to share with adults, siblings, and other family members. As previously noted, research suggests that home-reading programs can increase the amount of home reading children do (e.g., Koskinen, Blum, Bisson, Phillips, Creamer, & Baker, 2000).

To encourage at-home literacy efforts, Lynn Warren and Jill Fitzgerald (1997) feel it's important to establish a one-to-one relationship with parents and to show them that you are an expert who cares and wants success for their child. They recommend at-home activities that are well structured, concrete, and directly applicable to school success, but are not overly rigid. See the sample parent letter on the next page.

FOR YOUR INFORMATION...

Have Students Read Board Books to Little Ones

Looking for a way to encourage informational reading at home? Let children borrow, take home, and read simple informational board books to younger siblings, cousins, or playmates. There are many informational board books for young children. Here are just a few:

Dinosaurs, Dinosaurs by B. Barton. HarperCollins

Let's Look at Shapes. Lorenz Books, Anness Publishing

Tree Frogs. National Geographic Society

Around Town. Snapshot Books, Covent Garden Books

Do Monkeys Tweet? by M. Walsh. Houghton Mifflin

The National Wildlife Federation's *Wild Animal Baby,* a board book magazine, usually contains some informational text in addition to other genres. For subscription information, call 1-800-611-1599.

A Send-Home Letter to Help Garner Parent Support

Dear Parents:

We are working hard to include more information books in our classroom. Research shows that children benefit from listening to and reading a wide variety of books, even those that have a lot of facts in them. By reading with your child, you can help prepare him or her for the upper grades, where he or she will benefit from already knowing a lot about science, people and places around the world, and just about anything you and your child find interesting.

Because some parents appreciate having steps to follow when they read with their child, below are some general guidelines for you. Of course, feel free to add to or change the activities as you feel comfortable. We do, however, recommend having your child try to give the main idea of the selection and recall as much information as he or she can.

Step 1: Use a book that your child brings home from school, or use any book that interests your child and that he or she can or almost can read independently.

Step 2: Introduce the book; for example, "Let's read this book together. The title is (say title). Follow along with me as I read the book to you. When we're done, I'm going to ask you to tell me everything you can remember about the book."

Step 3: Point to the words as you read. Feel free to stop and discuss ideas or point out interesting things in the pictures.

Step 4: Ask your child to summarize or tell you "what this book was mostly about." If you read a book about spiders, an appropriate answer might be "this book was mostly about spiders and what they do." If your child has difficulty with this, you could say something like, "Since the book told us all about spiders, I think the book must be all about spiders and the things they do." Over time, your child should get better at this.

Step 5: Have your child tell you as much as he or she can remember about the book. This may be hard at first, but your child will improve over time. If your child seems to be having trouble, you can prompt him or her by saying "Remember what we learned about…" or "Tell me more about…." You can also ask for specific definitions: "Tell me about spinnerets."

Feel free to read the book again—your child will learn more on the second and third readings. And if your child is having trouble remembering at first, knowing that you will read the book together again takes the pressure off and lets you have fun!

Sincerely,

Inspired by Warren, L. and Fitzgerald, J. (1997). "Helping parents to read expository literature to their children: Promoting main-idea and detail understanding." *Reading Research and Instruction, 36,* 341–360.

THREE INSTRUCTIONAL STRATEGIES FOR INDEPENDENT READING

This section examines research-based strategies to consider for independent reading: repeated reading, creating incentives, and offering books on tape for school and home use.

Repeated Reading

When students engage in repeated reading, they practice a text orally until they can read it with ease and fluency. You can set up repeated reading in numerous ways. Texts can be read aloud to children initially and then practiced by children individually or with a partner. Choral reading is also suitable for repeated readings. Taped reading can also be adapted for use in repeated reading. These approaches are described below.

Repeated reading has been shown to improve word recognition, reading rate, and, to some degree, comprehension (National Reading Panel, 2000; Kuhn and Stahl, 2000; Meyer and Felton, 1999). Although we know of no published studies on repeated reading using informational text in the early grades, the benefits to students should be similar to those that are realized from using narrative text. Some points to consider, regardless of the type of repeated reading you assign, include the following:

Choosing a text. Use your best judgment in determining how much text each child can handle. Jay Samuels (1979) suggests using a text of around two hundred words for typical primary students. For older students and better primary readers, use longer texts.

Establishing students' word accuracy rate. Recommendations about the level of texts appropriate for repeated reading vary. We recommend using text that is initially at an instructional or low independent reading level for the child. (See box on page 115 on determining accuracy.)

Determining the number of readings. O'Shea, Sindelar, and O'Shea (1985) found that when normally-achieving third graders read a passage seven times, about 85 percent of the growth in rate happened after the fourth reading. Given this finding, it makes sense to have children practice a text about four times. Practice much beyond that point is not always necessary or desirable. In fact, requiring children to practice to perfection can be counterproductive and frustrating, especially if they are reading a lengthy piece. If children must read with a high degree of accuracy for a particular purpose—for example, if they are making a tape—you might want to assign separate passages to each child. That way, students can practice to perfection or near-perfection without becoming overwhelmed.

Ways to Carry Out Repeated Reading

In general, children enjoy practicing texts because each successive reading typically leads to a better overall performance. We've found, in fact, that children will elect to practice text well beyond their third reading. This type of commitment is most common among students

FOR YOUR INFORMATION...

Determine Reading Accuracy Rates

To determine their accuracy rate, have the student read the passage aloud. Count the number of words he or she reads incorrectly or not at all. Then divide the number of words read correctly by the number of total number words in section. So, if a child makes two errors in reading aloud a 100-word section of text, divide 98 words read correctly by 100 total words to get a 98% accuracy rate. (Note: For other purposes, more complex procedures may be appropriate, but for repeated reading this simple approach is probably sufficient.)

	Accuracy Rate/ Word Recognition
Independent: Child can read the text without support	96–99%
Instructional: Child can read the text with teacher support	92–95%
Frustration: Child struggles a great deal to read the text, even with teacher support; text is not appropriate for instruction in most situations	90–92% or less

Adapted from Lipson, M., & Wixson, K. (1991). *Assessment and Instruction of Reading Disability: An Interactive Approach.* New York: Harper Collins.

whose teachers find ways to make repeated reading a purposeful activity. Techniques for doing this include:

Choral reading. One second-grade teacher we worked with had groups of students read aloud their science text repeatedly together, in a choral fashion. Children worked together to make their group's reading sound as good as possible.

Tape-recorded reading. Have students practice a text and then tape it for use by other children in the class, by younger children, or by others. Many children will want to practice until their reading is very fluent. You might ask all children to practice the entire text and individual students to practice specific passages within the text to achieve a higher level of mastery.

Reading for the public. Many children will willingly read repeatedly if they know they are going to perform the piece for the class, a partner, or a special adult in the school. Some schools allow students to read brief texts they've practiced over the communication system every morning. These texts usually address topics of school interest, such as the mascot, the local economy, local history, material being covered in content areas, or seasonal themes. Providing children with opportunities to show off a practiced, fluent reading is a wonderful way to bolster their perceptions about themselves as readers. Bill Henk and Steve Melnick (1998) found that almost 20 percent of the children they surveyed were highly uncomfortable reading in public. Many children might fear negative judgment by other students, and oral reading is a primary way children make judgments about their performance relative to others. Allowing them to read texts repeatedly beforehand can decrease their anxiety significantly.

Reading with a partner. Many children look forward to repeated reading with a partner or paired reading (Topping, 1989). Like the other activities suggested in this section, paired reading provides children with a relatively safe forum for practicing text. To make it even safer, students might first practice the text individually. Hearing the text read aloud first might also help. If the text is relatively difficult for a child, the child could be paired with a somewhat stronger reader; if the text is relatively easy for the child, perhaps pair that child with a less strong reader. When reluctant readers know they will be partnered with students a grade level or two below them, and thus expected to be the "expert," they often rise to the challenge and work very hard to master the text beforehand. (For more about ways to promote fluency in oral reading, see Timothy Rasinski's *The Fluent Reader: Oral Reading Strategies for Building Word Recognition, Fluency, and Comprehension*, 2003.)

Creating Incentives

Offering incentives is another strategy for promoting independent reading. Although incentives have been criticized by many educators, their negative impact is not clearly based in research (McQuillan, 1997). In fact, a number of studies suggest that the judicious use of incentives for reading can be helpful under certain circumstances (Christmas, 1993; Gambrell, Almasi, Xie, & Heland, 1995; Harrop & McCann, 1983). Incentive programs have been used as a way to give children a taste of success in reading, paving the way for continued growth and better opinions of themselves as readers.

One program that works well for independent reading is called *Running Start* (Gambrell, Almasi, Xie & Heland, 1995). For ten weeks, children work toward reading 21 books. (For first graders, this total includes books they read or those that are read to them.) Children keep track of their reading in a log chart, using stickers to mark their progress. Literacy-related items, such as bookmarks, are also given out during the program. The final reward for reading 21 books is a book of the child's choice to take home.

A study involving more than 7,000 children found that the *Running Start* program resulted in increased motivation to read, as well as enhanced reading behaviors at school and at home. Children who took part in the program reported spending more time reading independently, talking more frequently about books with families, and taking a greater number of books home.

Reading to a former teacher or to the principal is also an effective incentive. This is especially desirable to children who admire and want to impress the adults around them. However, many teachers worry about intruding upon busy colleagues and setting a precedent

Designing an Effective Reward System for Reading

If you're thinking about weaving incentives into your reading program, be sure to:

Reward what really matters. A preferable incentive program is one that celebrates growth and increased competence, rather than one that gives out rewards for perfunctory completion of an activity. For instance, children might earn an incentive by practicing a text until they can read it with good expression.

Offer literacy-related incentives. In the *Running Start* program, incentives are literacy related—they contain positive messages about reading or help children interact with print in some way. In addition to stickers and bookmarks, children might earn more free-choice reading time, a read aloud of a book of their choice, or writing materials. Time reading with special adults is also a great incentive.

Cut costs by partnering. Purchasing incentives on your own can become costly, so try partnering with local bookstores. Managers may provide gift certificates, books, or other reading goodies. They also might offer their store as a venue for your students to read to an audience.

for doing so. While it is true that we are all busy, your coworkers are likely to welcome the opportunity to interact with a child around reading. The caring adults in your school who provide services that too often go unrecognized—the lunchroom, main-office, or custodial staff members—might also welcome a brief reading by a child.

Offering Books on Tape for School and Home

Audiotape support (Carbo, 1989; Koskinen, et al., 2000) provides an effective way of encouraging independent reading. Taped books can help when a text is too difficult for a child to read on his or her own, and research indicates that listening to books on tape can have a positive impact on reading skills. One study found that when linguistically diverse first graders (both native English and ESL speakers) took home books on tape, they made significant gains in

Get Started With Books on Tape

Few activities are more intriguing to young readers than recording their own voices. To do it successfully, though, they need the right space and materials. These include:

◆ a tape recorder/player: This does not have to be an expensive, school-grade model. An inexpensive recorder/player, with easy-to-manipulate buttons and a built-in microphone, will do.

◆ a microphone: If your recorder/player doesn't have a built-in microphone, or has one that creates low-quality sound, purchase an inexpensive external microphone at your local electronic supply store.

◆ 30-minute audiotapes: Buy these in bulk when you find them at a good price. Thirty minutes is more manageable and less wasteful than longer tapes.

◆ labels for the tapes.

◆ plastic bags for storing the tapes and books.

◆ a bell or some other signal to indicate "turn the page."

◆ a quiet spot with good acoustics to record. Think creatively: Possible spots might include behind your desk, in the hall, in the coat closet, inside a refrigerator box, even in the bathroom with a volunteer.

Once you have the space and materials, give students tips for successful recording. Remind them to:

◆ practice reading the text aloud until they are ready to record it. By practicing before recording, children build their ability to read clearly, with expression and confidence.

◆ read at a rate listeners will understand and enjoy.

◆ sound a bell or other signal when they want listeners to turn the page, as readers of commercially made books do.

◆ have fun! Listeners can tell if readers enjoyed the text by how they sound on the tape.

Writing these tips out for children may help them to remember. If they have trouble, invite them to listen to some commercially made tapes and talk about what the reader does to make it easier for listeners to understand and enjoy.

reading (Koskinen, Blum, Bisson, Phillips, Creamer, & Baker, 2000). Children who took home books with tapes made significantly greater progress than children who took home only books. And children who took home only books made greater progress than children who took home no books at all. According to teacher reports and parent surveys/interviews, students who used tapes were more likely to read for fun and spent more time talking about books to their families and friends.

There are relatively few information books on tape, but teachers can make their own by recording favorite titles.

Starting to use taped books in your classroom does not have to be an overwhelming task, especially in the early grades. Because ready-made books on tape can be expensive, and good informational texts on tape can be hard to find, we suggest recording many texts yourself. You could also ask children in the class or in the upper grades to make tapes. Children especially enjoy hearing books read by adults in the school and guessing the "mystery reader."

ASSESSING INDEPENDENT READING: FINDING OUT WHAT CHILDREN CAN DO

It's important to know how deeply students are processing text during independent reading. This doesn't necessarily mean administering paper-and-pencil multiple-choice tests or computerized quizzes. Two alternatives are asking students to give retellings and asking students to write reviews of their reading.

Retelling Informational Text

A retelling is an oral recounting of a text that has been read. A good retelling need not be a word-for-word or detail-for-detail account of a text, but it should capture the important aspects of the text. For example, with fictional narrative text a good retelling would normally include reference to the setting, characters, problem or plot, key events, and resolution. Over time, children who engage in retellings of stories develop better comprehension (Morrow, Gambrell, Kapinus, Koskinen, Marshall, & Mitchell, 1986). For example, in one study children who participated in oral retelling remembered more about what they had read than children who were asked traditional comprehension questions (Gambrell, Miller, King, & Thompson, 1989, as cited in Gambrell, Koskinen, & Kapnius, 1991).

We know of no research showing that oral retellings improve children's comprehension of informational text. However, there is evidence that teaching children particular approaches to summarizing informational text in written form builds comprehension. Summarizing is also part of certain effective instructional practices such as Reciprocal Teaching. (See Chapter 4.)

Evidence like this gives us good reason to think that children, even young children, *can* retell informational text. In a study conducted by Barbara Moss (1997), children listened to a read aloud of the book *How Kittens Grow* (Selsam, 1973). Then, they were asked to give a retelling of the text. Moss used a five-point scale to assess the retellings and found they were of a fairly high quality, with most coming in at level 3, and only two children scoring below that. (See box, next page, "Evaluating Children's Retellings of Informational Text.") This work indicates that retelling informational text is not beyond even first-grade children.

Although hearing and guiding children's retellings is a valuable practice, it is not always necessary to have children retell a selection only to you. You may want to pair up students and have them give retellings of informational text to one another. If you circulate during this time, children who are having difficulty should stand out. Practice does help (Gambrell, Koskinen, & Kapnius, 1991).

Evaluating Children's Retellings of Informational Text

Here are two approaches to evaluating children's retellings of informational text. The first is a five-point scale used by Barbara Moss (1997) in the study described on page 121 and presented in detail below.

Level	Criteria for Establishing Level
5	Student includes all main ideas and supporting details, sequences properly, infers beyond the text, relates text to own life, understands text organization, summarizes, gives opinion and justifies it, may ask additional questions, very cohesive and complete retelling
4	Student includes most main ideas and supporting details, sequences properly, relates text to own life, understands text organization, summarizes, gives opinion, fairly complete retelling
3	Student includes some main ideas and details, sequences most material, understands text organization, gives opinion, fairly complete retelling
2	Student includes a few main ideas and details, some difficulty sequencing, may give irrelevant information, gives opinion, incomplete retelling
1	Student gives details only, poor sequencing, irrelevant information, very incomplete retelling

From Moss, B. (1997). A qualitative assessment of first graders' retelling of expository text. *Reading Research and Instruction, 37* (1), 1–13. Adapted from Irwin, P. A. & Mitchell, J. N. (1983). A procedure for assessing the richness of retellings. *Journal of Reading, 26,* 391–395.

<table>
<tr><td valign="top">

Air

Air is all around us.
But we can't see it.
How do we know it is there?
There are many ways.
We can see what air does.
Moving air is called wind.
Wind moves plants.
Wind moves dirt.
Strong winds can move heavy things.
Strong winds can even move a house.
We can weigh air.
We can weigh two balloons.
The one with a lot of air weighs more.
We can see what air does.
We can weigh air.
Then we know it is there.

</td><td valign="top">

Retelling Scoring Sheet for Air

Main Idea

____ Air is all around us.

____ But we can't see it.

____ How do we know it is there?

____ We can see what air does.

Details

____ Moving air is called wind.

____ Wind moves plants.

____ Wind moves dirt.

____ Strong winds can move heavy things.

____ Strong winds can move a house.

Main Idea

____ We can weigh air.

Details

____ We can weigh two balloons.

____ The one with lots of air weighs more.

Main Idea Restatement

____ We can see what air does.

____ We can weigh air.

____ Then we know it is there.

Other ideas recalled, including inferences:

</td></tr>
</table>

Figure 5.1: An informational text passage and retelling scoring sheet from the *QRI–3*.

The other approach is from the *Qualitative Reading Inventory–3* assessment by Leslie and Caldwell (2001). The retelling portion of the assessment contains reading passages along with a preprinted list of main ideas and details for each passage. (See Figure 5.1.)

For the retelling portion of the *QRI–3*, the child reads the passage and gives a retelling. During the retelling, the teacher checks off, from the preprinted list, each idea or detail the child provides or numbers it according to the order in which it was given. (The first idea the child gives is marked with a 1, the second a 2, and so on). Examining children's retellings this way provides information about:

◆ whether the child has understood or recalled a substantial number of ideas and details.

◆ whether the ideas and details recalled are accurate.

◆ whether the child is sufficiently focused on main ideas. (Some children will give only or primarily details.)

continued on next page

◆ how the child orders the ideas and details she or he recalls, and to what extent that sequence matches the text.

It's also important to ask the child what she or he thought about the selection. This can reveal valuable information such as whether the child can be critical of or question what she or he reads. If possible, have students retell a selection to other children who are unfamiliar with the text rather than to you or someone else who is already familiar with it. We suggest this because:

◆ it makes the activity more authentic. Outside of school, we are more likely to retell or summarize a text for someone who has not read it than for someone who has.

◆ it may help the child think more deeply about what to include in the retelling, since he or she knows that listener has not read the text. And the listener might learn something in the process!

You don't necessarily need to use the *QRI-3* to assess children this way. You can choose texts yourself, create a list of main ideas and details from that text, and ask students to read it and give a retelling.

Writing Reviews in Response to Informational Text

Another way to find out what students are learning in independent reading is to have them write reviews of what they've read. Not only does this help you evaluate their understanding of the text, but it also encourages children to process the text more deeply. (See Figure 5.2.) And because reviews can be read by other children and used to guide their book selections and discussions, writing them is an authentic activity. As previously mentioned, children influence one another's book selections and social groups can form around particular titles. By asking students to write reviews, we provide another platform for children to share information and opinions about books with one another.

When introducing review writing, discuss why reviews are important and tell children that it's okay for them to say that they didn't like a book or something about it. We've found that as children become comfortable reading informational text and writing reviews, they become more discerning. For instance, a simple book on spiders might not appeal to a child who has read widely on the topic and, therefore, it may not receive a favorable review from that child. Or the child may conclude that the text is a good choice for a person who does not know a lot about spiders. This is an excellent exercise in thinking critically about text and audience. Reviews can be placed on a bulletin board, in a large index-card box, or on a class computer. They can also be posted on Web sites such as www.kidsreads.com, www.kidsbookshelf.com, www.spaghettibookclub.org, and www.amazon.com.

Although we are not aware of research on the impact of writing reviews of informational texts, in general, engaging children in writing in response to reading appears to have a positive effect on their reading and writing development. (See discussion of research in Chapter 6.)

> **The Coolest Cross-Sections Ever**
> **By Stephen Biesty**
>
> **147 pages**
>
> **This book is really cool. I liked it a lot. This book is about cross-sections. A cross-section is how something works. Take for instance, an eyeball. It shows how the eye works by taking the eye apart layer by layer. The artwork was very, very good. The artwork is realistic. I learned how people build spaceships. The best part probably was the section on "Working at Sea" because there was a page that showed amputations, or people's limbs getting cut off. Gross but cool. Even though it's a big book, it's pretty easy to read because it has little facts all over the pages and you can read just a little or a lot. I read a lot of pages. In fact, I read the whole book. It was interesting. I think you should read it.**
>
> **Dawson**
> **Grade 3**
>
> **Biesty, S. (2001). The coolest cross-sections ever! New York: DK Publishing.**

Figure 5.2: This third grader's review of an information book suggests that he understands and engages with the content and applies good strategies.

Concluding Thoughts

This chapter reviewed research related to independent reading in general and independent reading of informational text specifically. It presented many factors to consider in deciding whether, when, and how to conduct independent reading, including other activities it supplants and the kinds of texts children read.

It also showed how one teacher conducts independent reading and uses strategies for encouraging it in school and at home. We suggested repeated readings, incentive programs, and books on tape as ways to promote independent reading—and having students give retellings and write reviews as ways to evaluate their learning. Review writing sets the stage for the next chapter, which focuses on writing informational text.

CHAPTER 6

Writing

Teaching Children to Compose
Informational Text

BY DENISE MCLURKIN

"Milk is something people drink. Milk has vitamins. Milk is good for you. Milk doesn't have fiber." — Mark

"People make butter from cream. Butter is yellow. People can put butter on bagels and toast. Butter has [to] be in ref[r]igerator." — Derek

Based on their writing, can you guess which grade Mark and Derek are in? Third? Second, maybe? In fact, they're first graders. They wrote these texts as part of a project on food. Their teacher, Pam Richardson, asked each child to choose a kind of food, research it, write about it, and report their findings to classmates. We chose Mark and Derek's pieces not because they were the best, but because they represented typical writing in this class. According to Pam, they are her "middle-of-the-road kids. Mark even has a speech and language impairment for which he receives services. But that doesn't stop him from writing his heart out."

All of Pam's students were excited about the food project and other informational writing they did throughout the year. According to Pam, "The students brought a lot of background knowledge…to the table, and I used that as a bridge to get them to write more. It worked. They wrote more and I believe that it really helped them with their overall reading and writing skills." Pam reports that her budding informational writers were "…interested, excited, on-task, and they worked hard. What more could I ask for?"

We hope you share this excitement about informational writing. In this chapter, we:

◆ briefly discuss research related to informational writing in the primary grades.
◆ describe how two primary teachers include informational writing in their curricula.
◆ explore three research-based principles of developing children's informational writing.

INFORMATIONAL WRITING IN THE PRIMARY GRADES: WHAT THE RESEARCH SAYS

As explained in Chapter 1, there once was—and perhaps, still is—a widespread belief that young children cannot handle informational text, and that narrative text is more appropriate for them. In 1987, however, Thomas Newkirk published an article in *Research in the Teaching of English* entitled "The Non-Narrative Writing of Young Children." In this article, Newkirk provided compelling evidence that children not only can write non-narrative text, including informational and emergent informational text (such as lists), but that they often do so quite naturally, spontaneously, and even *before* writing narrative text. Two years later, Newkirk published a book on this topic entitled *More Than Stories: The Range of Children's Writing* (1989). Since then, dozens of other researchers have shown that young children are capable of writing informational text.

Some research has examined how informational writing abilities develop over time. These studies indicate that children increasingly differentiate among genres—their informational text looks more like what we think of as informational text, and less like other genres—as children develop (e.g., Boscolo, 1996; Donovan, 2001; Kamberelis, 1999). However, exposure to a variety of texts is key because there appears to be a close relationship between the kinds of text to which children are exposed and the kinds they choose to write and are able to write well (Chapman, 1995; Kamberelis, 1998). So children who are not exposed to much informational text are not likely to develop informational writing skills as quickly as children who are. In the Early Literacy Project, first graders in the experimental classrooms (children who were exposed to more informational text) were better writers of informational text by the end of the year than children in the other classrooms.

So far, little research has tested the effectiveness of a specific approach to teaching young children to write informational text. There is not an equivalent to reciprocal teaching in reading, for example. Rather, studies have tended to identify overarching principles related to informational writing development: that reading and writing are inextricably linked; that children may need help making information they've read and gathered "their own"; and that informational text has functions and features different from many other forms of text. Later in this chapter, we discuss how these principles can guide classroom instruction and offer several examples of techniques and activities for teaching informational writing.

INFORMATIONAL WRITING IN SECOND GRADE: TOBY FOWLER'S APPROACH

Toby Fowler teaches second grade in a low-socioeconomic status area, made up mainly of families living in small homes and trailer parks. Because she suspects that many of her students' access to books and magazines at home is limited, Toby has hundreds of books and magazines in her classroom library. Toby's library is very diverse. She thinks it is important for the students to have access to a variety of genres including narratives, poetry, biographies, informational text, autobiographies, and all sorts of magazines.

The variety of texts that Toby provides students has, in her view, made a big difference. For example, she notes that using informational text during social science has been very motivating to students and has taught them a great deal about communities, people, and places. Seeing how her students responded to informational text during read alouds and independent reading, Toby decided to try implementing informational writing during writing workshop. According to Toby, the students "were always so fascinated by me reading those types of books (informational books) that one day I thought, 'I wonder if they would like to write informational essays?' At first I was unsure, because you just don't see that many primary-grade classrooms loaded with informational books, [let alone] informational writing by the children. But then I thought, 'Hey, let's just give it a shot!' To my surprise, they really enjoy it and write just as much, if not more...."

Toby continues to include a great deal of informational writing, as well as other kinds of writing, in her writer's workshop. In fact, she even carries out a series of lessons in which children write informational text about a form of fictional narrative text—fairy tales.

The Fairy Tale Genre Study:
Writing Informational Texts About Narrative Text

For her fairy tale genre study, Toby has clear goals for her second graders. She wants them to:

◆ hear a variety of fairy tales.

◆ describe and compare the features of fairy tales.

◆ write about the features of fairy tales.

Toby helps her students meet these goals by following the plan described below.

Days One Through Five:
Reading Aloud and
Identifying Features

Toby starts by reading aloud a host of fairy tales, such as *Cinderella, Rumpelstiltskin,* and *Snow White.* (See Chapter 3 for more on read aloud.) She reads and re-reads the tales until the stories are familiar to the children. She wants them to get to the point where the children can tell her the beginning, middle, and end of the story. Then she expects them to be able to tell her about the setting, characters, and so on.

As children listen, Toby encourages them to think about the features of fairy tales. As she reads, she asks students to identify features and lists them on a chart. With each new fairy tale she introduces, she encourages children to identify new features, compare them to features they've already identified, and add to the list as necessary. (See sample list right.)

Features of Fairy Tales

1. Fairy tales start with "Once upon a time."

2. They end with "The End."

3. They end with "And they all lived happily ever after."

4. Fairy tales have princesses and princes in them.

5. Sometimes, fairy tales have castles in them.

6. Fairy tales sometimes have dragons in them.

7. They have witches and magicians in them.

8. Most of the time, they have magic in them.

9. They have different kinds of people in them, like dwarfs and hags.

Expect children to identify features of fairy tales such as these.

Day Six:
Copying and Discussing Findings With Peers

On the sixth day, Toby rewrites the list so that it's easier for children to read. The children then copy this list in their journals and talk further with a partner or in a small group about features of fairy tales.

Day Seven:
Assessing What Children Have Learned

To assess what the children have learned about the features of fairy tales, Toby has them write an informational essay on the genre. She asks them to write in their journals, providing about twenty minutes for them to write about what they know.

Attention to Content

Of course, Toby does not want children to think of fairy tales only in terms of their features, but in terms of their content, as well. One way she does this is by pairing traditional fairy tales with modern-day versions and encouraging students to discuss issues they raise related to, for example, gender, class, and ethnicity. She also asks her students to write their own fairy tales in response to her read alouds, and talks with them about the content of those, too.

INFORMATIONAL WRITING IN FIRST GRADE: PAM RICHARDSON'S APPROACH

Pam Richardson teaches in a socioeconomically diverse bedroom community. She has always included informational text because, according to her, "the children just love the pictures, and I just love what you can do with informational text."

Pam takes a writing process approach to all genres—she guides children through brainstorming, drafting, revising and editing, and publishing their work. Pam regularly models each of these phases and provides explicit instruction in particular writing skills and strategies, such as appropriate use of punctuation or brainstorming before writing.

When doing informational writing, Pam often guides her students through an additional phase: researching. She introduces this phase because it is frequently an important part of writers' processes, particularly when writing various kinds of nonfiction texts. Of course, it is challenging to teach young students to be effective researchers. So Pam often chooses topics that children are likely to have some knowledge of—a tactic that is especially helpful at the start. This allows the children to learn about researching without becoming overwhelmed by all that they need to learn. For example, the topic of food has worked especially well for Pam and her students, because all children already know something about food.

Food Products Lessons:
Writing Informational Texts Based on Research

For her series of lessons on writing about food products, Pam wants to:

◆ involve children in research for informational writing.

◆ introduce them to some characteristics of informational writing.

The schedule described below helps her meet these goals.

Day One:
Explicit Teaching, Modeling, and Shared Writing

Pam gathers children on the rug to model writing informational text. She begins by asking them about facts—what they are and what they are not. Students respond with comments such as, "It's true, not fake." "They're like for real." "Not an opinion." "It's not how you feel, but what really is."

After a lively discussion about facts, Pam reads aloud a book about food that contains facts, opinions, and points that can't be easily classified as one or the other. For example, "Ice cream is a yummy treat" is clearly an opinion. "Ice cream is made from milk" is a fact. And "Ice cream comes in many delicious flavors" is a bit of both. During the read aloud, Pam questions the children about whether certain statements are fact or opinion and asks for the reasons behind the answers. She also asks children for their thoughts on how the author might have found the information upon which the book is based, laying the groundwork for research they would be doing later on.

Pam also draws children's attention to some features that are characteristic of informational text. For example, she steers them toward words authors commonly use to qualify statements, such as *some, most,* and *often.* She points out how informational text authors tend to speak in universal terms about their topic, for example, about *all* carrots, rather than about one or two specific carrots. She tells them that authors of informational text generally don't include characters, the way authors of narrative text do.

Once Pam finishes the interactive read aloud, she introduces the food product that the class is are going to write about together—pickles—and asks what they already know about it. Here's what they say:

1. "They are green."
2. "They have soft seeds."
3. "They have little stripes that go down the side of them."
4. "Some are sour and some are sweet."
5. "They are made from cucumbers."
6. "Some are soft but most are really crunchy."
7. "They are oblong—kind of like little green footballs."

As the children call out their ideas, Pam writes them on a chart that is large enough for everyone to see, pointing out that the children are doing a great job of talking about the qualities of pickles in general and not just one or two pickles they remember.

After they generate their list of pickle facts, Pam and her students read and reread it. From there, she informs the children that they will be writing what she calls essays about a food product they are assigned. These essays will be read by other children in the class and by other children in the school at lunchtime, as they stand in line, and at other times of the day. Pam is careful to point out that their writing will look different from the list because it will be written in an essay format; she explains that their essays will contain paragraphs rather than numbered items.

Once she finishes introducing the assignment, Pam invites questions. Brian asks, "But what if I get a food I don't know anything about?"

Pam, understanding the value of collaborative learning, opens the discussion up to the class. "What do we do when we don't know something about a topic, boys and girls?" The children share what they do when they encounter an unfamiliar topic:

◆ "First you need to really think hard because you might know something about it and just forgot. Then after that, like if you really still don't remember, you can ask your colleagues at your table in a quiet voice."

◆ "You can ask your teacher or another adult in the class."

◆ "You can read around the room."

◆ "You can get on the computer and search the Internet with Pam."

Pam suggests some other ideas as well. Once the children feel comfortable with what they are expected to do in the coming days, Pam moves on to another subject. That afternoon, on chart paper, she writes an informational text about pickles based on the class-generated list, in preparation for the next day's lesson. (See sample text, right.)

> **Pickles are a kind of food made from cucumbers. Like cucumbers, they are oblong and have little stripes that go down the side. They are green and have soft seeds.**
>
> **There are different kinds of pickles. Some are soft, but most are really crunchy. Some are sour and some are sweet. Some people like only one kind of pickle, some like them all!**

Day Two:
More Explicit Teaching, Modeling, and Shared Writing

Pam begins the lesson by rereading the class-generated list of pickle facts from the day before. From there, she shows the class the informational text she wrote based on the list and reads it aloud. She then asks what the title of this piece should be. All of the children agree on "Pickles" because the piece is, after all, about pickles. After Pam writes the title at the top, she demonstrates how she converted the list to a paragraph. She also points out that she checked for misspelled words and correct use of punctuation. Finally, she tells the children that, since this was the final draft, she made sure she wrote neatly. She asks the children if they have any questions about the piece or her process of writing it.

Then Pam gives each child an index card with the name of a food product on it. Although research indicates that student choice is important (see discussion in Chapter 5), Pam chooses to assign topics for this lesson. This reinforces the point that no matter which topic a child gets, and how little the child knows about it, the child can still write about it as long as he or she does some research beforehand. She then encourages her students to brainstorm what they know about their assigned food in their journals, circulating and helping them get their thoughts down.

Day Three:
Researching Their Topics

Pam's students rely on a variety of sources to research their foods, including:

1. the World Wide Web (with screening and assistance)
2. books in the classroom
3. their peers (through discussions)
4. relatives (through interviews)

Pam encourages students to record what they learn in list form, as they did as a class on the first day of the study. Naturally, their notes are not as detailed or organized as older children's might be, but they do capture some of the most important and/or interesting things about their foods.

Day Four:
Writing Rough Drafts with Explicit Teaching and Coaching

On day four, the children convert the lists to paragraph drafts in their journals. Before they begin writing, Pam reminds students to refer to their list or notes as they write, to come up with a good title, and to use punctuation marks the class has been working on. As they write, Pam circulates around the classroom and coaches students individually. Specifically, she:

◆ works most closely with children who are struggling.

◆ refers children to the model list and informational text on pickles, which is posted on the wall.

◆ tells the children that what they write will be read by others who may not know much about their food. She encourages children to think about what readers might need or want to know most.

◆ focuses not only on content but also on language, praising children for using clear language appropriate to their topic and purpose (informational text language).

◆ holds children accountable for using writing conventions that have been previously taught.

This period of guided practice allows Pam to reinforce, reteach, or refine instruction that she provided in whole-class lessons. She tailors her responses to each child, trying to move each one forward.

Day Five:
Revising and Editing

Pam continues to work with children individually, asking them to read their drafts and commenting on what's working well and what's not. Her policy is to correct all spelling and punctuation, emphasizing the need for the writing to be polished in the final draft. Discussions revolve around the importance of writing clearly and tailoring the writing to the audience. Her students seem to be internalizing these instructions, because Pam observes them making many edits and revisions to their writing independently, with some commenting about their audience as they go.

Days Six and Seven:
Writing Final Versions
With Illustrations

Once they finish revising and editing, children write their final versions of their essays and draw an accompanying picture. Because the essays tell facts about their food, Pam encourages them to create realistic illustrations to support those facts.

When they complete their essays, Pam pastes each one to an 11-by-14-inch piece of construction paper. (See Figure 6.1.)

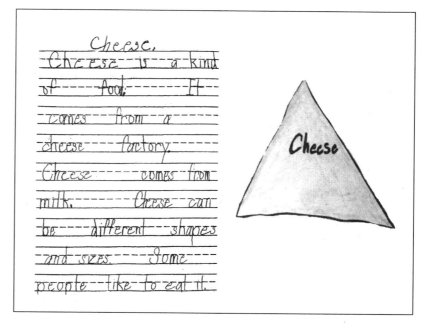

Figure 6.1: Here is an example of a child's writing that grew from Pam's food products lessons.

Day Eight:
Presenting and Posting Work

Pam gives the children the opportunity to come to the front of the class to present their findings. Each child reads his or her essay and shows the accompanying picture. Then Pam displays their essays on the wall just outside of the classroom. This allows the children in the class and other children in the school to read the essays when they are standing in line before and after lunch, or at other times of the day.

The Importance of Good Practices

Toby and Pam have much to teach us about effective informational writing instruction for primary-grade children. Their methods reflect the importance of engaging children in many phases of writing, of modeling and providing models of informational writing, of offering real purposes and audiences for writing, of giving children opportunities to write about what they know or are learning, and more. In the next section, we focus on three important principles for developing students' informational writing.

FOR YOUR INFORMATION...

Start Students Early

Lucy Calkins, one of the most noted figures in the field of writing education, is convinced that nonfiction—including informational writing—should be an important part of primary-grade curricula. In *The Art of Teaching Writing* (Calkins, 1994) she writes, "The impulse toward research and nonfiction writing needs to be nurtured during the early childhood years" (p. 432). "If children in the primary grades were examining, drawing, measuring, mulling over, and investigating milk pods or the blueprint of a building (or whatever else they brought in), this would provide a foundation for nonfiction writing. Out of what comes to school in children's pockets and backpacks, out of what they see and wonder about and poke into, their nonfiction writing emerges" (p. 432).

Build Writing Skills Through Research

Research involving Finnish kindergartners and second graders found that children can engage in research with text, provided they are given support to do so (Korkeamaki & Dreher, 2000; Korkeamaki, Tiainen, & Dreher, 1998).

Denise McLurkin is a former kindergarten teacher whose very young students were able to conduct research and write about their findings. They could do this largely because of Denise's ongoing, strong support. Below are three lessons she used to teach children about data gathering: observing, note-taking, and interviewing. Discussion is a big part of these lessons because, according to Denise, it gives children a chance to clarify unfamiliar things so that they can build on their learning. Discussion also gives Denise a way to gauge how much scaffolding children need to carry out the data-gathering activities, as well as how much conceptual knowledge the children have gained.

Lesson #1: Recording Science Observations

Objective: To help children become more comfortable recording science observations.

Preparation: Denise models observing and note-taking for the children prior to this lesson. She asks the children to observe the characteristics of something very familiar to them: a teddy bear. They investigate the bear's color, texture, and size, and share their observations. With the children sitting on the rug, Denise writes their observations on a sheet of posterboard and hangs it up for future reference.

The Lesson: Denise reads aloud several books on different types of trees. She then tells the children they are going to be scientists investigating trees in their community by paying close attention to their similarities and differences. Children are excited to go on this mini-field trip (one that is free and requires little planning!). Denise reminds the children that they are going to do the same type of activity that they did with the teddy bear, pointing to the list of observations on the back wall.

Once the children understand what they are to do, they go exploring, with their science journals in hand. As they observe the trees and discuss what they see with Denise and classmates, they write notes and draw pictures of their findings. The different shapes of

continued on next page

the trees they observe particularly fascinate children.

For the next couple of days, students write with Denise about the different shapes of the trees they observed, referring to their science journals as necessary. (See Figure 6.2.) The discussion is quite lively, as is the writing that results from it.

Lesson #2: Taking Field Notes

Objective: To help children understand that some scientists collect data by writing down field notes.

Preparation: To cap off a unit on the sea, Denise takes her students on a field trip to Sea World. Prior to the trip, she models how to take field notes by having selected children do various tasks, such as watering the plants, for approximately one minute, while the other children describe what they observe. Denise writes their observations on a sheet of posterboard for future reference.

Figure 6.2. Kindergartners write informational text about trees.

The Lesson: On the field trip, the children choose to observe what takes place during lunchtime at Sea World. Denise instructs them to write for two minutes in their science journals. After the time is up, the children discuss their findings in small groups while eating lunch. Then Denise engages them in a discussion on perspective—on how observers notice different things, depending on their viewpoint. The children compare their notes with an eye toward noticing differences, and are amazed.

On the next day, Denise and her students write together about their findings, drawing on their field notes and further discussion.

Lesson #3: Conducting Interviews

Objective: To help students understand the importance of talking with people around them in order to gain valuable information for writing.

Preparation: Michael, a custodian at the school, is someone Denise's students see often but know little about. So she decides interview him in front of the class, using an "interview protocol," which she writes on the chalkboard, as a guide:

Our Interview with Michael

Interviewer: _____

His Job:

    1. How long have you been working here?

    2. What do you have to do for your job?

    3. Do you like your job? Why or why not?

    4. Do you recycle our trash from school? Why?

    5. Do you recycle your trash at home? Why?

His Personal Life:

    1. Do you have any kids? How many?

    2. Do you have any pets? How many?

    3. Are you married? (a question followed by giggles)

    4. What do you like to do?

    5. What don't you like to do?

    6. What's your favorite food?

    7. What foods do you hate?

    8. If you could be anything in the whole wide world, what would you be?

Thank you!

The Lesson: With the children seated on the rug, Denise demonstrates how to use the protocol to guide the interview, how to listen carefully to responses, how to ask follow-up questions, and how to take notes on the interviewee's responses. She encourages the children to chime in during the interview if they think of questions that might make a biography of Michael more meaningful. A volunteer parent writes down the children's questions on the board as they are asked. As Michael speaks, children write down his answers on sheets with the questions photocopied on them. The interview lasts about twenty minutes.

    After the demonstration, the children discuss and write out or dictate questions that they feel would be interesting to include in their interviews of family members—the next assignment. They eventually conduct those interviews, draft biographies, and publish them in a class book.

THREE PRINCIPLES OF TEACHING INFORMATIONAL WRITING

As already noted, most research on informational writing and young children so far has focused on general principles for practice, rather than specific approaches. In this section we discuss three of those principles:

◆ Use reading to support writing—reading and writing are inextricably linked.

◆ Help children make information they've read and gathered "their own."

◆ Realize that informational text has functions and features that are different from other forms of text.

Principle #1:
Use Reading to Support Writing—Reading and Writing Are Inextricably Linked

According to Leonard Orr (1986), "No literary text is written in a vacuum. Besides the general culture surrounding the text and the author's own horizon (i.e., his [or her] experiences, prejudices, use of language system, 'worldview,' and so on), there are, perhaps more importantly, other texts, especially literary texts" (p. 814, quoted in Cairney, 1990, p. 480). Orr is discussing the notion of *intertextuality*: drawing from and making connections among multiple sources or texts (books, articles, Web sites, past experiences, discussions, interviews, observations, and so on) to inform and enrich one's own writing, reading, or response to text. Although we acknowledge the importance of all the different kinds of intertextual connections children make (oral text to oral text, oral text to written text, and so on), in this section we examine those between texts children read (or have read to them) and texts children write. (For a classic article on reading-writing relationships, and implications for instruction, see Shanahan, 1988.)

Some argue that primary-grade children are too young to make intertextual connections, but researchers have found this to be untrue (Marten, Flurkey, Meyer, & Udell, 1999). Some even argue that engaging primary-grade children in activities that require them to read *and* write is crucial to their reading and writing development (e.g., Moss, Leone, & DiPillo, 1997). For example, when a child is involved in an innovation (an activity described below), she is continuously referring back to the original text in order to inform the writing. Thus, the child is reading and rereading not only from a published text, but also from her own written product. Her reading of this text informs her own writing because it has intertextual connections to her writing. She sees the author's word choices, the author's treatment of information, devices, and so on, and may or may not apply them in her own writing.

How can we help children make intertextual connections as they write informational text? We offer these three strategies: exposing children to many models of informational text, engaging them in "innovations" based on informational text, and studying authors of these texts.

Expose Children to Many Models of Informational Writing

Perhaps the most fundamental way to promote intertextual connections is to expose children to many models of informational writing. As Yvonne Siu-Runyan (1998) writes, "If we want our students to develop into writers, they must hear and read excellent books from across all genres. And, it means that if we want our students to write nonfiction, we must read aloud and provide time for browsing and sharing well-written informational books" (p. 178). How different this is from exposing children only to textbooks and encyclopedias. Stephanie Harvey (2002) writes, "Authentic nonfiction writing is rich and full of voice. We teach our students that their best writing teachers are the authors they love, not the encyclopedias they need for beginning research" (p. 19). Siu-Runyan urges that by "massaging and combing" a text, the teacher and students learn aspects of informational writing, such as organizational structures and powerful language.

In his (2002) book *Is That a Fact?: Teaching Nonfiction Writing K–3,* Tony Stead points out the importance of including nonfiction texts in the classroom library as a means of supporting nonfiction writing development. He writes, "When I looked through my classroom library I found that 90 percent of the books were fiction stories. My read alouds and shared-readings were limited to the world of make-believe or personal narrative. No wonder my children wrote the same things every day and had become masters of these few forms. While I still believed that fiction and personal narrative were important, I realized they were only part of the bigger picture" (p. 7).

Figure 6.3: This simple text can provide a frame for informational writing: "_____ learn. They learn to _____. They learn to _____." and so on.

They learn to play.   They learn to hunt.

Subsequently, Stead began to include much more informational text in his classroom library, as well as in his read alouds, shared readings, and writing activities.

We agree that models of high-quality—and, for purposes of comparing and contrasting, low-quality—informational text are an important part of a writing curriculum. However, it is not always enough simply to expose children to these texts. Helping children to identify the characteristics they believe are found in quality writing and to develop their own stylistic preferences is critical. (For inspiration, see the box on pages 38–39 entitled "Criteria for Selecting Informational Text.") It's also important to help children apply their developing vision to their own writing. In the next sections, we discuss ways to do that.

Engage Students in "Innovations" Based on Informational Text

Innovations involve presenting children with a "frame" of a text from a particular genre. They then use this frame to create their own text in the same genre.

Figure 6.4: A more sophisticated text that could be used as a frame for informational writing.

Start by identifying a text with a clear pattern and organization to use as a frame. We have seen innovations done with quite sophisticated informational texts as well as very simple ones such as Pamela Chanko's *Baby Animals Learn* (1999), shown in Figure 6.3. One that works well is Devin Scillian's (2001) *A is for America*. In this book, each letter of the alphabet is connected to information about America or American history through poetry and prose. (See Figure 6.4.)

Read the text with the class, group, or individual who will be writing the innovation. You may need to help children identify the author's pattern and organization, so be prepared to provide assistance if they need it.

Have children write an innovation—in other words, their own version of the text. For example, an innovation based on *A is for America* might focus on the school: *S is for School*. Children would present the alphabet as Scillian did, but using things around schools to represent each letter: C is for the cafeteria, D is for days in school each year, and so on. When they are finished, have children share their innovations with a real audience, preferably one that would learn something from the text. They might share *S is for School* with parents or with children at kindergarten roundup, for example.

Try Paragraph Frames

Educators Evelyn Cudd and Leslie Roberts (1989) provide children with paragraph frames, which are much like the innovation frames described above, to teach them to write with various kinds of text structures. For example, for a sequential structure they recommend a frame such as, "Mother box turtles prepare for their babies in a very interesting way. First, _____. Next, _____. After this, _____. Finally, _____." (p. 395). First, Cudd and Roberts model how to write a paragraph using the frame. Then they provide students with a similar frame to complete on their own. Their hope is that, after enough practice, children won't need the frame and will be able to write a simple sequential text on their own.

Frames can be used to teach non-sequential text structures as well, as Cudd and Roberts show in this example: "Bats are unusual animals for several reasons. First, _____. Second, _____. Third, _____. Finally, _____. As you can see, bats are unique in the animal world." (p. 396). We do not recommend using paragraph frames for all informational writing that children do; if overused, they could lead to overly formulaic writing. But they are very helpful when introducing children to signal words and phrases (such as *first, next, is different than, are similar to,* and *is a kind of),* to text structures such as compare/contrast, or to rhetorical devices such as using an anecdote to capture the readers' attention.

Study Authors of Informational Texts

Typically, author studies focus on narrative writers such as Dr. Seuss and Eric Carle. However, there are authors of informational texts whose lives and work are well worth exploring. Some information book authors are prolific; their work can teach children much about the writing process, craft, style, and so on. (See box at right for twenty of our favorites.) You can investigate where authors get their information and how they verify its accuracy. You might also examine how authors represent their beliefs and values in their texts— for example, how Gail Gibbons expresses her commitment to the environment.

Principle #2:
Help Children Make Information They've Read and Gathered "Their Own"

"Excuse me Miss M., can you please hold this book down while I copy this stuff about the duck-billed platypus?" This child is sweet and hardworking, but guilty of a common problem: plagiarism. We've all read children's reports that sound exactly like an encyclopedia, dictionary, or Web site.

Researchers have found that children do copy, often word for word. What's even more troubling is that some children continue to plagiarize even if they're

Twenty Authors of Informational Text Worth Studying

◆ Aliki

◆ Melvin Berger

◆ Franklyn Branley

◆ Joanna Cole

◆ Allan Fowler

◆ Rita Golden Gelman

◆ Gail Gibbons

◆ Linda Glaser

◆ Ruth Heller

◆ Barnabas and Annabel Kindersley

◆ Patricia Lauber

◆ Milton Meltzer

◆ Charles Micucci

◆ Ann Morris

◆ Ifeoma Onyefulu

◆ Mary Pope Osborne

◆ Jerry Pallotta

◆ Laurence Pringle

◆ Seymour Simon

It may also be worthwhile to study writers from your students' favorite magazines, CD-ROMs, or other informational text sources.

aware that they should not and can give reasonable explanations for why they should not (Lewis, Wray, & Rospigliosi, 1994; Wray & Lewis, 1992). Suggestions for alleviating the problem include (Lewis, Wray & Rospigliosi, 1994, and Read, 2001):

◆ Have children do at least some informational writing based on what they already know, on topics such as school, favorite animals, and games they enjoy.

◆ Steer children toward some sources that can't be easily copied, such as interviews.

◆ Ask children to respond to informational text using a graphic organizer such as a grid, a chart, a tree diagram, a flow chart, a Venn diagram, or even a map, instead of writing out their responses in prose form. This technique is known as Text Remodeling (Lewis, Wray, & Rospigliosi, 1994).

◆ After children have studied their topic, consider having them write about it in a genre that's different from the original source but still appropriate to the purpose, such as a letter. This technique is known as Genre Exchange (Lewis, Wray, & Rospigliosi, 1994).

◆ Have children draw pictures or diagrams after reading but before writing. This technique is known as Pictorial Forms (Lewis, Wray & Rospigliosi, 1994).

◆ Before writing, distance students from any one source by using multiple sources and discussion (Read, 2001). For example, Sylvia Read had her students read several books on the same topic, held discussions with them about what they found in the books, and then asked them to write about their findings. Read noted that her students' writing was not only more their own, but that the content was richer as well.

For teachers who spend considerable time on informational writing, and connect it to the larger curriculum or to children's experiences, copying is often not a major problem. By engaging in the practices outlined in this chapter, you can significantly diminish the likelihood of it happening in your classroom.

Principle #3:
Realize That Informational Text Has Functions and Features That Are Different from Other Forms of Text

Functions

As mentioned in Chapter 1, the function of informational text is to convey information about the natural or social world, typically from someone presumed to know that information to someone presumed not to know it, but who wants or needs to know it. So that's just what we should encourage children to do as they write informational text: a) convey information about the natural or social world, b) from a position of knowing this information, c) to someone who wants or needs to know it. However, too often, we don't encourage students to do that. Think of the traditional state report, for example. These often look and sound very different from informational texts we find in children's sections of libraries or bookstores, with teacher's name and date on the cover and the standard opening line, "My report is on…." These reports are usually not written because someone wants or needs to know those things about the state. They are written for the teacher—and, chances are, she isn't all that interested in the state's bird, flag, and flower. However, there are ways to have students write informational text for the purpose for which it is intended. For example, children could write about daily class routines for children who are new to the school. They could write a letter about animals they'd like to see displayed at their local zoo and send their wishes to the person in charge. One teacher we know had her kindergartners write books about stars to share with parents, classmates, school personnel, and others who expressed an interest in learning about that topic. A struggling third grader prepared an informational text about snakes—along with phonics games, activities, and worksheets related to snakes—for a first-grade class.

You can probably think of examples, too, in which children have written in a real genre for a real purpose and audience—perhaps thank-you notes to a class visitor, invitations to a class party, get-well cards to an ill classmate or staff member, pen-pal letters, written requests to the office, recipes to include in a cookbook to raise money for the school, and so on. Even very young children seem to understand that someone may read their writing, and that that should affect what and how they write.

Features

To serve their function, informational text has many distinct features. We believe that knowing about these features may make teachers more sensitive and responsive to children's developing informational writing. Several researchers have analyzed informational texts written for children to identify their features (e.g., Duke & Kays, 1998; Pappas, 1986; 1987; 2002; Purcell-Gates & Duke, 2001). It is not possible to discuss the results of all of these studies in this chapter, but some of the features researchers have found include:

◆ an opening statement/general classification (e.g., "Ants are a kind of insect.")

◆ a general statement/closing (e.g., "Ants are interesting to study.")

◆ description of attributes/components (e.g., "Ants have six legs.") and/or characteristic events (e.g., "Ants eat sugar.").

◆ frequent repetition of the topical theme (Ants... Ants... etc.)

◆ timeless verb constructions (Ants *carry* sand as opposed to *carried, are carrying,* etc.)

◆ generic noun constructions (*Ants* carry sand as opposed to *the ant, Joe,* or *that ant* carries, etc.)

◆ specialized vocabulary *(thorax, colony)*

◆ classifications and definitions

◆ text structures such as compare/contrast, problem/solution, cause/effect

◆ headings

◆ labels and captions

◆ index and/or (less common) table of contents

◆ boldface and/or italicized print

◆ graphical elements such as diagrams, tables, charts, and maps

◆ realistic illustrations or photographs

Not all informational texts have these features, and the absence of one or more of them doesn't necessarily make a text less desirable. The features of a text should be appropriate to its purpose, content, and style. For example, many of Seymour Simon's books seem to be written to be read from beginning to end. They resemble coffee-table books more than encyclopedias. As such, Simon often chooses not to include features such as headings and indexes.

We do not yet know to what degree, if any, it is helpful to actually teach children these features explicitly. Victoria Purcell-Gates and Nell Duke are currently conducting research to address this question, and preliminary results suggest that it is helpful only in some cases

(Purcell-Gates & Duke, 2003). However, much more information is needed. Be on the look-out for research in this area and, in the meantime, use your best judgment about when and how to teach children about features of informational text.

ASSESSING INFORMATIONAL WRITING: FINDING OUT WHAT CHILDREN CAN DO

Few tools have been developed to assess informational writing of primary students. In fact, we had to develop our own tool for the Early Literacy Project: a relatively simple rubric for assessing the writing of first and second graders. A modified version is presented on pages 152–155. Use it on its own or as a basis for developing your own rubric.

RUBRIC FOR ASSESSING INFORMATIONAL WRITING IN THE PRIMARY GRADES

Not Applicable

◆ Nothing on paper, no attempt to produce written text, drawing may be present

0

◆ Letter-like strings, all or almost all incomprehensible text

1

◆ No part has a function or features of informational text
◆ May be an entirely other genre such as narrative text, descriptive text, or listing

Example: A bee, A grasshopper, A fliiy (fly), A ant, A beetle A butterfly
Rationale: This is a listing and does not convey any information.

Example: I like ladybugs and I like bees and I like babese (baby) bees. I like sprdrsds (spiders)
Rationale: Doesn't convey information about insects.

Example: The insects is a insects. The insects is very ceut (cute). They very funny and ceot (cute).
Rationale: Descriptive of the illustrations without conveying any information.

2

◆ Has some function and features of informational text
◆ Writer seems to have an idea of what constitutes informational text
◆ May be mixed with features of narrative, descriptive, or listing
◆ Repetitive sentence patterns with minimal changes

Example: I like flies. Bugs like to eat other bugs. My bug is a bed bug.
Rationale: Some informational text, but is mixed with personal feelings about bugs.

Example: Ants is a big help. But flis (flies) ant (ain't or aren't) and bees are a big help to (too). But gasshopper (grasshopper) ant (ain't or aren't) a big help.

Rationale: Indicates an awareness that the purpose is to convey information, although the amount of information is relatively low.

Example: Insects fly. Insects eat. Insects croll (crawl). Insects hop.

Rationale: Simple repeating pattern in sentences. Conveys some information but not a great deal; not much variety.

3

◆ **Has the function and features of informational text to a moderate degree**
◆ **May reflect function or include features of other genres, but to a lesser extent than texts rating a 2**
◆ **May still include some features of oral language**
◆ **Overall, more varied in sentence structure**
◆ **Conveys more information than a 2**

Example: A insects have six legs. Ladybugs fly. I saw one. Beyfor (Before) ants are good works. Grasshopper always jump. Dragonflies are in the jungle. Flys (Flies) – I try not to kill them. Hunoey (Honey) bees allywas (always) make honey. Butterflys (Butterflies) are good. Noboty (Nobody) are insects. No insects are clgin (children). Bugs can get in your hair.

Rationale: Functions to convey information to a moderate degree. Sentence structure is somewhat repetitive, but the sentences are more varied and more information is provided. Describes components (insects have six legs), characteristic events (honeybees always make honey), and general statements (Beyfor ants are good works). Uses the word *always* to describe the degree to which an insect engages in particular behavior. The word *your* also appears to be a sort of generic *your*. Still has features not characteristic of informational text, such as use of the word *I* and the oral language of "flys- I try not to kill them"

Example: Insects ar (are) cool. But some insects are pusanis (poisonous)! Insects help us, but some insects do not. Other insects eat bugs and other insects. Some insects are harmless, but some are not. Watch out! for pusanis insects. The End.

Rationale: Functions to convey information to a moderate degree. Begins with a general opening statement ("insects are cool"). Includes specialized vocabulary (poisonous, harmless) and the words *some* and *other*, common in informational text. Shows contrast of helpful insects with those that are not. More varied sentences; includes more information than papers rating a 2.

4

◆ **Mostly or entirely has the function and features of informational text**
◆ **Considerable information is conveyed and many features are used**
◆ **Has few, if any, features of oral language**

Example: Insects have six legs. They have three bodt (body) pars (parts). A abdmin (abdomen) and a hede (head) a Thoraet (thorax). Insects sach (such) as a latybug (ladybug) haves six lags too. But sume (some) bug ar (are) not insects. But sume bug have eight lage (leg). Bug ar halpfl (helpful) too us. Sume bug halp (help) us. They crall (crawl) and crrep (creep) around the....

Rationale: Has some specialized vocabulary (abdomen, thorax) and refers to them as specific components (body parts). Organization of that section is tighter— the list of body parts immediately follows the information about body parts. There is also use of constructions common to informational text (e.g., "But sume bug ar not insects."). Mostly functions as informational text.

Example: Fruit is vary (very) good for you. Pepel (People) by (buy) fruut (fruit) because they like it. Our (Or) they now it is good for you. Pepel grow fruits not only because they tink (think) it tast (taste) good. But because it is good for you. Pepl (People) at supermarkets don't sell fruit just to get mony (money) they sell fruits because ther (they're) hethy (healthy). Farmrs (Farmers) don't grow fruit to eat they grow fruit because it is hethy. Thet's (That's) wy (why) you should eat fruits.

Rationale: Begins with a general statement (fruit is very good for you). Use of the word *people* to refer to people in general. Repeats topical theme of fruit, especially the idea of fruit being healthy. Conveys a lot of information. Content is structured: "People don't grow fruits just because it tastes good. People don't sell fruits just to get money." There is specialized vocabulary (supermarkets, farmers).

Example: Did you know that flis (flies) can bite? After a bee stings you it dis (dies). Grass hopts (hoppers) mace a cliing (clicking) sound at night. The mssetto (mosquito) sucs (sucks) you're blud (blood). when ant bits you're skin it dusint (doesn't) hrt (hurt). But what about the red anf? It herts (hurts) dusin (doesn't) if? Some other insect can bite and sting too. Do you now (know) the life sicle (cycle) of evry (every) insecf? what... evry (every) life sicle (cycle) or jut (just) one. The ladybug has six legs. If you're an insect you have six legs. Can you think of eny (any) more?

Rationale: Includes hooks that are often used in the opening sections of text. Asks a question, then conveys information pertinent to that topic (biting and stinging). There is specialized vocabulary (life cycle, mosquito). There is also a distinction between ants in general and red ants. Use of words common to informational text (some, other, too). Conveys a lot of information.

5

◆ **Entirely or almost entirely has the function and features of informational text**
◆ **Considerable information is conveyed and many features are used, with features including an organized structure, topic sentences, support sentences with additional details, and summary sentences**
◆ **Has few if any features of oral language**

Example: Fruit has lots of tastes and are good to eat. Many people make many things with fruit such as apple or cherry pie. Many people make and use fruit as snacks. Sometimes people eat small seeds of fruit, such as watermelon, pears, apples, grapes, or cherrrys. Fruit is a popular snack all around the world. Here in America, people eat all kinds of fruit.

Rationale: Has many characteristics of informational text and conveys considerable information. Has a topic sentence ("Fruit has lots of tastes and are good to eat."). Writer supports and clarifies statements with examples: making many things to eat—apple and cherry pies, snacks; eating fruit that has seeds—watermelon, grapes. Writer sums up with idea that fruit is popular and people eat all kinds of fruit.

CONCLUDING THOUGHTS

Adding informational writing to primary-grade curricula is not only possible, it's also exciting. It's important to remember that young children need instruction and support to develop as informational writers. You can provide this by exposing them to models of informational text, connecting reading and writing through activities such as innovations and author studies, helping children conduct research and make information their own, providing real purposes and audiences for informational writing, and being aware of the distinct features of informational text. Indeed, writing informational text need not be put off until children are older, but can be embraced joyfully even as early as kindergarten. The next chapter explores how reading and writing informational text can be integrated into content area instruction.

CHAPTER 7
Content Area Reading
Using Informational Text to Build Children's Knowledge of the World Around Them

BY EMILENE VOGEL

Do the endless "Whys?" and "Hows?" of preschoolers have to turn into what older children too often say: "Do I have to do this?" "I don't get why we have to learn this stuff…" "I'm just not good at it."? Of course not. We all constantly process information, from birth to death, and we can keep the natural curiosity and joy of learning flourishing in our students.

Science, math, social studies, health, art, and music help children discover ways to connect with and make sense of their world. Quality informational text is one tool we can use to ensure that our content area teaching is exciting and productive. In this chapter we:

◆ briefly discuss research related to using informational text in content area instruction.

◆ describe how several teachers have used informational text in content area instruction.

◆ discuss some special considerations for locating and selecting books for content area instruction.

◆ explore three research-based instructional strategies for using informational text in content area instruction.

This information is designed to offer new insights on how to use informational text to enhance your students' understandings of concepts across the curriculum.

INFORMATIONAL TEXT IN CONTENT AREA INSTRUCTION: WHAT THE RESEARCH SAYS

There is quite a lot of research related to the use of informational text in content area instruction. Some researchers have looked at textbooks—their readability, accuracy, and role in developing or failing to develop children's understandings. (See Beck & McKeown, 1991, for a discussion.) Of greatest interest to most primary-grade teachers, however, may be research on integrating trade books into content area instruction. Studies have looked at using trade books—usually both narrative and informational, but sometimes only one or the other—in science, social studies, and even mathematics. *Every* study we have encountered indicates that using trade books in this way has a positive impact on children's learning—specifically, on their content area learning, literacy learning, motivation, or some combination of these (e.g., Bristor, 1994; Guthrie, Van Meter, McCann, Wigfield, Bennett, Poundstone, et al., 1996; Guzzetti, Kowalinski, & McGowan, 1992; Levstik, 1986; Morrow, Pressley, Smith, & Smith, 1997; Smith, Monson, & Dobson, 1992; see Gavelek, Raphael, Biondo, & Wang, 2000 for a review of many of these and other studies). Although most of these studies were conducted with upper-elementary students, there is every reason to think that using information trade books in content area instruction benefits younger students as well.

We especially like the way Annemarie Palincsar and Shirley Magnusson (2000) talk about integrating text in science instruction. They discuss firsthand and secondhand investigations as part of scientific inquiry. Firsthand investigations involve real-world or hands-on experiences; secondhand investigations involve the use of written text. Palincsar and Magnusson argue that both types of investigations are a part of scientists' work and, therefore, should be part of children's science education.

Another study, by Emily Anderson and John Guthrie (1999), supports that argument. They looked at four approaches to science instruction: hands-on experiences only, text-based experiences only, both types of experiences, and neither type of experience. They found that the combination of hands-on and text-based experiences was most educational for children. Throughout this chapter, you will see how teachers use a combination of firsthand and secondhand investigations, along with children's prior knowledge and experiences, to foster content area and literacy learning.

Incorporating Informational Text into the Content Areas: A Few Teachers' Approaches

Once teachers have quality information books, they tend to look for ways to integrate them into the content areas. The teachers described in this section use informational text especially well. They create a synergy between print, technology, and real-world experiences that leads to powerful learning for children.

Margaret Barker, Kindergarten Teacher

Margaret Barker has been teaching kindergarten for 18 years in a small town. She has completed some graduate work beyond her master's degree in elementary education. About 40 percent of her students receive free or reduced lunches. About 15 percent have parents who commute to the large city about thirty miles away, to jobs that pay better than those they might find locally.

"I've seen a lot of changes in curriculum since my first year of teaching kindergarten," says Margaret. "We had half days then. Our main goals were to get the children used to the school structure—sitting still to listen to a story, standing in line, getting along with others, and maybe a few manners. We would then add a little reading readiness, which was mostly learning the names of letters, nursery rhymes, songs, and poems. We would do some counting and number recognition, and call it good. Our only textbook was for penmanship.

We do a lot of content area work now. We have a science, social studies, and math curriculum, and of course literacy development. This is our fourth year of children coming all day, every day."

Recently, Margaret's school revised its science curriculum, and she was responsible for updating the kindergarten section. "We will mostly be covering the earth sciences—the weather, the seasons, the environment (reduce, reuse, recycle), and fossils. The children get excited learning about real things they are able to see, touch, and experience."

Instead of a science textbook, Margaret uses the leveled "little books" that are part of the Newbridge *Discovery Links* series. The children like the books' bright colors and fascinating photographs. Margaret likes the fact that the publisher provides multiple copies of each book, so she can engage more than one student at a time in reading them. For social studies, Margaret uses the Wright Group books to augment the textbooks. Her school library has an excellent collection of information trade books, which she also uses for classroom instruction. She displays information posters around the classroom to convey science, health, and social studies concepts.

Margaret uses these resources in a variety of ways. She reads books aloud to her students, stopping for discussion to make sure the children understand the concepts. Often she skims more complicated books—skipping around, looking at pictures, and concentrating on a single concept. When she teaches how to find answers to questions, she lets children know that they don't have to read every page and she models how to use the table of contents and index.

Seizing every opportunity she can to teach literacy, Margaret exposes her students to a variety of genres. She makes sure that they have lots of opportunities to explore books they select on their own, for their own purposes. She shows the children how to use their library computer to find books on topics that interest them. Whether they're interested in frogs, freight trains, or fairy princesses, she wants them to experience the thrill of learning through reading.

Many of Margaret's students relate better to the informational text than to traditional storybooks. "Sometimes the storybooks go over their heads…they just don't get it," she says. "The children haven't had enough experiences to make the connections."

"Our Seasons Are Changing" Lesson

Margaret wants to help her students understand the concept of the changing seasons. Specifically, she wants them to be more aware that when seasons change, so does their world. So she conducts a lesson entitled "Our Seasons Are Changing." To introduce the lesson, she engages the whole class in a discussion about the daily activities calendar. Her students' comments include:

"We are in the summer season. Soon we are having a change."

"We will be changing our season box from summer to fall."

"Today is cloudy. That is a change from all our other sunny days."

The class then discusses the word *change* and concludes that it means "something is different."

Next, Margaret has the children form small groups. She tells them that she has some "special books" to look at and shows them four information books from Newbridge's emergent reader series: *In Summer* (Parkes, 1997), *Fall* (Nayer, 1997a), *Winter* (Trumbauer, 1997), and *In Spring* (Nayer, 1997b). (See Figure 7.1.) She then asks the children to look at each book's cover and tell her which season it represents. Pointing to the titles, she asks the children to read the names of the seasons. She then assigns each group a season and gives it the corresponding set of books, making sure that every child has a book to examine. Finally, Margaret instructs her students to "look for things that let you know it is summer, fall, winter, or spring," depending on their group. They know that they will be reporting back to the whole class about characteristics of their season. She goes on to tell them, "Turn those pages. Look and think! Look and think!"

Figure 7.1: Covers of the four books about seasons that Margaret uses with her kindergartners.

As students explore the season books, Margaret visits groups individually. The children are excited; they want to show her the neat things they notice. (See Figure 7.2.) She validates their feelings of enthusiasm with responses such as, "How interesting!" "Yes, that is cool!" "Wow!"

After a while, Margaret tells the children it's time to let the rest of the class see what they have discovered. Starting with the summer group, she asks the children what they saw that let them know that it was summer. Below is an excerpt from the discussion. Notice how Margaret asks questions that encourage children to reveal their findings. She then jots down their findings on a chart as they speak. (See Figure 7.3.)

Figure 7.2: Margaret's students share interesting things they notice in information books about seasons.

MARGARET: What's in your picture, Tina?

STUDENT: They are playing in the sand.

MARGARET: What's over her head, that red and white thing?

STUDENT: An umbrella.

MARGARET: It doesn't look like it's raining. Why would she need an umbrella?

STUDENT: Cause it's too sunny out!

MARGARET: Oh, good reason. [Pauses.] So there is more than one reason to use an umbrella. That's cool!

[After discussing more about summer, such as how hot it gets outside, Margaret moves on to another group.]

MARGARET: Okay, where's my fall group? What did you see that lets you know it's fall?

STUDENT: Pumpkins growing.

MARGARET: Pumpkins growing, interesting. What holiday has pumpkins in the fall?

STUDENT: Halloween?

MARGARET: Now you guys said it was really, really hot in the summer right? How is the weather in fall? Does it change? Is it any different?

Figure 7.3: Margaret records her students' observations.

photo: Emilene Vogel

The discussion continues, with children taking increasing responsibility for the discussion. They talk about how leaves change color and eventually fall off the tree, and why this happens. They discuss ways the weather changes, why some animals store food, and why some birds fly to a warmer place.

Margaret then moves the conversation to the winter group by asking the children what season follows fall, and what changes it brings. The children discuss snow and the need for warm coats. They point out "little birds" that stay for the winter and where they might find food and shelter. Because the children had been introduced to the concept of hibernation the previous week while studying bats, they connected the concept to bears and talked about how the two animals' hibernation patterns are similar and different. From the winter group,

Margaret moves on to the spring group with a discussion of how the world changes because of the weather and season.

The success of this lesson on changing seasons is due in part to the books that Margaret gave her students. They provided an important source of new information on seasons and triggered connections to what the children already knew about seasons from their own experiences.

Marcia Barnes, First-Grade Teacher

Marcia Barnes, a teacher in a large urban school district, tells us that she and her students love using information books to learn about their world. Marcia has taught for over twenty years; she is in her fifth year of teaching first grade. "The kids at this age are so eager to learn," she says. "They want to know all they can about everything!"

Many of Marcia's students have skills far below grade level and come from low socioeconomic backgrounds. Despite that, Marcia does not accept excuses from students, and she does not baby them. She demands performance, reminding them often, "You are here to learn and you will!" Her students know that she cares for them and their learning. On one of our visits to the class, when we asked a new student to read, she said, "I can't read. At our old school, all I did was color. In this class, I'm gonna learn!"

Informational text is one of Marcia's favorite teaching tools, and she is particularly fond of trade books on nature and science. She often gives book talks—that is, she previews books for the class before putting them in the reading bins or book display. She discusses the book's topic and asks the children what they know about it. She might read a few pages. Together, she and the students look at some of the pictures and illustrations. She says that this serves dual purposes. First, it acquaints the children with the subject to activate their prior knowledge. Second, it lets her know what gaps in their knowledge she needs to fill in. Such book talks can also incite student interest. (See Chapter 5 for more information.)

"For the last three years, I've been using more and more information trade books to teach science. I have found that they are a good resource for teaching reading and writing skills, too…. Students cannot relate to ideas in typical textbooks. However, I find that the information books and videos with real pictures put the child there. Indirectly, they give the child a *real* experience. Once the interest is there, involvement in reading, writing, and discussion build upon each other."

Motivating Students in Content Area Instruction

One striking aspect of Marcia's classroom is how motivated the children are—they're motivated to think, learn, write, and read.

Motivated to think. Marcia emphasizes that students should make connections—from what they know to new things they encounter, from cause to effect, from one text to another. She asks children many questions about what they think and why they think it. Her questions help them discover relationships and push them to think hard. And Marcia really listens to their answers. She has a real gift for communicating with students; she talks to and with her students, not at them. Above all, she encourages and praises good thinking.

Motivated to learn. "The children are so eager to learn about their world," says Marcia. She goes on to tell us that her students want to read information books because they find these books so fresh and exciting. The colorful pictures and inviting graphics let them see beyond their immediate surroundings to a world of wonder. "Things changed when I brought information books into my classroom. The students' vocabulary increased. They searched in their own homes and yards for examples of what we had discussed in our plant and animal studies. They also started bringing information trade books back from the library to share with the rest of the class. Parents commented that when flipping through channels, the students now stopped on educational science programs. Reading and learning is becoming a focal point in their lives. They have a curiosity for science. They now lead discussions and incorporate their ideas in their writing."

Motivated to write. Marcia has noticed that the children pay attention to details and are more focused when it comes to writing. They know what they want to say and are more willing to work to sound out the words and learn the mechanics of writing. Quite often they will type the final draft on the computer. Marcia adds that the children are so proud to have written something "real." Marcia makes sure children feel they have a lot of world knowledge to bring to their writing. She helps children see how much they already know about the world around them. If there's an area in which they have little knowledge, she builds it. For example, when they studied the ocean, none of the children had ever been near an ocean. She set up an exhibit of seashells, ocean fossils, fish netting, and a real sponge along with some beautiful ocean books: *Amazing Animals of the Sea* (Rinard & O'Neill, 1981) and *Our Ocean Home* (Nelson, 1997) were two of them. She also painted some windows to look like an ocean scene.

Motivated to read. On one visit some of the children read their "Under the Sea" texts that they had previously written and edited for their principal. Here is an example:

> *Some fish are camouflaged. They*
> *blend in with the sea floor. Some*
> *other fish are normal.*
> *The blue whale is the biggest*
> *animal of them all. It is not a fish. It*
> *is a mammal.*

The principal expresses surprise as these students who are typically labeled "nonreaders" read their essays perfectly. After praising them, the principal asks how they got to be such good readers. One child answers, "We like reading our own words!"

Marcia succeeds in creating a classroom in which children are proud of what they do and are motivated to do more.

Learning About How Things Live and Grow in the Wild

To provide real-life experiences for her students, each year Marcia takes the class on a field trip to her country home, which is surrounded by a pond, forest, and wetlands. During the two weeks prior to their trip, she focuses her instruction on how things live and grow in the wild. She reads and makes available information books on insects, seeds, snakes, frogs, small wildlife, and ecology. With the students, she discusses what they see in the books and what they hope to see on their trip. Any topic is fair game: how seeds travel, why spiders make webs, where ants build their homes, and the variety of animals that live together in ponds.

On the day of the trip, the children experience nature firsthand, many for the first time. They look for and find seeds, anthills, spiderwebs, a bird's egg, butterflies, snails, and a woolly caterpillar. Marcia gives the children fake-fur leggings to wear as they as they walk about, to simulate how animals naturally spread seeds through their fur as they travel. At the end of the trip, the children are fascinated to see the seeds on their leggings. Some take the seeds home to see if they will grow in their yards.

Figure 7.4: After exploring information books on insects, this child investigates an anthill.

The children find dragonfly skins, which are shed like snake skins, as they explore around the pond. They also find a bullfrog hiding in the grass. One student notices that its skin matches its surroundings almost perfectly and shouts, "It's camouflaged!" Other students collect acorns from an oak tree. Some take a paddleboat ride to get a closer look at aquatic life.

These first graders see themselves as the young scientists that they are. They observe. They explore. They discover. They experience what they have read about. They learn.

Anna Vogel, Second-Grade Teacher

Anna Vogel is just two years out of college, with a bachelor's degree in elementary education. She is teaching second grade in a suburban school close to a large metropolitan area. Her class consists of 21 students from diverse ethnic and economic backgrounds.

Anna views informational text as a fundamental resource. She believes that incorporating it into her learning community is essential to helping students comprehend, analyze, and evaluate conceptual understandings of how their world works. So naturally, she values helping children use informational text as a tool for being "researchers of their world."

Becoming "Researchers of Their World"

Teaching research processes is important to Anna. One way she does this is by reading aloud trade books that relate to topics her class is studying—a practice she loves. She does not always read the whole book; sometimes she reads only sections that relate to questions that she or her students have raised. She talks through her process of locating information and how she determines whether it relates to her questions.

Anna has students carry out research independently. For example, when students asked, "Why do leaves change color in the fall?" she found about ten books on the topic and told students that the answer could be found in them. She wanted the students to find the information on their own—not only to get an answer to their question, but to see firsthand the value of using texts as resources. She explains, "I do this because, in the real world, if they have a question or are just curious about something, they will have to conduct research to find their answers. While they were searching, I would pick up a few of the books and real aloud some of the facts. I did this to model how to find information in books to help answer questions."

The Internet is an important research tool in Anna's class, too. "We log on to the Weather Channel [www.weather.com] every day to find out about the day's weather. After gathering our data, we graph it. We also use educational Internet sites to find information on topics we are studying, such as dinosaurs and Australia. Using technology such as the Internet and even education software [*Compton's World Encyclopedia* (Broderbund, 2000) and *Exploring Where and Why* (Nystrom, 1999)] really motivates students to learn."

Anna also subscribes to a children's news magazine each year, such as *Time for Kids*. Her students use it not only as a source of information for answering specific research questions, but also for general learning and pleasure reading. According to Anna, "The value of having these resources is that kids find out about current events that are important to them. They see that articles hold factual information that can help them understand and be more aware about their world. Students also discover that graphs and organizers are used in real-life publications to communicate information."

It is important for her students to conduct research in groups. For example, in the social-studies center, students explore different nonfiction books about countries they are studying. They then work in groups to write five facts they learned and illustrate the one they find most interesting. Anna also incorporates information books in her reading groups, which she and the children use to discuss how to use tables of contents, glossaries, page numbers, and indexes to pick out information from texts.

A Research Unit on Farming

Anna engages students as researchers of their world in her two-week unit on farming. She uses both fictional narrative and informational texts related to animals and raising crops, and she also uses objects from real farms. Key parts of this unit include making a KWL chart, reading aloud, making fiction-nonfiction connections, and guided reading.

KWL chart. To find out what the children already know about farming and to help them link that knowledge to new knowledge, Anna kicks off the unit by creating a KWL chart with the students (Ogle, 1986). For more information on creating KWL charts and an example of one that Anna created with her students, see pages 190–191.

Read Aloud. On the same day the class creates the KWL chart, Anna reads part of James Cooper's (1992) information book, *Great Places to Visit: Farms.* She models how to use the table of contents and glossary to check out facts and find information. The students and Anna refer to their KWL as they find information in the text. They learn where their food and milk come from. They learn that "Farms are the places where domestic animals, like cows and pigs, and food crops like grain and vegetables, are raised" (Cooper, 1992, p. 23). They discuss the word *domestic* to make sure that everyone understands that domestic animals are those raised by people. They learn about specialty farms that raise fish, rabbits, minks, llamas, bees, and even ostriches. They put checks by any understandings on their chart that are verified by the text.

Anna shows the students photographs of her parents' dairy farm, which support some of the book's information. She emphasizes the importance of checking out facts by saying "you have to think and make sure you believe the right things." In Cooper's book, it states, "Most dairy farmers use electric milking machines" (p. 11). Anna passes around some photographs of her father using electric milking machines to milk cows, which spurs more questions. For example, one student asks, "What do cows do when people are milking the cows?" After the discussion, Anna encourages students to learn more about farms by checking out the many information books she has displayed in the classroom.

Making fiction-nonfiction connections. Anna believes that it is important for children to recognize differences between nonfiction and fiction texts, so she reinforces the point all year. One way she does this is by using stickers to color code fiction and nonfiction books in her classroom library, so that children can distinguish them at a glance. Juxtaposing related fiction and nonfiction texts is another strategy she uses.

On the first day of the farm unit, Anna read aloud the first chapter of the fictional narrative text *Charlotte's Web* (White, 1952). On this second day, she reads aloud an information book about pigs and students compare facts in it to the description of Wilbur in *Charlotte's Web*. Specifically, students sort out what is true about all pigs including Wilbur (e.g., "They weigh between x and y pounds.") and what is unique to Wilbur (e.g., "He can talk"). Anna jots down their thoughts on chart paper. Then she reads aloud a passage from *Charlotte's Web*: "Wilbur was allowed to live in a box by the stove in the kitchen" (p. 8). She asks if anyone remembers a fact he or she learned that would relate to this. One boy quickly replies, "They need warm places to live!" Eventually in the story, Wilbur is moved to a pen, just the way a real pig might be, according to the information book. This, too, is pointed out by the students. Other fictional narrative texts used in this unit include *Click, Clack, Moo: Cows That Type* (Cronin, 2000) and a book from the district reading series about two sisters who grow and sell vegetables.

Guided reading. Anna next conducts guided reading using a set of books called *From Farm to Table* (e.g., Anton, 1998). Children read about and discuss how corn is grown, harvested, and processed as well as how it is used as food for people and animals. They decide to look at food labels at home to see how many products contain corn as an ingredient.

As a cooperative learning activity, Anna organizes students into groups of three and gives each one a different "farm fact card"—a card containing a photograph of a farm scene with a brief, simple description. (See Figure 7.5.) She asks groups to discuss their card and then report back in their own words what they learned from it. To model the activity, she chooses a card showing a farmer planting wheat, reads the description, and discusses the meaning of the text and the picture. Then she has the groups try it on their own.

As Anna walks around the room, she overhears a student in one group say, "I got my fact. Silos are round and big." At one point, members of that group have trouble with the word "spoiling":

"What does it mean?" a child asks.

"When something goes bad," another responds.

"Like sometimes my baby['s] milk, it be spoiled, and she can't drink it anymore. They [her parents] have to get a new one," another child adds, clearly excited about making a connection to her own life.

Anna moves to a different group in which the children are reading about how farmers store chopped corn in silos. She asks if they know what the word "silo" means.

A child responds, "Yes, 'cause I read it with you in the other book!"

As the group reads the next fact on the card, one member asks what shelled corn is. "Like dried corn, I think," another student responds.

Anna asks, "How do you know?"

Silos are big round structures that hold feed.

Silos keep rain, snow, and dirt out of the feed.

They keep the feed from spoiling.

Figure 7.5: A sample fact card that Anna used for guided reading during the farm unit.

"From the book we read … dried corn was filled up in silos for storage."

By monitoring each group, Anna helps children to access information they gained from other texts and to use it to check the "facts" on their fact cards. This is an excellent way to promote understanding of concepts and reinforce research strategies that students will continue to use.

Wrapping Up the Unit on Farming. As one culminating event for the farm unit, Anna has students independently write about what they have learned about farms and create their own farm fact card to share. (See Figure 7.6.) Anna also brings in some ears of unhusked field corn, chopped corn, and soybean plants with the roots and beans still intact. The children are thrilled to handle these real crops and make connections with what they've read. They open what they describe as soft, caterpillar-like soybean pods, plucked from the plant. One student exclaims, "I never knew soybeans looked like this. I thought they were just beans." The students also are impressed with the corn; many are surprised by how hard and dry it is. In fact, a few of them think it isn't real. But Anna sets them straight by telling them it is a different kind of corn than they would eat (i.e., sweet corn). She explains, "This is corn that cows eat."

Introducing real crops to students is a great way to end the unit, Anna concludes. It allows children to see, firsthand, that what they learned about in books and from one another is, in fact, a real part of the world.

1. Birds help farmers by eating worms and bugs.
2. Mother pigs are called sows.
3. The milk that is in a cow is store in the udder.
4. Corn can grow taller than a fith grater
5. In fall corn is chopped

Figure 7.6: This child has learned some information related to farms. Anna's next step will be to move him to organizing the information topically.

Susi Meagher, Third-Grade Teacher

Susi Meagher is about halfway through her master's degree in elementary education. Language arts was her undergraduate major. On her journey to teaching, she lived in many places and had an "endless array of jobs," from managing a doctor's office to driving a cab. A life filled with the laughter of children, as well as a chance to change the world one child at a time, has kept Susi teaching third grade for 11 years. She says, "Childhood is a time for practicing who we are going to be…and I love helping my students to practice being good, thinking people." In addition to being a teacher, she is a child advocate for her county's mental health department.

Informational text is at the heart of almost all of Susi's instruction. She says with today's information-driven society, this is a necessity: "The ability to glean information from the printed word is an absolutely essential life skill." Furthermore, she believes that story-based reading programs do not prepare students for the real world. She maintains, "Fiction certainly has its place, but we need nonfiction abilities to survive in this world. I am extremely excited by the world around me… the everyday miracles of our body systems or the mechanics of flight or so many other things…nonfiction is a way to get a glimpse of (and into) the causes and workings of those miracles. Learning is power!"

Using and Applying Information Through Multiple Genres

Susi doesn't just have children read and refer to informational texts, she has them use, apply, even transform information. For example, after reading *Body Battles* by Rita Golden Gelman (1992), a trade book that Susi uses to introduce the body systems unit that she is required to teach, she has the children pick favorite defensive body weapons (such as white blood cells) and write hero stories that chronicle adventures they have with uninvited "bad guys" (such as germs).

Similarly, she combines material from the Internet with other kinds of informational text

---

FOR YOUR INFORMATION…

Help Kids Search the Internet With These Resources

Susi highly recommends Jean Armour Polly's (2001) book, *Net-Mom's Internet Kids & Family Yellow Pages,* which contains over 3,000 URLs arranged in alphabetical order, by topic: astronomy, space and space exploration, sports, music, history, computers, and others. It's great for research projects. Kids can explore official state home pages, for example, and move onto sites for countries outside of the United States. Another fun resource that Susi uses for "quickie" research projects and "three-minute book reports" is Moira Butterfield's (1992) *1,000 Facts About Wild Animals.*

for art projects. For example, she has children look up information on the Web about birds and make illustrated *Birds in Our Backyard* take-home books. Her class also studied the characteristics of information books and made a handbook. The students discovered that information books may have captions, subtitles, glossaries, indexes, photographs, charts, and graphs. To create their handbook, they assembled examples of each of those elements and wrote descriptions.

"Core Democratic Values" Lesson

Susi teaches a social studies lesson on core democratic values, a grade level required unit in her state. At the beginning of the lesson, she tells the children about a little boy who loves to sing "America the Beautiful" with his hand over his heart because he is so proud to be an American. She then asks the children which value the boy embraces.

On the wall hangs a big poster that Susi's principal, David Averill, made, listing the values of "life," "liberty," "pursuit of happiness," "justice," "common good," "equality," "truth," "diversity," "popular sovereignty," and "patriotism." There are also simple descriptions of each value to help young children understand. For example, for diversity, David wrote, "Differences in language, dress,

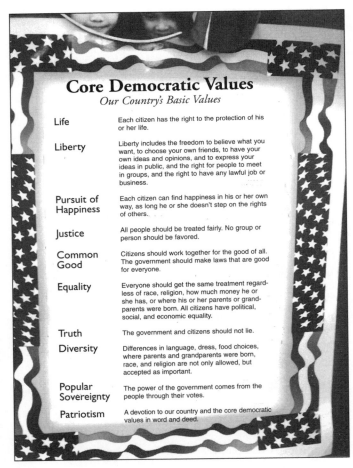

Figure 7.7: A poster on core democratic values that Susi uses in her teaching and displays in her classroom.

READING & WRITING INFORMATIONAL TEXT IN THE PRIMARY GRADES

food, where parents or grandparents were born, race, and religion are not only allowed, but accepted as important." (See Figure 7.7.)

Students answer Susi's question about the boy. One says "life." Another says "pursuit of happiness." After reading and discussing each value on the poster, Susi's students conclude that "patriotism" is the value that the boy is most clearly displaying. She reminds the students that they practiced patriotism during their September 11 observances and they talk about the patriotic things they did that day. After this introduction to the core democratic values lesson, the class moves onto read aloud, discussion, and writing.

Read aloud. Once Susi is confident that the students have a basic understanding of values, she reads aloud a fictional book that reinforces what they've learned. She says, "Now I'm going to read a story. I want you to listen and listen hard. See if you can find some of these values. Ask yourself, 'Is it a really good example of life, liberty, justice, and so on, or is it more like an example of when somebody takes away democratic values?'" Susi then presents Yoshiko Uchida and Joanna Yardley's (1993) historical fiction book, *The Bracelet,* about a little Japanese-American girl, Emi, who is forced to leave her home in Berkeley, California, to live in an internment camp.

Before reading the book, Susi gives the students some information about World War II and the attack on Pearl Harbor. She tells them that people were afraid, just like they were on September 11. She tells them how we put the Japanese-American people in internment camps. Then she reads the sad story.

Discussion and writing. After finishing the book, Susi and her class discuss some of the rights that Emi and her family were denied. The children recognize that there are many "bad" examples of liberty, freedom, justice, equality, pursuit of happiness, and the other values. Susi then has each child choose a value that Emi was denied and write about it, focusing on what the value means and what makes them think Emi didn't have it. (See Figures 7.8 and 7.9.)

By using a combination of informational and narrative text (i.e,. the poster and the storybook), Susi helped the students come to deeper understandings and insights—ones that they may not have come to if she had used only one text or the other.

JUSTICE

I think Emi didn't get justice. Justice means all people should be treated fairly. No group or person should be favored. We put her in prison camp. And then took her to a desert camp. After 46 years we new it was wrong. And we gave them a few dollars to show that we were sorry.

Liberty

I think that Emi didn't get liberty because we did bad things to them. Like we sent them to a raectrack and they had to live in a horse stand. I feel sad that we did that to them. I feel the same as Emi did. Liberty means freedom. We didn't give Emi freedom.

Figure 7.8 and Figure 7.9: Children wrote about values that were denied a character in *The Bracelet*.

Jan Newman, Title I Reading Teacher

Jan Newman has been teaching for 34 years. She is a Title I reading teacher in a rural school district made up of only five hundred K–12 students. She helps elementary-level children improve their reading skills by working with them individually, in small groups, in large groups, and sometimes as a whole class. She loves children and good literature. In fact, she has a large collection of books that she lends to teachers and students. Though partial to using narrative-information books in her teaching, she is using more non-narrative information books than she has in the past. (See Chapter 2 for a discussion of narrative-information books.) She attributes this to the growing number of quality information books, as well as to the growing need for students to learn from many sources.

Jan's philosophy is that we learn by doing, so she feels that the best way to teach reading is to engage children in it. The more children read, the better readers they become. The more they love to read, the more they will read. It sounds simple, and, like many expert practitioners, Jan makes teaching look that way. However, we all know that getting some children interested in decoding and comprehending text is far from simple.

Because Jan works exclusively with students who struggle, she often sees frustration and anxiety in them. To help them overcome those feelings, she encourages them to read, read, and read some more. She treats them like the capable readers she wants them to become. She makes sure that their progress is obvious to them. Jan emphasizes, "There is no room for failure. It's negative and I don't allow negativity!" With each success, Jan's students become more confident, and they use that confidence to gain even more success. "A successful interaction with text is enjoyable, and an enjoyable interaction is a success," she says.

Jan knows her students well. She is genuinely interested in what they think and say, and she uses that information to find books that spark their curiosity. She maintains everyone's attention in discussions because she includes everyone in the discussions. All opinions are accepted, so children are free to explore ideas without fear of ridicule.

Cross-Age Reading

Jan is always on the lookout for authentic ways to help her students apply their learning. She finds that her students work harder if they have a good reason for doing the work in the first place. One way she does this is by having her older students teach younger students. For example, her third graders recently came to the aid of first graders who were studying outer space and space travel. Their job was to find interesting, informative texts on the topics in the classroom library—texts that they felt they could read. The third graders practiced reading to each other and discussing anything they didn't quite understand, then they read the texts to small groups of first graders.

After reading, the third graders evaluated their performances in group discussions. One student was grateful that she practiced because, as she put it, "It was harder than I thought it would be!" Other students commented on how nervous they were. And some expressed doubt about the success of their reading. When that happened, classmates were quick to jump in to offer reassurance. Jan's students experienced the pride of a job well done.

"Children can accomplish so much more when they have a sense of purpose," says Jan. She believes that children can figure out processes and procedures when they have a need to do so. Consider sequencing as an example. Many authors of information books use a sequencing structure to present their main ideas in an orderly way. When students learn to recognize that structure and identify the main ideas within it, they tend to understand and remember those ideas. Jan has discovered that when she asks her older students to "teach" younger students this concept, rather than presenting it to them in a lesson, they are more likely to grasp it.

Hosting Author/Illustrator Visits

To get and keep her students excited about the books they read, Jan asks published authors and illustrators to come and speak to the entire school.

One recent visitor was Shelley Gill, who writes about the Alaskan wilderness. Some of her books include, *The Egg* (2001), *Alaska's Three Bears* (1990), *Thunderfeet: Alaska's Dinosaurs and Other Prehistoric Critters* (1997), *Swimmer* (1995), and *Kiana's Iditarod* (1992). Ms. Gill told students about the beauty and glory of Alaska. She showed them slides of its people, places, and animals. She talked about the variety of people that she knows and loves who live there—the tough old prospector, the rugged shopkeeper, the famous explorer, the Iditarod racer, the people who come to Alaska for adventure, and those who come for peace and tranquility. She spoke about the Inuit, who were Alaska's first inhabitants. Her passion convinced the audience that Alaska is the most wonderful place on earth. Ms. Gill also conveyed her passion for writing. She spoke about her process, letting the children know that it takes a long time to research information to make sure her books are accurate. And then it can take months to find just the right words to convey her message in just the right way.

Tom Woodruff brings history alive through his illustrations for books such as *Great Lakes and Great Ships: An Illustrated History For Children* (Mitchell, 1991), *Prehistoric Great Lakes: An Illustrated History For Children* (Mitchell, 2000), and *Michigan: An Illustrated History For Children* (Mitchell, 1987). Jan invited him to talk about the history of the Great Lakes to the whole school community—not just students, but teachers, administrators, and parents, too. During his presentation, Woodruff created drawings of great ships and then encouraged audience members make their own, while he provided guidance and inspiration.

Jan's students benefit from their interactions with real creators of books. Author/illustrator visits help students connect texts to their world. They put a face to the ideas. They get students excited about the concepts and inspired to learn more. They spur reading and writing. Students come to realize that ordinary people, just like them, are creating wonderful, informative works.

Selecting Books for Content Area Instruction

Chapter 2 presented general guidelines for selecting informational texts for instruction. Here, we discuss these guidelines specifically as applied to texts for content area instruction.

Accuracy and Authorship

Carol Donovan and Laura Smolkin, who have written extensively on selecting trade books for content area instruction, assert that accuracy of information is essential (2002). Information book author and photo illustrator Bruce McMillan (1993) states that it is the author's responsibility to make sure the text is accurate, "with no misstatements or errors of omission… free of value judgments… an interesting read" (p. 98). He says that young readers need concise, simple descriptions of concepts. Facts need to be checked and rechecked to make sure they are up-to-date and verifiable. Often, what was considered true yesterday is no longer accepted as true today (Bamford & Kristo, 1998; McMillan, 1993; Rice, 2002).

But students have some responsibility as well. Carol Avery (1998) encourages her first graders to question what they hear and read, and when they recognize conflicting information, to find more sources and identify strategies to resolve the issue. This kind of critical reading requires children to look to other texts, to themselves, and to the world around them. Children theorize, clarify, revise their thinking, and ask more questions when they are asked to be critical readers. In short, they do things that good readers do when they read. (See Chapter 3 for more information on the strategies that good readers use.)

In science, it is especially critical that children learn what Donna Rice (2002) calls "good science," rather than the science misconceptions that she finds too frequently in textbooks, trade books, and classroom teaching. Once learned, these misconceptions are hard to eradicate. Rice feels that this problem is due in part to the fact that, too often, teachers as well as students believe that if it's in the book, it must be true. The printed word gets the benefit of the doubt. In fact, in a study by Annemarie Palincsar and Shirley Magnusson (2000), the researchers found that some teachers did not want to use text in the beginning stages of their science investigations because they feared students would put too much faith in it. They didn't want children accepting the text conclusions as answers rather than attempting to arrive at their own. It is important to teach children not to assume that if it's in the book it must be true.

In social studies, it is important to expose students to primary sources (Zarnowski, 1998). Real letters, diaries, and newspaper articles not only provide students with information, but also give them a glimpse into the life of the writer and his or her motivation for writing the piece. Try asking students to investigate who wrote the document, just the way a historian might. What was the writer's purpose? Is he or she telling the truth? Why or why not? How do we know? Zarnowski reminds us that reading and writing in response to the ideas in quality informational text promotes critical thinking skills that benefit the reader and society alike.

Accessibility, Appropriateness, and Appeal

Style and structure are important features to consider when selecting informational text, because they determine its accessibility, appropriateness, and appeal for a reader. Young readers need clear, simple, yet interesting text that helps them understand key concepts. The text should supply adequate background information on the topic, while revealing clear differences between the main ideas and their supporting details (McClure, 1998).

Informational text can be organized in many ways, and children need to be made aware of them. The author may compare and contrast ideas, put events in sequence, or describe categories of information if sequence is not important. He or she may present an idea as a problem that needs solving, or as a cause that has an effect. What is most important is that the text has a clear, recognizable structure that children can understand (Blachowicz & Ogle, 2001).

Learners sometimes bring little prior knowledge to a reading of a text. They may find it difficult to sort out the important concepts and relevant information. Well-written informational text keeps the reader's attention on the main idea and contains supporting details that help to maintain that attention, rather than detract from it (Alexander & Jetton, 2000). To create such a text, the writer takes into account the audience's prior knowledge, includes enough details to explain the concept, links the main ideas and supporting details, explains technical terms, and offers additional sources.

Rosemary Bamford and Janice Kristo present a number of suggestions for selecting useful informational text in *Making Facts Come Alive: Choosing Quality Nonfiction Literature K–8* (1998). In that book, Anthony Fredericks reminds us that not all science-related trade books are "satisfactory in terms of information or presentation" (p. 113). They may contain accurate facts, but lack voice and vibrancy. Fredericks feels that the passion of the writer must come through to support the wonder and the awe of the reader. The student needs to see a connection to his or her own life; the science must matter to the student.

Science is not a set of finite facts, points out Fredericks. Rather, it is "an application of processes that aid in the discovery and learning about the world in which we live" (p. 116). Quality information books advance this process. They encourage divergent thinking and offer students opportunities to observe, predict, and experiment. Providing a variety of quality informational text helps students realize that science is an unending process that enables them to investigate, discover, and make sense of their world (Fredericks, 1998).

Similarly, Myra Zarnowski (1998) asserts that information trade books used in social studies must not only be accurate but also interesting, well structured, and inviting. In addition, they must help readers visualize the social world. They should provide a structure to support students' attempts at building understanding. In quality informational text, connections between the reader's world and the text are obvious. And information about who, what, when, where, and some possibilities as to why, are clearly presented.

THREE STRATEGIES FOR HELPING STUDENTS READ IN THE CONTENT AREAS

Patricia Alexander and Tamara Jetton (2000) point out that today's children are "faced with a knowledge explosion" (p. 285). With the seemingly endless flow of information bombarding them, they need guidance to help them sort the facts from the frill. It stands to reason that if children are to become independent learners, they must have the necessary skills to learn from text. In this section, we present several techniques for teaching vocabulary and organizing information. We also present a critical reading strategy known as Questioning the Author.

Building Vocabulary

Informational text often contains a great deal of technical vocabulary (Duke & Kays, 1998)—vocabulary that may be unfamiliar to students, yet is important to understanding the topic at hand. Fortunately, there are a number of techniques for building vocabulary that have been validated through classroom research. (For recent reviews of research on vocabulary instruction, see Blachowicz & Fisher, 2000; National Reading Panel, 2000; or Stahl, 1998.)

Children's vocabularies grow when we immerse them in words in a variety of ways and get them personally involved in constructing word meanings. Children learn by encountering words repeatedly in many contexts (Blachowicz & Fisher, 2000).

Explicitly teaching word meanings is also an effective way to build vocabulary. Of course, we do not have time to explicitly teach children all the words that we want them to know. Therefore, we recommend choosing words that are likely to appear frequently in their content area studies, such as *era* for history or *experiment* for science (Beck, McKeown, & Kucan, 2002).

In the past, many teachers have relied simply on having children look up word meanings in dictionaries and glossaries, and, perhaps, asking them to copy the definition and write a sentence to go with it. However, research suggests that we should move away from this approach to approaches that focus on making connections among words. Specifically, this means we should encourage students to connect new words to known words and build a wider understanding of a single word by exploring its variations. The more connections students make to a specific word, the better they understand it (National Reading Panel, 2000). Several ideas for doing that are described below.

Semantic Word Maps

Semantic word maps encourage students to make connections (Rupley, Logan, & Nichols, 1999) by grouping words into categories. So if Anna, the second-grade teacher discussed previously, wanted her students to learn farm-related words, she would first ask the children to generate a list of words relating to the farm, such as *silo, tractor,* and *feed*. She would then group the students to work together to sort the words and place them in categories such as animals, crops, equipment, or products to sell. (She might initially provide these categories, but over time children should become capable of generating their own.) Blachowicz and Fisher (2000) indicated that it is even better to go beyond the "relatedness of words" and provide activities that require the students to "recognize that relatedness." One way to do this is by labeling the semantic word maps or webs (Blachowicz & Ogle, 2001). Anna's students might create a graphic organizer like the one shown below to organize the words into categories and show connections between categories. (See Figure 7.10.) Finally, each group would explain its semantic map to the class. (It is important to remember, however, that the process of creating the map is at least as important as the finished product.)

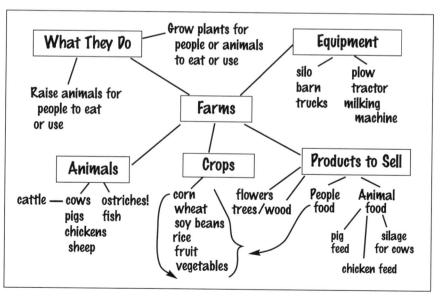

Figure 7.10: A semantic word map on farms, with words grouped into categories and labeled.

Concept Wheels

Another way children can be encouraged to learn new word meanings is by making a concept wheel (Rupley, Logan, & Nichols, 1999), a graphic organizer that helps define new words by linking them to known words. Margaret, the kindergarten teacher previously described, might use one to help her students gain understanding of the

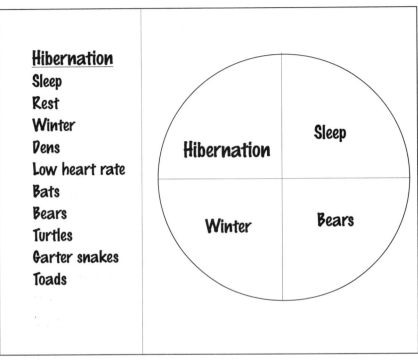

Figure 7.11: A concept wheel for the word *hibernation*

word *hibernation*. After their study of bats and the seasons, she could ask the children what words come to mind when they hear *hibernation*. (See Figure 7.11.) She would list their responses on the board, chart paper, or an overhead. She would then give students big paper circles to fold in half, and then fold in half again. Then students would unfold their circles and draw lines on the creases to create pie-shaped quarters. In the upper-left quarter, Margaret would ask them to write "hibernation" and then select three words that they think best convey the concept for the other three sections. Younger children might draw pictures representing words, with the teacher writing them in; older children might write the words themselves, referring to the word list as needed.

Concept of Definition

Concept of Definition is another strategy for clarifying word meanings when teaching in the content areas (Rupley, Logan, & Nichols, 1999, originally developed by Schwartz & Raphael,

1985). This strategy involves mapping the meaning of a word, such as *ants,* within a framework of categories (What is it?), properties (What is it like?), and examples/illustrations (What are some examples?). Once children fill in the framework, they compare the word to similar words, such as *bees, wasps,* and *termites.* Then they write their own definitions of the word. (See Figure 7.12.)

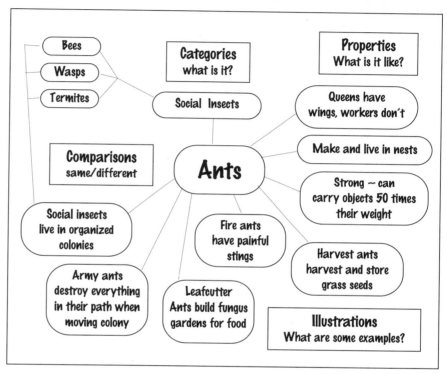

Figure 7.12: Concept of Definition graphic organizer for the word *ants*

Explaining Words in Context

Scholars suggest that it is not always beneficial to introduce young children to vocabulary words from informational text before they have encountered those words in the text (Beck, McKeown, & Kucan, 2002). One reason for this is that children's background knowledge on the topic may be so limited that they have little or nothing to connect the introduction to. Another reason is that young children have limited recall and may not remember the unfamiliar word when they later encounter it in the text.

Isabel Beck, Margaret McKeown, and Linda Kucan (2002) suggest that it may be best to explain a new word as children encounter it in text, when they are more apt to integrate word meaning and concept meaning, and, as a result, achieve a better understanding of both. When children are provided with a student-friendly explanation of the word the first time they

Activities to Get Students Thinking About Words

There are many additional techniques for building vocabulary—more than we can cover here. To learn more, one book we recommend is *Bringing Words to Life: Robust Vocabulary Instruction* (Beck, McKeown, & Kucan, 2002). The authors' recommended techniques include:

Word Associations After presenting vocabulary words, have children answer questions, using the words as answers. Then have them explain why they chose each word.

Examples:

◆ Which word means "not standing straight?" (e.g. *tilted*)

◆ Which word means you sent a message somewhere? (e.g. *transmitted*)

◆ Which word goes with light? (e.g. *shines, brightest*) (The follow-up discussion could be interesting, given the two possible answers.)

Have You Ever…? Link new words to children's personal experiences by giving them prompts that mean something to them.

Examples:

◆ Describe a time when you did something to <u>affect</u> your family.

◆ Who is the most <u>powerful</u> person you know?

Applause, Applause! Have children clap in response to how they would like to be described, using a certain word. For example, if they would like to be described as <u>powerful</u>, they would clap a lot. If they would not like to be described as <u>debris</u>, they would not clap at all. Then ask, "Why do you feel that way?"

Idea Completions Provide children with sentence stems that require them to put words into a context.

Examples:

◆ Jimmy said that his new toy was <u>exactly</u> what he wanted because …

◆ I <u>commit</u> to study more because…

Activities presented in Beck, McKeown, & Kucan, 2002.

encounter it, they are less likely to form misconceptions. For example, for the word *hibernation,* a teacher might say, "Some animals, like bears and turtles, sleep through cold seasons," rather than giving a lengthy explanation about how the animals' metabolisms slow down for a period of time as they live off of their acquired fat. Sleep is something the children can relate to; complex body systems may be a little out of reach. When children don't understand something, they may fill in the mental blanks inaccurately. And as already stated, misconceptions are hard to eradicate (Rice, 2002).

Even though it is best to explain words as children encounter them, there are times when that simply isn't practical—such as when children are reading independently. In cases like those, Beck, McKeown, and Kucan suggest introducing and explaining word meanings before the child begins reading, rather than waiting until after he or she has finished.

Teaching Use of Context Clues

Figuring out the meanings of words from the context in which they appear is another effective vocabulary-building practice. Teach children to look out for "clues" such as definitions, restatements, or examples provided around the word. For example, in the sentence "It seemed that cowpox gave a person <u>immunity</u>, or protection, from smallpox" (Phelan, 2003), there are strong clues to the meaning of the word *immunity*. Of course, there are many cases in which direct clues like these are not available. Take this sentence, for example: "He left <u>cultures</u> of chicken cholera germs with his lab assistants." When teaching this strategy, use texts in which the author provides strong, easily recognized clues to word meaning.

Introduce the strategy of using context clues by modeling it. Then have students try it on their own, intervening to point out relevant clues as necessary and ensuring they don't get off track (Beck, McKeown, & Kucan, 2002).

Interestingly, research suggests that good and poor readers do not differ much in their ability to determine the meaning of words from context. Because good readers do so much more reading than poor readers, they are exposed to new words more frequently, which helps them to crack words both in isolation and in context (Stahl, 1998). This underscores the importance of combining wide reading with explicit vocabulary instruction.

Organizing Information

Semantic word maps and concept wheels are examples of graphic organizers that are useful in building vocabulary. Here we present graphic organizers designed to serve a somewhat different purpose: to help children organize information and concepts from text. (For reviews of research on using graphic organizers to teach content area information and concepts, see Banikowski & Mehring, 1999; Duke & Pearson, 2002; and National Reading Panel, 2000.)

Generally speaking, the better children understand the structure of the text, the more likely they are to understand the concepts it contains (Duke & Pearson, 2002). Graphic organizers help children recognize structures. Graphic organizers also help them deepen their understanding and memory for information and concepts. Indeed, research suggests that information conveyed visually (through images) as well as verbally (through a text or discussion) is remembered better than information that is only conveyed in one of those ways (Banikowski & Mehring, 1999; Robinson, 1998).

Venn Diagrams

A Venn diagram is a graphic organizer often used for informational text that involves comparing and contrasting. (See Figure 7.13.)

Hierarchical Maps

Hierarchical maps are especially helpful for texts or concepts that are organized in a highly structured way. For example, information from a book about

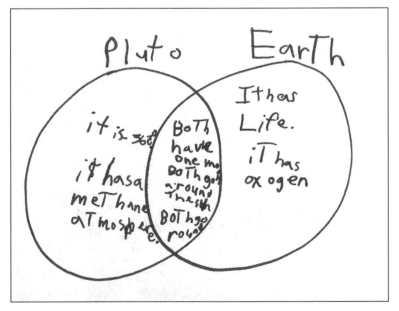

Figure 7.13: A child's Venn diagram illustrating how individual planets are similar to and different from one another.

mammals, which addresses different categories of mammals as well as specific types of mammals, and so on, would be a good candidate for a hierarchical map. (See Figure 7.14.) When children are actively involved in making hierarchical maps, they are forced to think and rethink information and the relationships among it. Knowledge, comprehension, and memory reinforce one another to improve learning (Duke & Pearson, 2002).

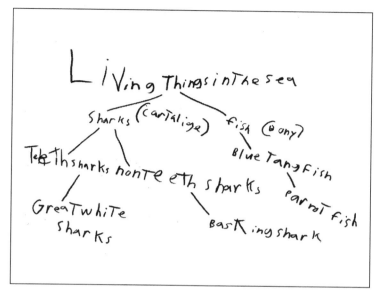

Figure 7.14: A child's hierarchical map on sea life, with an emphasis on sharks.

Flow Charts

Flow charts are especially useful for organizing cause and effect, problem-solution, and sequential structures and concepts, such as those that address historical events or life cycles. (See Figure 7.15.)

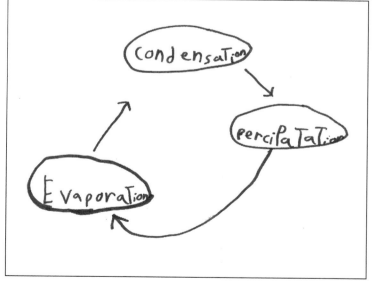

Figure 7.15: A child's flow chart of the water cycle.

Lists

Lists can be a form of graphic organizer, too. As a follow-up activity after their lesson on the seasons (see page 161), Margaret and her kindergarten class made a chart. On the top, Margaret wrote out the four seasons. Then she asked her students to help her make a list of characteristics of each season. She also wrote the terms *compare, contrast, predict,* and *make conclusions* on the chart. After explaining the terms, she used them in season-related questions to the children. For example, when asked, "What do you predict the weather will be like on Christmas?", the children concluded that it would probably be cold and it might snow.

KWL Chart

A KWL chart is a popular device for helping students make connections between their prior knowledge, their purposes for reading, and the texts they read (as does the E-T-R technique

FOR YOUR INFORMATION...

Check Out These Symbols for Creating Flow Charts

Microsoft Word™ and other software programs have "Autoshapes," symbols you can use to create flow charts:

described on pages 54–55). Before a lesson or unit, teachers and students work together to create a three-column chart, listing what students *know* and what they *want* to learn in the first two columns. When the lesson or unit is finished, they go back to the chart and list what they did *learn* in the third column (Ogle, 1986). They may also return to the Want to Know column with more questions. (See Figure 7.16.) Some teachers use a modified KWL chart called KWWL, which includes a column for *where* the child can learn the information (Bryan, 1998).

Charting children's prior knowledge helps us get in touch with their experiences and misconceptions. When we know where they are coming from, we can guide children to where they are trying to go. If prior knowledge is limited or nonexistent, you may be able to provide it by offering hands-on experiences, artifacts from history, objects from nature such as the crops that Anna uses in her farm unit, real or virtual (such as through *Reading Rainbow* videos) field trips such as those used by Marcia—anything that learners can "tie" to the new learning (Banikowski & Mehring, 1999).

Questioning the Author

Questioning the Author (QtA) is another strategy for improving children's comprehension of content area texts and building their content area knowledge, developed by Isabel Beck, Margaret McKeown, Rebecca Hamilton, and Linda Kucan (1997). QtA has been tested in research and found to be effective at developing fourth graders' comprehension (Beck, McKeown, Sandora, Kucan, & Worthy, 1996). We have reason to believe that a modified version can

KWL Chart on Farming

What We Know	What We Want to Know	What We Learned
Horses, pigs, goats, and chickens all live on farms.	How do they get the milk out of the cows?	Farms are places where domestic animals live.
Ducks also live on farms.	How do we get the milk?	Domestic animals are animals such as cows, pigs, ducks, goats, and horses. They are raised by people.
They grow corn and vegetables on farms.	How do they get the "stuff" to grow?	
They grow fruit and hay.		Food crops are grown on farms.
Some children live on farms.	Where does food come from?	Specialty farms raise animals like fish, rabbits, and ostriches.
Pumpkin and sheep are found on farms.	What foods have corn in them?	
They have cows that give us milk.	Why do they need tractors?	Farmers plant seeds to get their crops.
Farmers need to have food to feed their animals.	What do animals eat?	The crops need sun, dirt, water, and time to grow.
Farmers use tractors.		Farmers use electric milking machines to get the milk out of the cows.
Peacocks and ostriches can be on farms.		Farmers put chopped corn and hay in silos to feed their cows.
Pens keep the animals inside.		Refrigerated milk trucks take the milk from the farm to places that put the milk in containers for us to buy in stores.

Figure 7.16: Part of a KWL chart that Anna and her students created for their research unit on farming.

be used to enhance comprehension for younger children. When carrying out QtA, students are actively involved in the text. They question its concepts and ideas as they read, asking themselves and each other, "What is the author trying to say?" "What does she really mean when she says this?" "Why would he say it this way?" Children "think, learn, and explain, rather than memorize, dictate, and forget" (Beck, McKeown, Hamilton, & Kucan, 1997).

A key premise in QtA is that authors are fallible. They don't always present their ideas in a clear, forthright way. In fact, sometimes they present ideas in a way that makes comprehension difficult, if not downright impossible. So it's important for us to tell children that they should not necessarily blame themselves when they have a difficult time making sense of a text; sometimes it's the author's fault. Maybe he or she isn't giving us enough information. Maybe he or she isn't helping us to see how ideas are connected. Maybe he or she has made it difficult to figure out the main ideas. When we explain why a text may be difficult to understand, children are less likely to accuse themselves of not being able to "get it."

QtA can be conducted in small groups or with the whole class. Regardless of the number of students participating, though, it's vital that everyone is involved in discussion.

The main focus of QtA is to teach children how to question the ideas and concepts the author is trying to convey in the text as they read it. Students work to make what they read understandable. They interpret the text information until it makes sense. The focus is not on learning specific facts; instead, it is on developing an understanding of the concepts presented.

For example, Susi's third graders may know that "justice" is one core democratic value. They may know that the definition on their poster says, "All people should be treated fairly. No group should be favored." They may even be able to state all or part of that definition in an assessment. However, students may not truly understand what "a core democratic value" means to all Americans and what it means to them. Why is it important? Why is the term "core" used? Does it have any connection to an apple core? An apple core has seeds. Does that mean a core democratic value has seeds? What could these seeds represent? The teacher facilitates these discussions by helping to guide conversation to advance understandings of the concepts.

When it comes to the definition of justice in particular, children may ask, Why did the author say all people should be treated fairly? What does "all" mean? Are people from different cultures part of "all people"? Are people who look or act weird to be treated fairly? Are people without power to be treated fairly? What about children? Are they part of "all"? Should they be treated fairly? Are bad people part of "all"? Why would the author want bad people to be treated fairly?

After students actively discuss these types of questions, they have a much deeper understanding of how "justice" relates to them and the people around them. This type of questioning is called a "query-driven discussion."

Carrying Out a QtA Discussion: Steps to Follow

1. Identify Major Understandings and Potential Problems. In advance, on your own, read the text to be discussed. As you read, look for major concepts that you want students to discuss. Also look for areas where concepts are not clearly presented or that might require more background knowledge than students have.

2. Segment Text. Decide on the section or sections you and your students will read, where to stop reading, and when to start discussions.

3. Develop Queries. Plan some initiating queries to start the discussion and some follow-up queries that might be used to focus and drive discussion. (See Figure 7.17 on page 195 for examples of queries.)

4. Introduce the Text. Once planning in steps 1 through 3 has been done, the lesson can begin, perhaps with students reading or, if they've read the text earlier, rereading the text.

5. Facilitate the Discussion. Make a number of "discussion moves" during discussion. Below are some sample moves, with specific examples from Beck, McKeown, Hamilton, and Kucan (1997):

- **Marking:** Draw attention to the idea or concept to be emphasized.
  Example: "Good point. It's important to know that stopping ships was seen as such a terrible act that the United States declared war because Great Britain was doing this." (p. 82)

- **Turning Back:** Give the responsibility of building understanding back to students. Students return to the text to keep on track or clarify ideas.
  Examples: "Wait—if what's upsetting Ralph is what Brad *said about him, why does Ralph keep talking about how unfair* Ryan *has been to him?" (p. 83)*
  "But is going back to the hotel a real option for Ralph? What did the author tell us about why Ralph asked Ryan to take him to school in the first place?" (p. 84)

- **Revoicing:** Rephrase ideas to clarify thinking.
  Example: Student: "The way this was going, they weren't going to make it because they didn't

do it on their own. They had to depend on the Indians." Teacher: "It seems you are saying that because the settlers depended on Native Americans for food and didn't learn how to grow their own food, there were going to have a hard time surviving." (p. 85)

- **Modeling:** Demonstrate a response, thought, or feeling.

  Example: "Okay now, when I was reading this, I understood that in the first sentence, the author said most people in developing countries had to make a living by farming. But later the author said, 'However, there is a shortage of food.' Well, if everyone makes their living by farming, why would there be a shortage of food? What's going on here?" (p. 92)

- **Annotating:** Fill in information that is not provided in the text.

  Example: "The author didn't tell us, but the Whiskey Rebellion was a real test of the new government. President Washington's decision to send troops to put down the rebellion was a message to the entire country." (p. 91)

- **Recapping:** Summarize ideas to reinforce students' understanding, so they can move on.

  Example: "Those were great ideas. You figured out why Eskimos moved so often in the winter, even though the author did not explain it in the text." (p. 92)

Queries to Guide Questioning-the-Author Discussions

Goal	Queries
Initiate the discussion	What is the author trying to say? What is the author's message? What is the author talking about?
Help students focus on the author's message	That is what the author says, but what does it mean?
Help students link information	How does that connect with what the author already told us? How does that fit in with what the author already told us? What information has the author added here that connects to or fits in with____?
Identify difficulties with the way the author has presented information or ideas	Does that make sense? Is that said in a clear way? Did the author explain that clearly? Why or why not? What's missing? What do we need to figure out or find out?
Encourage students to refer to the text either because they've misinterpreted a text statement or to help them recognize that they've made an inference	Did the author tell us that? Did the author give us the answer to that?

Figure 7.17: Examples of queries (Beck, McKeown, Sandora, Kucan, & Worthy, 1996, page 389)

A Close-Up Look at Informational Text in the Content Areas

Each year, first-grade teacher Jackie Smart carries out an owl unit that spans the content areas. In small groups, her students use informational text to investigate different types of owls, their characteristics, their habitats, and their eating habits.

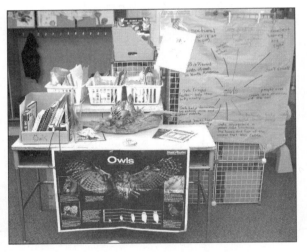

1 Jackie provides information books, graphic organizers, and posters as research sources for her students.

2 As Jackie's students collect information on owls, they store it in folders, which they decorate themselves.

3 To investigate what owls eat, Jackie's students dissect owl pellets, the coughed-up remains of digested prey. (For owl pellets and supplies, contact Pellets, Inc., at www.pelletsinc.com.)

4 Tools for the owl pellet investigation include a probe, magnifying glass, measuring tape, tweezers, rubber gloves, and a chart that illustrates the bones of various animals that the owl may have devoured— a rodent, shrew, mole, or bird.

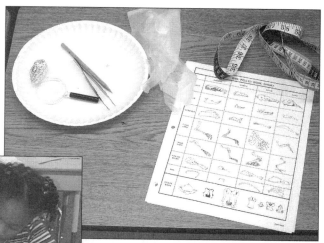

photo: Jackie Smart

photo: Jackie Smart

6 Children compare the skeleton to information on a web they created earlier in the unit, which builds their understanding of the owl's eating habits.

5 Once the children have determined the animal, they match and glue the bones to a diagram to recreate a skeleton.

photo: Jackie Smart

7 Once they have finished their research, the children create life-sized pictures of their owl in its natural environment, often using information books for inspiration.

CONCLUDING THOUGHTS

Informational text can play a central role in content area learning. The teachers profiled in this chapter use informational text in a variety of ways to inspire, enhance, and even transform children's learning. They engage children as researchers of the world around them, exposing them to experiences in and outside the classroom. They also expose children to different genres, and set up situations for them to apply their learning in a variety of ways.

Well-written information books for young children focus on explaining meaning in a simple, interesting way. The author is considerate of the prior knowledge of the reader, provides enough details to explain the concept, and links main ideas with those details. Accuracy of information is vital. Teachers and students alike should be vigilant about evaluating texts for it, as well as for biases, agendas, or questionable perspectives that the author brings to the text.

Development of vocabulary and concept knowledge build upon each other. Research suggests that combining direct instruction in vocabulary with wide reading of a variety of texts is the best way to build children's word knowledge. Research also indicates that using graphic organizers with students increases their understanding and retention of concepts. Practices like these make learning content a wonderful journey. Enjoy the ride!

CHAPTER 8

The Classroom Environment

Integrating Informational Text in the Print-Rich Environment

There is a trend in grocery stores to display produce right near the entrance, presumably to give the impression that everything in the store is fresh and healthy. We know, too, that first impressions are critical in other situations, such as buying a home or interviewing for a job. Our classrooms work the same way. What is the first thing a child sees when he or she walks into your room? To find out, get down on your knees and take a look. Does the child see a long list of rules for behavior or a welcoming message? More commercial posters than classmates' writing and artwork? Are books and writing materials abundant and accessible to children, or are they stashed in a corner for use only under your supervision? What does your room say about what you value? The classroom environment should say something to and about its inhabitants. Creating it means more than decorating it. It means transforming the room into a space that supports rich teaching and learning. In this chapter, we show you how to create an environment that supports children's reading and writing of informational text.

As you may recall from Chapter 2, the genre-diversification framework calls for including substantial amounts of informational text not only in classroom activities, but also on classroom walls and other surfaces and in classroom libraries. Chapters 3 to 7 focused primarily on classroom activities. In this chapter, we focus on the classroom environment. Specifically, we:

◆ briefly discuss research related to the importance of the print environment and informational text in that environment.

◆ describe how some teachers have incorporated informational text into their environments.

◆ identify three research-based ways to incorporate informational text into your environment.

The classroom environment has a significant impact on what goes on in a classroom and sets the stage for interactions with a variety of genres.

THE PRINT ENVIRONMENT AND INFORMATIONAL TEXT: WHAT THE RESEARCH SAYS

"Print environment" refers to the written language that surrounds children in their class-rooms. This includes print on classroom walls and other surfaces (such as desktops and other furniture within the classroom), and books and other materials in the classroom library. Many major documents, including the International Reading Association and the National Association for the Education of Young Children joint position statement on literacy (1998), stress the importance of the print environment. They call for literacy-rich classrooms, with lots of materials for children to read for real purposes. Lesley Morrow (1989) and Susan Neuman and Kathleen Roskos (1993) found that classrooms that were rich in environmental print artifacts inspired more realistic, literacy-focused dramatic play. For example, the children used signs, symbols, and writing to act out post office play. And when provided with real products, children playing "grocery store" read the labels as their parents did at home.

Almost no research has examined print environments with an emphasis on informational text. As reported in Chapter 1, Nell (Duke, 2000a) found that there was very little informational text on classroom walls and other surfaces or in classroom libraries, particularly in low-socioeconomic settings. For the Early Literacy Project, which is described in Chapter 2,

photo: Emilene Vogel

Figure 8.1: This print-rich classroom includes a variety of informational texts including books, posters, and students' dioramas and accompanying reports.

we included informational text on walls, on other surfaces, and in classroom libraries. However, it's difficult to separate the effects of doing that from the effects of other decisions we made, such as increasing the use of informational text in classroom activities. Similarly the study by Mariam Dreher and Ann Dromsky (2000), described in Chapter 5, examined the impact of including more informational text in classroom libraries, but this was combined with more read-aloud of informational text. So again, we cannot isolate the effects of altering the print environment. In any case, based on what we do know about print environments, it seems that informational text should be included in significant ways.

INCORPORATING INFORMATIONAL TEXT INTO THE PRINT ENVIRONMENT: A FEW TEACHERS' APPROACHES

We have had the pleasure of working with creative teachers over the years who have found many ways to incorporate informational text into their classrooms. Some of their ideas are presented in this section.

Beefing Up the Library

All of the teachers in the Early Literacy Project added materials to their classroom libraries. (See box "Five Ways to Build a Better Classroom Library," page 212.) Several made a conscious effort to make materials more accessible by putting them out for children to "get their hands on." Many filled bins with books of various genres and placed the bins on worktables. One teacher reported that children sought out informational texts for independent reading— so much so, in fact, that once when all of the informational texts had been snatched up by classmates, one child complained, "All we got are storybooks."

Research suggests that children gravitate toward books that are displayed (Martinez & Teale, 1989, cited in Fractor, Woodruff, Martinez, & Teale, 1993). So in addition to placing books in bins, some teachers used display racks that held many books, including Big Books, with covers facing out. This not only enhanced the print environment, but also made books easier for children to browse and select. (See box "Great Idea, But Where Do I Put All This Extra Text?," page 205.)

Displaying Children's Work

When the children in our study wrote informational text of three or more related sentences, their pieces became candidates for display. Teachers posted the pieces on bulletin boards, classroom and hallway walls, and other surfaces. As a result, children were exposed daily to multiple examples of informational text which they and

photo: Emilene Vogel

Figure 8.2: First-grade teacher Marcia Barnes displays children's informational writing about ocean animals.

their friends had written, which was more compelling than published text. (See Figure 8.2.)

Science on the Move

A few years ago, Susan taught a K–6 class in rural Alaska. Part of the science curriculum required students to observe changes in the environment over time. So she gave each child a long piece of string and asked them each to stake out a four-foot-square patch in the woods, near the play yard. The children visited their patches once a week, carrying clipboards for making notes about any changes they observed, such as fallen pinecones, growing fungi, and traces of animal tracks. Back in the classroom, they documented changes across the patches. Susan asked the children to report their findings in complete sentences and then she wrote them down on chart paper. These group-created summaries formed a picture of the biosystem that even the youngest learners in the group could appreciate. Susan posted the summaries throughout the classroom to support children as they reflected on and discussed their understandings of how the environment changes over time.

Increasing Children's Awareness of The Print Environment

The print environment becomes more meaningful to children when we make conscious efforts to increase their awareness of it. After all, there is not much value in posting text just for the sake of posting it—we want children to read the text, to look forward to generating the text, and to view their room as a place for rich literacy learning.

There are many ways to increase children's awareness of the print around them. One teacher we know sends students on environmental-print scavenger hunts during field trips. Before the trip, she prepares a sheet containing a list of objects that students must locate by reading environmental print. For example, on a recent trip to a museum, things the children had to find included something made of stone, something from Egypt, and something more than one-thousand years old. They worked in small groups, reading captions on museum objects and writing down findings on their lists, which were attached to clipboards. This approach can transform an ordinary field trip into a rich literacy experience. Not surprisingly, the chil-

"Great Idea, But Where Do I Put All This Extra Text?"

Most of us think about bulletin boards and bookshelves as the primary classroom areas for displaying text. We all know how quickly they can fill up, though. If we are committed to displaying children's work and a variety of genres, there always seems to be a shortage of space. Here are some ideas for finding more. Note: Fire regulations may prevent you from carrying out some of these ideas, so check with your administrators.

◆ Hang a clothesline across your room and clip children's writing or other informational text to it.

◆ On each cluster of tables or desks, put a bin of books in a variety of genres. Also make sure you provide time for children to use the books!

◆ Hang posters and work in areas where children typically wait in line, whether for recess, the drinking fountain, or the lavatory. The backs of classroom doors, hallway walls, and bathroom stalls make especially good spots. And any genre is fair game!

◆ Use long hallway or bathroom walls to post the text of books that you've used in shared reading. One way to do this is to type out the text from each page of the book and have children illustrate the pages. Display the pages in order along the hallway, at the children's eye level. The lead page should provide the title, author, and

continued on next page

photo: Lynn Beard

Kindergartners brainstormed a picture glossary of winter words during a unit on winter. Their teacher affixed the words on the classroom door for all to see and use as needed.

young illustrators—for example, "*Dinosaurs, Dinosaurs* by Byron Barton, illustrated by Ms. Jones' first-grade class."

◆ Display posters, newspaper clippings, or examples of children's writing at the ends of bookcases. Be sure to rotate pieces regularly.

◆ To create a holder for books, affix a length of rain gutter (which can be purchased inexpensively at most hardware stores) to the edge of your chalkboard's chalk tray. Line books up, covers facing out.

◆ Pin posters or children's work to window drapes.

◆ Keep posted webs, maps, notes, or other material you've written on chart paper during lessons so that children can revisit them. Large "sticky note" chart paper makes this easier, but it isn't necessary. Good, old-fashioned tape works just as well.

◆ If the coat-closet door is prominent, use it as a surface for children's work.

◆ If your windows provide less-than-compelling views of the great outdoors, consider using some of them to display text.

Even narrow, out-of-the-way spaces can showcase information.

◆ If you have a special spot for reading in your room, look for ways to display the dust covers of books. Try laminating the covers and posting them around the area. It makes a striking display and invites children to explore the books themselves.

◆ The next time you chant, sing, or choral read a text as a class, write out the text, post it, and have one child track the words for all to see. Leave the text up for children to enjoy after the activity.

When children are surrounded by words and see them in use, they begin to use those words independently…even when you aren't looking!

dren are energized about seeing objects that might not normally grab their attention. (The Detroit Institute of Arts offers its own version of a scavenger hunt to families. Museums near you may offer one, too.)

Some teachers encourage children to "read around the room"—that is, to circulate around the room, reading material on classroom walls and other surfaces. Others have them record environmental print they notice outside the classroom. All of these techniques help to increase children's awareness of the print around them.

Using the Internet and Community Resources

If you are short on material to post in the classroom or include in the classroom library, consider tapping into the Internet or community groups for help. (See the box entitled "Think Outside the Book" on page 209 for more ideas.)

The World Wide Web is full of free information for young children. Experts on nearly any topic are just a click away—though a lot of nonexperts are, too. Be sure to choose your sources wisely! You can find an institute or organization that specializes in nearly any topic you want to study. These groups often offer print materials for classroom use, such as posters, informational pamphlets, and promotional material. A quick search by topic should generate many groups eager to share information. Local groups might have information, too, and might even be happy to send a speaker to your class. For example, Susan was surprised to learn that The Bat Conservancy, a national organization (members.aol.com/obcbats/batinfo.html), was just one town away. When her class studied bats, the Conservancy sparked passion among her students by providing topic-related materials and a speaker who brought a couple of bats into her classroom.

When considering whom to contact, don't overlook charity organizations. For instance, Heifer International (www.heifer.org), an organization dedicated to providing farm animals to people in need throughout the world, has a free program that promotes reading called Read to Feed (www.readtofeed.org). It includes a book, a video about two children who received animals through the project, multiple copies of bookmarks, posters, a curriculum for teachers, and other support materials offering opportunities for reading and learning. In one school, the materials were used as part of a cross-curricular, building-wide effort to raise funds to purchase farm animals for children around the world. The project sparked interest in the partici-pating countries, the animals that would be donated, and the issue of world hunger. Further, it promoted literacy throughout all the classrooms.

You might also consider a community gardening project. The Internet is a great source for seed and plant catalogs, as well as many informational sites related to gardening and garden design. Members of the local garden club or parents with knowledge of gardening or farming could visit your classroom and share their expertise. Children could use the many print materials you and they gather to create a plan for a garden near your school or in a nearby park. The possibilities for gaining information for study units or service proj-ects are limitless.

THREE STRATEGIES FOR INCORPORATING INFORMATIONAL TEXT INTO YOUR CLASSROOM ENVIRONMENT

The classroom library, literacy-enriched play environments, and outside funds of knowledge can all be used to incorporate informational text into the classroom. Since the research on enriching classroom environments with informational text is limited, the following ideas are based on research involving all kinds of texts. As you read about these strategies, think of informational text as one component of an enriched environment.

Create a Rich Classroom Library

Research tells us that access to print varies across communities and socioeconomic status. Some communities are rich in libraries and bookstores, while others have virtually no resources for acquiring reading material (Neuman, Celano, Greco, & Shue, 2001). Classroom libraries pro-vide hope. Lesley Morrow and Carol Weinstein (1986) found that children are more likely to use books and participate with others in literacy-related experiences when there is a special place in the classroom to enjoy those books. Several recommendations from that study point

Think Outside the Book

Often when we think of reading, we think of books. But for many genres, especially informational genres, text comes in many formats. Here are some examples of nonbook informational texts that we have seen in classroom libraries and on walls and other surfaces.

Magazines Subscribe to magazines that contain a great deal of information, such as *Ranger Rick, My Big Backyard* (www.nwf.org), and *Dig* (www.digonsite.com), an archaeology magazine for kids. Popular magazines such as *Time, Discover,* and *National Geographic* offer versions for children. Go to www.timeforkids.com, www.kidsdiscover.com, and www.nationalgeographic.com/kids/ respectively for details.

Cobblestone Publishers, who bring us the excellent *Cricket* and *Ladybug* magazines, offer three informational magazines for the primary level: *Appleseeds* (a social studies magazine), *Ask* (a science magazine), and *Click* (a combination of science, history, and other areas). All are available at www.cobblestonepub.com.

Newspaper Articles Find news articles on topics your class is studying and post them in prominent places for children to see. Establishing a spot in the room labeled "In the News," where you rotate newspaper articles on a regular basis, encourages children to look for posted items and bring in items of interest to share. There are even some newspapers written especially for children, such as *Scholastic News* (teacher.scholastic.com/products/classmags.htm).

The Internet Even if your classroom doesn't contain a computer with Internet access, children can probably get online somewhere in your school. Many Web sites are kid-friendly. A favorite search engine for children is Yahooligans (www.yahooligans.com), which sends surfers to kid-appropriate sites exclusively, without denying certain key words. For example, a search on the word "sex" generates sites dedicated to cell division, animal biology, and so forth, and not sites a standard search engine would generate. Additionally, many informational sites, including the CIA (www.odci.gov), National Geographic

continued on next page

(www.nationalgeographic.org), PBS (www.pbs.org), and the World Health Organization (www.who.org) have sections that contain information and games for kids. When children email the White House (www.whitehouse.gov) about an issue that they've researched, they get instant confirmation of receipt on very fancy "letterhead"—mail from the president!

Children's Work Having twenty or more examples of informational text on the same topic is hard to come by. But if each of your students has researched the topic and written a mini-report about it, you have as many examples of informational text as you have students. Children love to read each other's work—and knowing that will happen may motivate them to do their best.

Commercial Posters There are many sources of commercial informational posters, including those catalogs you receive at your school from publishers such as Scholastic (www.teacher.scholastic.com) and Carson-Dellosa (www.carsondellosa.com). There are also Web sites such as www.creativeprocess.net/moreposters, www.junglewalk.com, www.thegiftshop.info/posters/education/, and http://print-a-poster.p-rposters.com/educational-posters.htm. And don't overlook the free posters that you can get from organizations such as The Dairy Council or your state's Department of Natural Resources. When selecting from the lot, consider how the content relates to what your class is studying; the size of text; the quality of the writing; and the accuracy, appeal, and attractiveness of the illustrations. Hold posters to the same selection standards that you would for other resources in your room. (See "Criteria for Selecting Informational Text" on pages 38–39 for guidelines.)

Teacher-Prepared Materials Sometimes it's easier to write your own informational texts than to try to find ones at the right reading level and with the right content for your students. You may want to rewrite excerpts of a favorite or important published informational text so they are large enough for children to see. Your morning or afternoon messages can include informational text, be posted, and be left up throughout the day. You can also add children's dictation, KWL charts, and group reports to the informational print in your room.

toward the importance of creating a cozy but active literacy space. Sadly, however, classroom libraries in wealthier schools continue to be far better stocked than those poorer schools, with more of all kinds of text, including informational text (Duke, 2000a, 2000b). Filling classroom libraries in all schools with a range of materials is an important step toward helping all children interact with informational text. (See box on page 212, "Five Ways to Build a Better Classroom Library", for suggestions.)

Consider Literacy-Enriched Play Environments

Traditionally, children were taught literacy skills in a carefully defined language arts block that had little spillover into other parts of the day. A newer view sees literacy as the foundation of a classroom, where reading and writing become the framework on which every classroom experience is based. (See Chapter 7 for a discussion on integrating literacy across content areas.) With this in mind, play experiences become opportunities to support literacy development. As noted previously, Susan Neuman and Kathleen Roskos (1993) found that classrooms rich in environmental print inspired more realistic, literacy-focused dramatic play. Children in these classrooms demonstrated greater literacy competencies. (See "Themes and Texts for Dramatic Play Areas," page 213.)

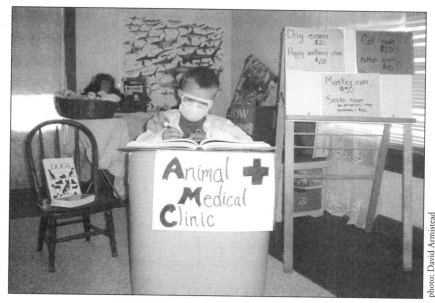

Figure 8.3: During a kindergarten unit on pets, the dramatic play area becomes an animal medical clinic that includes medical props, stuffed-animal patients, posters and signs, a clipboard for taking down information on incoming pets, beloved animal encyclopedias, and some dog care and breed guides.

Five Ways to Build a Better Classroom Library

The backbone of a literacy program is the classroom library. We use it to access materials for read aloud and shared reading, and to offer materials for guided and independent reading. Studies have shown, however, that primary-grade classroom libraries are typically limited in terms of range of levels and genres. When establishing or expanding your library, consider the following tips:

1 Offer Multiple Genres We suggest including narrative (such as traditional stories from a variety of cultures), fantasy, concept books, predictable books, informational texts, biographies, poetry, procedural texts (such as cookbooks and science experiment books), humor (joke books and cartoons), and other genres.

2 Offer Multiple Formats Some children will be drawn to magazines, others to books, and still others to newspapers. (See "Thinking Outside the Book" on page 209 for more ideas.)

3 Offer Multiple Reading Levels A good rule of thumb is to include some materials that are two grades above your class's level, and some that are two grades below its level. That means in a second-grade classroom, you would have materials for kindergarten, first-, second-, third-, and fourth-grade reading levels.

4 Offer Enough Materials to Go Around Irene Fountas and Gay Su Pinnell (1996) recommend that a classroom library have between 300 and 600 books. More conservative estimates suggest seven books per child, with new books being added all the time (Neuman, Celano, Greco, & Shue, 2001). Since many of us buy our own materials, these numbers can seem daunting. One strategy, of course, is getting donations and searching yard sales and public library sales. Some teachers use book club bonus points to build their libraries. Others rotate their books with other teachers in their building, so there is a constant influx of "new" books in the classrooms. Using nonbook materials (see "Thinking Outside the Book" on page 209.) can also be a help, as can borrowing materials from the public library. Most of us use a combination of these sources to add to the overall availability of text.

5 Offer Mostly Quality Materials While it may be tempting to shop yard sales to bulk up your library, keep an eye on the quality of what you make available to children. (See Chapters 2 and 7 for guidelines on selecting quality informational texts.) More is not necessarily better. Consider using quality public library materials in your room if you don't own what you need.

Themes and Texts for Dramatic Play Areas

If you have a dramatic play area in your classroom or are thinking about creating one, be sure to change the props each time you begin a new theme or unit of study. The following chart contains some typical themes and informational text materials to support those themes.

Theme	Suggested Informational and Other Texts
Camp-Out (Can also be a base camp for a paleontological or archeological dig.) Include tent, campfire, binoculars, coffee pot, pans, etc.	Guidebooks on birds (or reptiles, dinosaurs, fish, or whatever you're studying), posters with examples of habitats (available free from the Department of Natural Resources) with labeled features, blank journal for documenting finds
Doctor's Office Include lab coats, cotton swabs, bed, tongue depressors, X-rays, refrigerator for storing medicines, baby doll patients, etc.	Book on the human body, posters with body parts on them (available free from doctors' offices and drug companies), "stay healthy" posters (also available from drug companies as well as health departments), empty prescription medicine bottles with labels, appointment books, clipboard for charting patient progress
Flower Shop Include silk flowers, sand table filled with potting soil, clay or plastic pots, trowels or spoons for planting, vases, ribbon, etc.	Seed packets with labels, FTD book for placing orders for arrangements (get out-of-date ones from your local florist), order forms to take orders, posters of flowers and their names, price lists for arrangements
Grocery Store Include grocery bags, cash register or scanner, money, receipts, purses and wallets, carts, etc.	Real containers from food, grocery store circulars with prices and descriptions, posters of fruits and vegetables, poster of butchering guides, charts of different fish, sale price signs
Airplane Include chairs in a row, a headset and control panel for the pilot, windows with clouds on them, refrigerator and stove for serving food, suitcases, etc.	Travel brochures (available free from travel agencies), travel diaries, books and magazines on a variety of countries or states, maps, flight manual (created by you or borrowed from an airline), passports

In Lynn Beard's kindergarten class, children are treated as literacy learners in dramatic play areas. Throughout the day, they have opportunities to read narrative and information books, write stories, sing along to songs written on charts, and even jot down their orders in "Papa's Pizza Parlor." Lynn's students perceive themselves as readers and writers

Figure 8.4: Kindergarten teacher Lynn Beard changes the dramatic play props weekly. This week, "PaPa's Pizza Parlor" is stocked with a cookbook containing recipes for and information about pizzas, order forms, menus, pizza fixings, and a sign to tempt the customers.

because they are, in their play and other activities. Informational text is one piece of a rich array of literacy resources in her classroom. (See Figure 8.4.)

Tap into Funds of Knowledge

Researcher Luis Moll suggests that students' home environments are often undervalued for what they can contribute to classrooms (1992). The Latino families that he studied, for example, had rich knowledge on a wide range of topics such as agriculture, medicine, religion, and cultural heritage. Moll suggests using this knowledge in our classrooms to engage learners and enrich the classroom experience. By encouraging children to bring in artifacts from home, you help to make the classroom a familiar place and provide resources for learning. For example, if you were beginning a unit on local wildflowers, you could invite a child's grandmother to come in and share her knowledge of medicinal herbs. A chart showing various herbs and their uses would reinforce the conversation and act as a reminder of the time that special person came to teach.

You might also have parents and other members of the community send in tools of their trade, such as a nurse's medical equipment or a mechanic's tools. Create a display and have the children label the object with its name and function. This idea coordinates nicely with home-to-school themes such as "plants in my yard or neighborhood," "occupations in my family," "holidays we celebrate at my house," and so on. The point is to draw on the wealth of experience and knowledge in children's homes. Once they reach school, artifacts can provide springboards for engaging in discussions, reading related books and other materials, creating signs or posters, or writing other informational texts.

A Close-Up Look at Informational Text in the Print-Rich Environment

When you enter Jackie Smart's classroom, you enter a world of informational text in action. In addition to posting informational text on the walls, Jackie ties activities to that text, creates graphic organizers to help children understand concepts, and displays books everywhere. Children have many opportunities to interact with materials and make information their own.

Jackie stores books in various places throughout her classroom—in the library, in the listening and science centers, and in bins on the tables. Here, students read aloud to favorite stuffed animals.

Linking art projects to literacy projects is important to Jackie. This student admires the globe she created to accompany her fact book about the world.

On the wall outside her classroom, Jackie displays all kinds of weather-related information—a daily weather graph, illustrated vocabulary words, a sample weather journal—which she updates regularly. Children enjoy exploring the information as they come and go from class.

For a unit on Native Americans, Jackie asked her students to create a model hogan, a traditional Navajo lodge. They used illustrated information books as references.

This graphic organizer, which compares characteristics of different types of bears, is at the center of a display that also includes students' reports on bears and "trioramas" depicting bears in their natural habitats. Using a pointer, children "read the room" together.

photo: Jackie Smart

After reading several fairy tales together, and studying them for title, setting, good and evil characters, and magical events, Jackie and her students created this information chart. Jackie leaves charts like this posted for children to review and reference.

Even Jackie's alphabet frieze contains information. It not only helps children learn their ABCs, but also a thing or two about animals.

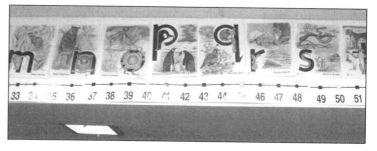

CONCLUDING THOUGHTS

The classroom's environment is like a book's table of contents. It lets children know what is in store for them. It may contain spaces that show children that reading and writing are important activities in the room. It may contain abundant and diverse materials that let children know that they are likely to engage in a wide range of reading and that, regardless of their interests or abilities, there will be something that appeals to them.

A print-rich classroom invites students to engage in literacy learning. It is visually appealing and dripping with resources such as books, magazines, posters, newspapers, and access to the Internet. Opportunities for children to interact with all of these resources are a core part of the language learning experience. As you have seen throughout this book, there are many ways to use informational text across your day. Having an environment that supports your work is key.

CHAPTER 9
Challenges of Using Informational Text
Finding Ways to Deal With Them

BY MARY KAY JOHNSON

You might think that the teachers you've read about in this book work in unusually supportive environments, are especially energetic and inventive, or are even a bit daring. And, to some degree, you're right. At the same time, many of the teachers are typical. They range in age, in background knowledge, and in years of experience from one year to over thirty years. They work in a range of schools, many serving primarily low-socioeconomic status children. They face the struggles and daily challenges of most teachers in American public schools. Yet because of their efforts, ingenuity, and willingness to take risks, they inspire us to try new things, such as incorporating more informational text into our classrooms. In this chapter, we:

◆ identify challenges common to many teachers.

◆ describe how some teachers deal with these challenges.

◆ discuss some important considerations and implications for changing practice.

Hopefully, this discussion will inspire you as you implement the ideas we've presented so far. Reading about challenges other teachers have faced may help you anticipate challenges you might face, and envision strategies for meeting them.

THE DIFFICULTIES WE TYPICALLY ENCOUNTER

Teaching is extraordinarily complex, especially teaching literacy. While there is considerable research on what effective teachers and schools do to promote literacy achievement (Taylor, Pressley, & Pearson, 2002a), there is less research on the kinds of barriers teachers face when trying to move toward more effective practice. During the data-collection phase of the Early Literacy Project, we learned about things that made diversifying genres difficult, particularly those related to incorporating more informational text. Using a survey, a formal interview, classroom observations, and informal conversations, we asked teachers to tell us about the challenges they faced. Two that seemed to come up again and again were:

◆ finding the time and energy to diversify genres

◆ diversifying genres in a mandated curriculum

Individual teachers faced other challenges as well, such as locating informational texts and feeling uneasy about change. We discuss these challenges and others in this chapter.

Finding the Time and Energy to Diversify Genres

Diversifying genres requires many efforts, including:

◆ identifying genres that need better representation in the classroom environment and curriculum.

◆ finding high-quality texts in those genres.

◆ linking texts to existing curriculum and activities.

◆ creating new curriculum and activities around the texts.

All of these efforts take time and energy. It's not unusual for teachers to take a year or even several years to accomplish them. In fact, many find it easier as time goes on. For them, getting started is the number-one challenge.

As teachers, we constantly weigh the importance of factors competing for our time and energy. If an approach does not pay off, it isn't worth the cost. Does diversifying genres pay off? Is it worth the cost? Teachers in the Early Literacy Project agreed that it was worth it for two primary reasons: It made a difference for their students, and it changed their teaching in a positive way. Many reported that children became interested in a wide variety of texts. Several noted children's—both boys' and girls'—engagement and excitement over informational text. Some noticed that children were reading more, for longer periods with fewer behavior disturbances, and were exhibiting higher levels of motivation. So while there are no easy answers to the time and energy it takes to diversify genres, it seems that that time and energy is well worth it.

Diversifying Genres in a Mandated Curriculum

A second challenge we have seen many teachers face is trying to incorporate diverse genres into a mandated curriculum, especially if the curriculum includes a basal reading program. Studies suggest that informational text, as well as other nonfiction genres, make up only a small portion of text in basal reading programs. An analysis of five first-grade basal reading programs from the early 1990s found that only 12 percent of its selections were nonfiction; an analysis from the late 1990s found that 16 percent were informational literature (Hoffman, McCarthey, Abbott, Christian, Corman, Curry, et al., 1994; Moss & Newton, 1998). So it's impossible to meet the target of one-third informational text without moving away from the basal, at least to some degree. In our experience, novice teachers are often the least comfortable moving away from the basal. So, incorporating diverse genres may be most challenging for them.

Supplement Your Basal Strategically

As an example of the challenge of supplementing basal units, consider one teacher from the Early Literacy Project whom we will call Amanda. Amanda wasn't a new teacher in the sense that she was just beginning her career—she had taught middle elementary for a number of years. But she was new to first grade. She was also new to the building, unfamiliar with the curriculum, and short on print materials and instructional supplies. She needed support to find ways to include more informational text in her new classroom.

Early in the year, we joined Amanda to take a closer look at her basal program's units. Specifically, we analyzed the genres they contained, as well as the opportunities they offered students for reading and writing connected text. (We also looked at activities in other parts of Amanda's day—for example, how she integrated reading and writing into science.) We could see, as we suspected, that the basal alone would not meet the "one-third informational, one-third narrative, one-third other" target. That finding left us with two options: Eliminate the basal entirely or supplement it with other materials. Given that Amanda was a new first-grade teacher and her district placed heavy emphasis on basal-based curriculum, we chose the latter option—supplementing the basal units to approach the one-third, one-third, one-third targets.

To determine how to supplement the basal program, we reviewed each unit for the amount of each type of text it contained. From there, we could decide how much informational, narrative, and other text to add. For example, a memo from February focused on parts of two upcoming units. The memo notes that the section had little informational text, but much text in the "other" as well as "narrative" categories. Suggestions for supplementing the basal during that unit included:

◆ doing primarily informational text read alouds.

◆ using informational text for partner time.

◆ encouraging selection of information books during DEAR (Drop Everything And Read) time.

◆ asking children to check out information books on their trip to the library that week.

Amanda's instructional time could also include informational text. For example, the focus on letter-sound relationships for /igh/ and /y/ could be practiced not only through materials provided in the basal, but also through *The Seed Song* (Saksie, 1995) and *What's the Weather Today?* (Fowler, 1991), two informational texts available to students in their classroom. The weather book might also link to calendar time.

Some basal units were easier to supplement with informational texts than others. For example, the unit on community, while including almost entirely narrative text, linked nicely to many information and "other" category books that Amanda had in her classroom, such as *Let's Take Care of the Earth* (Lanczak Williams, 1995b), which she had children take home to read. For other units, it was more challenging to find ways to connect informational texts in meaningful ways.

Based on this work with Amanda, we recommend using these three strategies to supplement basal units:

◆ Use informational texts on topics represented in the basal. For example, if a unit is on "communities," use informational texts on communities.

◆ Use informational texts that support practice in skills that are emphasized in the basal. For example, if the basal lesson emphasizes /igh/ and /y/, use an informational text that has a lot of words with those patterns.

◆ Use a somewhat higher proportion of informational text when the teaching activity isn't directly linked to the basal, such as during read aloud or independent reading.

Using these strategies, Amanda found ways to incorporate more informational text in her first-grade classroom, without neglecting important skills addressed in the basal or literacy standards that guide what we teach.

Collaborate With Your Colleagues

Another route to incorporating more informational text into a mandated curriculum is to get help from colleagues, and offer help in return. Whether it's the teacher down the hall, the school librarian, or the reading specialist, everyone benefits from collaboration with other professionals. You can make connections both in and out of school to enliven your teaching and supplement your materials. One teacher expressed the desire to "share what they've done, how they used materials or themes" by planning a gathering where she and colleagues would trade and discuss books they've used successfully.

Other Challenges of Diversifying Genres

Many challenges to diversifying genres go beyond time, energy, and a mandated curriculum. Below, we discuss a few of them: locating informational texts, accessing technology, feeling isolated and uneasy about change, and measuring success.

Locating Informational Texts

Many teachers have a hard time acquiring informational and other neglected kinds of text. As one teacher noted, "… it's hard to get enough stuff and the stuff is important!" Although there is no easy answer to this problem, Chapter 8 identifies a number of strategies, such as using the Internet and connecting with community resources, to deal with it.

Accessing Technology

A related challenge many teachers encounter is having a lack of adequate access to computers and other forms of technology that fuel our "information age." Many teachers want children to read more informational text from the Internet and CD-ROMs, but they have difficulty obtaining the software and support they need to make that happen.

Again there are no easy answers to this problem. If technology is important to you, consider appealing to local businesses for their used technology. Unfortunately, what's considered obsolete in for-profit companies is often considered state-of-the-art in schools. You might also consider applying for grants. (See Burke and Prater's *I'll Grant You That*, 2000, for an excellent guide to finding sources and writing proposals.) If you are politically inclined, speak to the state and local school board, legislators, and others who might be persuaded to appropriate more funding for technology. An increased emphasis on informational literacy across the grades hopefully will inspire administrators and politicians to devote more money and attention to technology in years to come.

Feeling Isolated and Uneasy About Change

Many teachers feel unsure or anxious when working to diversify genres. They're torn between going with the status quo and taking the risk of trying something new. As one teacher we worked with said, "I just think that people get used to doing things a certain way and it's hard to change."

Furthermore, these feelings of unease can be compounded by feelings of isolation. Several teachers have told us about debates they've had with others—teachers, administrators, even a librarian—who have argued for a story-based curriculum. Too often, the debates result in isolation because, by incorporating a lot of informational text into her classroom, the teacher is seen as doing something "radical." And sometimes the isolation can be harsh. For example, one teacher who participated in the Early Literacy Project explained, "I have smart-alecky teachers who are saying to me, 'Oh well, [she] is the reading expert,' and that is so not true. But they think because I am doing this… or I have a little tip for them here or there… I don't want to come off like some know-it-all either, but I feel like I've learned a lot."

A more subtle, but perhaps equally difficult situation is when a teacher's excitement over innovation is not shared or valued by peers. At the same time, this may spur the teacher to learn more and take on positions of leadership. We found this among Early Literacy Project teachers. Many of them were committed to getting into positions of leadership by, for example, obtaining a master's degree in reading or getting more involved in curriculum development and decision-making in the district, in part to support others in diversifying genres.

Chapter 10 provides many ideas for combating isolation around diversifying genres. Beyond those ideas, hopefully the many, many teachers around the country who are also working to diversify genres, as well as the recent increase in research and professional writing in this area, will be an inspiration to you. And, of course, we hope that this book will inspire you to take risks and innovate in this area.

Measuring Success

When we try something new, it's often hard to figure out whether it worked, didn't work, or needs to be changed. There are so many factors at play every day in classrooms: the quality of the curriculum, the aptitude and attitudes of the students, the daily schedule, the amount of support, the size of the class, the experience of the teacher. How do you decide what's working and what isn't? To what do you attribute success—and failure? One teacher summed it up well: "Maybe it's because I did use the [home reading] program [more] and I made sure the reading bags went home more than I have other years… maybe it is the informational reading. I have no way of knowing, you know. Yeah, my kids could not write this well [in past years]. This is the best group of writers I think I have ever had—it really is… [but] I don't know if it's the kids or the program."

Again, we do not have easy answers, but we hope the research cited in Chapter 1 and elsewhere in the book provides guidance. Visit the ERIC Clearinghouse at www.eric.ed.gov for links to some of the research publications cited in this book and to many others as well. You might also consider conducting research of your own. See Chapter 10 for some resources for getting started.

CLOSING THOUGHTS

Teachers in the Early Literacy Project, as well as other teachers we have known, have found many ways to confront the challenges outlined in this chapter. They meet the demands of time and energy by implementing change slowly, by mapping informational text onto their current curriculum and practice, and by making cross-curricular connections. They consider their time and energy well spent if they make a difference for their students and change their practice in a positive way.

To address the demands of a mandated curriculum, the teachers focus on and address the goals of that curriculum, while incorporating informational text and other genres. Collaboration makes the task more manageable; sharing ideas and resources is key.

Teachers deal with many other challenges, including locating and acquiring texts, dealing with technology shortages, feeling anxious or reluctant about trying something new, feeling isolated from colleagues, and experiencing difficulties in evaluating what's working. We hope we have conveyed a realistic but optimistic picture. You may have a different philosophy or work in a different context from the teachers described in this book, but you probably share at least some things with them. They have hope and vision—those qualities equip all of us to succeed in the face of any challenge.

CHAPTER 10
Professional Discussions and Development

Exploring Informational Text in Study Groups and Other Activities With Colleagues

BY EBONY M. ROBERTS

Teachers from Winans Elementary School. From right to left: Paulette Hospenthal, Dorothy Best, Adrienne Dunkerley, Candy Chatfield, Cecilia Stajos, Debora Start, and Donna Seney.

photo: Randee Smith

I f we have done our job well, you are now convinced (if you weren't already) that diversifying the genres in primary classrooms is important to children's early reading development. You also have many ideas and resources to help you incorporate informational text into your own classroom. In this chapter, we discuss some ways in which this book might be used as a professional development tool in your school. Specifically, we:

◆ briefly discuss research on teacher professional development.

◆ identify study groups as one forum for meaningful professional development.

◆ discuss study groups on incorporating informational text into primary classrooms.

The goal of this chapter is to help you create a professional learning community around the ideas and strategies discussed in this book.

TEACHER PROFESSIONAL DEVELOPMENT: WHAT THE RESEARCH SAYS

While most teachers participate in some form of professional development each year, the format does not always lend itself to rich learning. For example, many workshops are presented in a lecture format in which participants sit passively (Lieberman, 2000). Often teachers are not given the opportunity to discuss the ideas provided in these workshops with their colleagues and do not receive ongoing classroom support as they attempt to implement the ideas (Foster & Peele, 1999).

This stands in sharp contrast to what research shows about *effective* professional development. Effective professional development:

◆ is ongoing and collaborative

◆ invites active involvement from teachers

◆ often includes opportunities to observe practices as well as to hear and read about them

◆ engages teachers in trying new strategies, receiving coaching or feedback, and trying them again

◆ fosters a reflective stance toward teaching (Berne, 2001; Clark, 2001; Lieberman, 2000; Cochran-Smith & Lytle, 1999; Lord, 1994)

Increasingly, schools have begun to offer more meaningful professional development experiences, such as encouraging dialogue and collaboration across teachers, grade levels, and departments (Lytle, 2000). Collaborations with universities (e.g., professional development schools), inquiry or study groups, school-wide improvement or reform projects, and teacher networks are examples of other emerging, promising approaches to professional development. Each of these is organized quite differently and serves a different purpose, yet all speak to the

FOR YOUR INFORMATION...

Make Time and Space for Meaningful Professional Development

It is one thing to value meaningful professional development, but it is another to find the time to engage in it. The many demands on our time often provide few opportunities to collaborate with colleagues. Add to this the isolation we often feel within the four walls of our classrooms, which, to a large extent, has shaped the image of the "self-made teacher" who doesn't need support from colleagues (Labaree, 2000). Unfortunately, this image leaves little room to create a "shared professional culture for teachers across classroom domains" (p. 230).

However, there are ways to make time and space for meaningful professional development. Here are a few ideas:

◆ Ask your principal to designate one faculty meeting a month to small discussion groups for the purpose of professional development.

◆ Ask your district to set aside one professional development day where teachers can meet in small groups to discuss professional readings. (Teachers can submit a list of what they will read if district personnel are concerned about how the time will be used.)

◆ Ask the reading specialist to devote time to observing, coaching, and talking with interested teachers.

◆ Ask your principal for substitute teachers so that you and your colleagues can observe one another teaching at least once a month and discuss what you notice.

power of teacher collaboration as an ongoing part of meaningful professional development.

Research has shown that the conversations teachers have with one another around their practice can lead to creative and inventive transformations in the classroom (Clark, 2001; Berne, 2001; Burbules, 1993). Building collaborative relationships with colleagues empowers teachers to change the culture of their classroom. As Lieberman (2000) argues, participation in creating and sustaining a group that supports their professional identity, interests, and learning brings "great power and energy" to teachers (p. 223). While such groups often have different goals, they provide a meaningful source of support for teachers, create a sense of community, and encourage learning.

STUDY GROUPS AS A FORUM FOR MEANINGFUL PROFESSIONAL DEVELOPMENT

If we want to grow professionally, we must create opportunities for experiences that encourage inquiry and reflection around our practice. In a recent analysis of five large-scale studies on effective high-poverty elementary schools, researchers found that the schools shared a focus on professional development. Teachers in these schools learned together to improve their instruction (Taylor, Pressley, & Pearson, 2002a). In the company of colleagues and in the context of inquiry and reflection, teachers are more likely to try new instructional strategies and research questions that arise from their efforts.

Study groups are an increasingly popular forum for professional development, one that supports a reflective stance toward teaching (Lord, 1994). Study groups can take many forms. In some cases, they resemble book clubs or literary circles. Autobiography discussion groups, for example, have been studied as a way for both beginning and experienced teachers to explore issues of culture and identity (Florio-Ruane and deTar, 2001; Florio-Ruane, 1994; Reischl, 1999).

Other study groups focus on specific instructional practices, such as student-led book clubs (Smith, 1996; McMahon & Raphael, 1997). Whatever form they take, study groups provide a means for intellectual and social interaction in which participants can share ideas, thoughts, feelings, and reactions (Flood & Lapp, 1994). In recent years books such as *Mosaic of Thought* (Keene & Zimmerman, 1997) and *Strategies That Work* (Harvey & Goudvis, 2000) have been discussed in many study groups interested in comprehension processes and instruction. For many teachers, the interactions between the reader and the text, and between the reader and other readers, make study groups a powerful tool for increasing understanding and improving practice.

Barbara Taylor and her colleagues created the *School Change Framework*, which provides a structure to develop and implement high-quality literacy instruction in elementary schools. Study groups are an essential component of this structure. Teachers meet regularly in small groups, within grades and across grades, for about one hour a week to discuss aspects of classroom reading instruction. Members are encouraged to discuss issues that arise in their literacy instruction, to help solve instructional dilemmas, and to develop action plans that lead to productive changes in their instruction. Group members often observe one another's practice, study video clips of effective practice, and read and discuss books and articles on research-based practices. When learning any new skill or strategy, we need to build a knowledge base sufficient to sustain commitment and see change through. Studying in small groups with other colleagues is one valuable way to build that base. For more information on the *School Change Framework,* go to www.ciera.org/library/reports/inquiry-2/2-016/2-016a.pdf.

STUDY GROUPS ON INCORPORATING INFORMATIONAL TEXT INTO PRIMARY CLASSROOMS

Study groups provide an excellent forum for discussion as you diversify genres in your classroom. The following are some of the activities that you and your colleagues could do together:

Engage in a self-study of genre use. What genres are included on classroom walls and other surfaces, and in what proportions? What genres are in and on display in the classroom library? What about genres used in classroom activities involving written language?

Keys to Successful Study Groups

A number of researchers have studied study groups (Roberts, 2002; Taylor, Pearson, Clark, & Walpole, 2000; Reischl, 1999; Murphy & Lick, 1998; Florio-Ruane & deTar, 1995). Below is a round-up of their recommendations for creating and sustaining these groups:

Participation should be voluntary. Traditionally, professional development is required by school districts, which means that teachers often go along reluctantly. Willing participants in a study group, however, are more likely to be committed to the group's goals and work to sustain its energy. And a successful study group might eventually draw in teachers who were not inclined to participate initially.

The number of teachers should not exceed eight. The larger the study group, the more difficult it will be to find common, convenient meeting times for all participants. Additionally, with smaller groups each member is able to participate more in discussions and is more likely to take greater responsibility for the organization and direction of the group.

Goals should be established early and shared by all group members. It is important for the group to set goals at the start to increase the likelihood that everyone is on the same page. What does the group want to accomplish by meeting? What will be the focus of the group's studies? If participants feel that they have played an important role in addressing these questions, they are more likely to remain committed. Of course, goals may evolve as the group becomes more settled, but a shared understanding from the beginning is essential.

All members should play an integral part in structuring and leading the group. A study group should be a joint enterprise in which members share responsibility in deciding on the particulars, such as selecting books and preparing discussion questions. Participants should take turns facilitating the group's discussions and should not be made to feel intimidated by other members. When responsibility is shared, a sense of ownership grows. Participants feel more connected to the group and invested in its success.

Writing can be an important component of reflection. Writing in a journal provides a space for participants to reflect on readings, curriculum issues, classroom observations, and points raised in previous meetings. Group members might write in their journals before they meet, and then again following the meeting to reflect on changes in their ideas prompted by the discussion. This encourages participants to be reflective practitioners.

Underlying many of these recommendations is the belief that effective study groups require teachers who are true collaborators, critical colleagues, and inquirers (Fecho, 2000; Lord, 1994). Sadly, though, most schools and districts don't provide teachers with the resources they need to move in that direction. We hope that many of you will provide the special leadership and support that is necessary.

Inventory one another's classrooms for genres. It helps to have a fresh pair of eyes examine your classroom and curriculum. Ask a colleague to identify areas of strength and weakness in how you're diversifying and teaching various genres.

Review curriculum materials for genres represented. To save time, different members of the study group might be responsible for examining different types of materials, such as the district basal reading series and district-provided trade books. And don't overlook assessments—examine them with respect to genre, too.

Read books and articles related to genres in general and informational text in particular. In some cases, having everyone do the same reading, chapter-by-chapter or article-by-article, works well. In others, it may make more sense to have members of the group read different chapters and articles. For inspiration, see the discussion of the jigsaw approach on page 97.

Consider having each group member develop expertise in a different area. One member might become an expert in informational text read aloud, another in informational text writing, and so on. Each expert could be available as a consultant, a model to observe, and a leader of discussions in that area.

Videotape one another using informational text or other genres in instruction. View excerpts of the videotapes together and discuss strengths and weaknesses. As professionally produced videotapes on informational text in the primary grades become available, consider purchasing or renting them.

Devote a portion of each meeting to sharing new texts you have found. As discussed throughout this book, these texts can include not only books but also downloaded material from the Internet, pamphlets, newspaper and magazine articles, and a variety of other non-book texts. As discussed in Chapter 7, be sure to give these texts a critical eye.

Work together to create "products" that showcase what you are learning. For example, offer a workshop to other teachers in the school or district, present your work at a professional conference, or submit an article for publication in a professional journal.

Pool resources to build a library of materials on using informational text in the primary grades. You might subscribe to professional journals that are likely to include pieces on informational text, purchase books and other materials, take turns contributing photocopied articles and other writings to a file or binder, and so on. Also, consider purchasing a small set of high-quality informational texts and keeping them in a central location or book bin to share among colleagues as needed.

Create a book club in which you read informational texts for adults. Examine your own reading processes and think about the lessons this experience might hold for teaching students to read informational text. If the book club is successful, consider creating a writers' group in which members write informational texts.

Devote some meetings to taking on the roles of various stakeholders. For example, in one meeting, you might focus on parents and how diversifying genres pertains to, affects, or is affected by them. In another meeting, you might play the role of critical theorists, thinking about and discussing how to promote socially critical reading and writing of informational or other texts (Kempe, 2001). (See "Ask the 'Critical' Questions" on page 180.) In another meeting, you might play the role of content-area expert and discuss how learning in various subjects is being affected, for better and for worse, by including a greater diversity of genres.

Communicate with administrators about the importance of funding and supporting your efforts. Some administrators have simply not thought about the types of text to which children are exposed, especially in the early grades. Many are unaware that there has been research on genres and young children. But once that awareness is built, many of them support diversifying genres—particularly incorporating more informational texts— in primary classrooms.

Regardless of what you do in study groups, we hope that research forms a basis for many of your discussions and activities. Research today is often conducted in real classrooms with real teachers, real students, and real challenges. It speaks to the "whys" and "hows" of what we do or want to learn to do. Of course, many questions are not yet addressed in research, but

If You Have to Go It Alone

There may not be a group of teachers in your school or district with whom you can collaborate around incorporating informational texts in the primary grades. If this is the case, you may find it helpful to keep a professional journal in which you reflect on your work in this area—your trials and triumphs, frustrations, and questions. You might also consider doing a careful study of your own practices as a means of providing self-feedback and information. Your classroom can become a laboratory, in a sense, in which to study questions that arise from your teaching. *The Art of Classroom Inquiry* by Ruth Shagoury Hubbard and Brenda Miller Power (1993) is a good resource for budding teacher-researchers. Web-based discussion groups are another, such as www.educationworld.com/science, www.nsta.org, and www.school.discovery.com. There may be other forums that allow you to network with teachers beyond your school or district. Look into the possibilities.

new research—especially in the area of informational text—is being conducted every day. We hope you will look for it and that researchers will also keep their eyes open for your work. A marriage of accumulated professional wisdom and accumulated scientific research will serve our field and our students well.

CONCLUDING THOUGHTS

Too often, professional development experiences are not productive, nor are they consistent with what we know about how we grow as teachers. Teacher study groups can provide a forum for meaningful professional development. This chapter offered a number of suggestions for implementing study groups. In collaboration with your colleagues, we believe you will find many inventive and productive ways to incorporate informational texts into your primary classroom.

APPENDIX A
Resources for Locating Good Information Books for Young Children

PROFESSIONAL BOOKS

These books are especially helpful in providing guidelines for selecting texts wisely. For books on incorporating informational text into the curriculum, see Appendix B.

Checking Out Nonfiction K-8: Good Choices for Best Learning by R. A. Bamford and J. V. Kristo, Christopher-Gordon Publishers

Making Facts Come Alive: Choosing Quality Nonfiction Literature K–8 edited by R. A. Bamford and J. V. Kristo, Christopher-Gordon Publishers

Eyeopeners II: Children's Books to Answer Children's Questions About the World Around Them by B. Kobrin, Scholastic

The Best in Children's Nonfiction: Reading, Writing, and Teaching Orbis Pictus Award Books edited by M. Zarnowski, R. M. Kerper, and J. M. Jensen, National Council of Teachers of English

NONFICTION AND INFORMATION BOOK AWARDS

There are several awards given each year for nonfiction books in general or information books in particular. Here are six you may want to watch:

The Eve Pownall Award for Information Books, awarded by the Children's Book Council of Australia annually for a book written by an Australian or resident of Australia. **www.cbc.org.au**

The Orbis Pictus Award, awarded by the National Council of Teachers of English annually. Up to five honor books are also named. **www.ncte.org/nctetoyou/2003/ 2003-orbis-pictus.shtml**

Children's Book Awards, the Nonfiction Book for Young Readers category, awarded by the International Reading Association. **www.reading.org/awards/children.html**

The Boston Globe–Horn Book Award for Outstanding Nonfiction, awarded annually. **www.hbook.com**.

The Robert F. Sibert Informational Book Award, awarded annually by the American Library Association for a book written by a citizen or resident of the United States. To access the award page, go to **www.ala.org**, click on the site map, then click "Award Winners" and scroll down to find the Silbert Medal link.

The Washington Post/Children's Book Guild Nonfiction Award, awarded annually by the *Washington Post* to an author or author/illustrator who has "creatively produced books that make a difference" in the nonfiction world. **www.childrensbookguild.org/2003award.htm**

GENERAL BOOK AWARDS OR HONORS

Many awards or honors do not focus specifically on nonfiction but may include it among other genres. Here are a few to consider:

- ◆ American Library Association Notable Children's Books
- ◆ Coretta Scott King Award
- ◆ Hornbook Fanfare of Highly Recommended Books
- ◆ Notable Social Studies Trade Books for Young People
- ◆ Outstanding Science Trade Books for Children

- ◆ School Library Journal Best Books
- ◆ Teachers' Choices and Children's Choices, International Reading Association and Children's Book Council

PUBLISHERS' CATALOGS

We have seen a great increase in attention to nonfiction among educational publishers. Many catalogs now have extensive sections devoted to nonfiction texts. Perusing these catalogs, visiting exhibitions at conferences, and asking for samples may help you find the information books you are looking for.

COLLEAGUES

Your best resource for locating good information books for young children will likely be your colleagues within your school, district, or other professional networks. If you have a study group, consider including time to share notable information books you've come across. If you are looking for information books on a particular subject, ask your colleagues, your local librarian, or a listserve for help. If you have developed a good set of books on a particular topic or theme, consider telling others about it; this might inspire recommendations from others to come your way.

APPENDIX B
Professional Books on Incorporating Informational Text in the Primary Grades

If you wish to learn more about incorporating informational text in the primary grades, check out these resources. All of them address the topic to varying degrees.

Exploring How Texts Work by B. Derewianka, Australian Print Group

True Stories: Nonfiction Literacy in the Primary Classroom by C. Duthie, Stenhouse Publishers

Infotext Reading and Learning by K. M. Feathers, Pippin Publishing

A Matter of Fact: Using Factual Texts in the Classroom by P. Green, Eleanor Curtain Publishing

Nonfiction Matters: Reading, Writing, and Research in Grades 3–8 by S. Harvey, Stenhouse

Make It Real: Strategies for Success With Informational Texts by L. Hoyt, Heinemann

Exploring Informational Texts: From Theory to Practice edited by L. Hoyt, M. Mooney, and B. Parkes, Heinemann

Info-Kids: How to Use Nonfiction to Turn Reluctant Readers into Enthusiastic Learners by R. Jobe and M. Dayton-Sakari, Pembroke Publishers

Introducing Nonfiction Writing in the Early Grades by J. W. Mahoney, Scholastic

Young Researchers: Informational Reading and Writing in the Early and Primary Years by M. Mallett, Routledge

I See What You Mean: Children at Work with Visual Information by S. Moline, Stenhouse

Exploring the Literature of Fact: Children's Nonfiction Trade Books in the Elementary Classroom by B. Moss, Guilford Press

Finding Out About Finding Out: A Practical Guide to Children's Information Books by B. Neate, Winchester, UK: Infopress

More Than Stories: The Range of Children's Writing by T. Newkirk, Heinemann

Nonfiction Craft Lessons: Teaching Information Writing K–8 by J. Portalupi and R. Fletcher, Stenhouse

The Research Workshop: Bringing the World into Your Classroom by P. Rogovin, Heinemann

Vital Connections: Children, Science, and Books by W. Saul and S. A. Jagusch, Heinemann

Discovering Nonfiction: 25 Powerful Teaching Strategies Grades 2–6 by H. F. Silver, R. W. Strong, and M. Perini, Canter and Associates.

Is That a Fact? Teaching Nonfiction Writing K–3 by T. Stead, Stenhouse

Concept-Oriented Reading Instruction: Engaging Classrooms, Lifelong Learners by E. A. Swan, Guilford Press

Starting with the Real World: Strategies for Developing Nonfiction Reading and Writing, K–8 by A. Trussell-Cullen, Dominie Press

This list is not exhaustive, and the absence or presence of any title is not meant to be a commentary about the value of the work. We've assembled this list simply for your convenience should you wish to explore additional readings in this area.

Professional References Cited

Alexander, P. A., & Jetton, T. L. (2000). Learning from text: A multidimensional and developmental perspective. In M. L. Kamil, P. B. Mosenthal, P. D. Pearson, & R. Barr (Eds). *Handbook of reading research* (Vol. 3, pp. 285–310). Mahwah, NJ: Lawrence Erlbaum Associates.

Anderson, E., & Guthrie, J. T. (1999, April). *Motivating children to gain conceptual knowledge from text: The combination of science observation and interesting texts.* Paper presented at the annual meeting of the American Educational Research Association, Montreal, Canada.

Anderson, R. C, Wilson, P. T., & Fielding, L. G. (1988). Growth in reading and how children spend their time outside of school, *Reading Research Quarterly, 23,* 285–303.

Armbruster, B. B., Lehr, F., & Osborn, J. (2001). *Put reading first: The research building blocks for teaching children to read.* Washington, DC: Partnership for Reading.

Aronson, E. (1978). *The jigsaw classroom.* Beverly Hills, CA: Sage.

Avery, C. (1998). Nonfiction books: Naturals for the primary level. In R. A. Bamford & J. V. Kristo (Eds.), *Making facts come alive: Choosing quality nonfiction literature K–8.* Norwood, MA: Christopher-Gordon Publishers.

Bamford, R. A., & Kristo, J. V. (1998). *Making facts come alive: Choosing quality nonfiction literature K–8.* Norwood, MA: Christopher-Gordon Publishers.

Bamford, R. A., & Kristo, J. V. (2000). *Checking out nonfiction K–8: Good choices for best learning.* Norwood, MA: Christopher-Gordon Publishers.

Banikowski, A., & Mehring, T. (1999). Strategies to enhance memory based on brain research. *Focus on Exceptional Children, 32,* 1–16.

Beck, I. L., & McKeown, M. G. (1991). Social studies texts are hard to understand: Mediating some of the difficulties. *Language Arts, 68,* 482–490.

Beck, I. L., McKeown, M. G., Hamilton, R. L., & Kucan, L. (1997). *Questioning the author: An approach for enhancing student engagement with text.* Newark, DE: International Reading Association.

Beck, I. L., McKeown, M. G., & Kucan, L. (2002). *Bringing words to life: Robust vocabulary instruction.* New York: The Guilford Press.

Beck, I. L., McKeown, M. G., Sandora, C., Kucan, L., & Worthy, J. (1996). Questioning the author: A year-long classroom implementation to engage students with text. *The Elementary School Journal, 96,* 385–414.

Berne, J. (2001). *Connected teacher knowing: An examination of a teacher learning network.* Unpublished doctoral dissertation, Michigan State University, East Lansing, MI.

Blachowicz, C. L., & Fisher, P. (2000). Vocabulary instruction. In M. L. Kamil, P. B. Mosenthal, P. D. Pearson, & R. Barr (Eds.), *Handbook of reading research* (Vol. 3, pp. 503–523). Mahwah, NJ: Lawrence Erlbaum Associates.

Blachowicz, C., & Ogle, D. (2001). *Reading comprehension: Strategies for independent learners.* New York: The Guilford Press.

Block, C. C., Gambrell, L. B., & Pressley, M. (Eds.). (2002). *Improving comprehension instruction: Rethinking research, theory, and classroom practice.* San Francisco: Jossey-Bass.

Block, C. C., & Pressley, G. M. (Eds.) (2002). *Comprehension instruction: Research-based best practices.* New York: Guilford Press.

Boscolo, P. (1996). The use of information in expository text writing. In C. Pontecorvo, M. Orsolini, B. Burge, & L. B. Resnick (Eds.), *Children's early text construction* (pp. 209–227). Mahwah, NJ: Lawrence Erlbaum Associates.

Bristor, V. J. (1994). Combining reading and writing with science to enhance content area achievement and attitudes. *Reading Horizons, 35,* 31–43.

Britton, J., Burgess, T., Martin, N., McLeod, A., & Rosen, H. (1975). Schools Council Research Studies Series. *The Development of Writing Abilities* (11–18) (rpt. 1977 ed.). London: Macmillan Education Ltd.

Brown, R., Pressley, M., Van Meter, P., & Schuder, T. (1996). A quasi-experimental validation of transactional strategies instruction with low-achieving second grade readers. *Journal of Educational Psychology, 88,* 18–37.

Bryan, J. (1998). K-W-W-L: Questioning the known. *The Reading Teacher, 51,* 618–624.

Burbules, N. C. (1993). *Dialogue in teaching: Theory and practice.* New York: Teachers College Press.

Burke, J., & Prater, C.A. (2000). *I'll grant you that: A step-by-step guide to finding funds, designing winning projects, and writing powerful grant proposals.* Portsmouth, NH: Heinemann.

Cairney, T. (1990). Intertextuality: Infectious echoes from the past. *The Reading Teacher, 43,* 478–484.

Calkins, L. M. (1994). *The art of teaching writing* (new ed.). Portsmouth, NH: Heinemann.

Carbo, M. (1989). *How to record books for maximum reading gains.* Syosset, NY: National Reading Styles Institute.

Carlisle, J. F., & Rice, M. S. (2003). *Improving reading comprehension: Research-based principles and practices.* Timonium, MD: York Press.

Carver, R., & Liebert, R. (1995). The effect of reading library books at different levels of difficulty upon gain in reading ability. *Reading Research Quarterly, 30,* 26–48.

Caswell, L. J., & Duke, N. K. (1998). Non-narrative as a catalyst for literacy development. *Language Arts, 75,* 108–117.

Chall, J. S. (1983). *Stages of reading development.* New York: McGraw-Hill.

Chapman, M. L. (1995). The sociocognitive construction of written genres in first grade. *Research in the Teaching of English, 29,* 164–192.

Christmas, J. (1993). *Developing and implementing a plan to improve the reading achievement of second grade students at Woodbine Elementary School* (Ed.D. Research Report). Florida: Nova University. (ERIC Document Reproduction Service no. ED 359 493)

Clark, C. M. (2001). *Talking shop: Authentic conversation and teacher learning.* New York: Teachers College Press.

Cochran-Smith, M., & Lytle, S. L. (1999). Relationships of knowledge and practice: Teacher learning in communities. *Review of Research in Education, 24,* 249–305.

Copple, B. (2002). Shelf determination. *Forbes, 169,* 130–142.

Cudd, E. T., & Roberts, L. (1989). Using writing to enhance content area learning in the primary grades. *The Reading Teacher, 42,* 392–404.

Cunningham, P., Hall, D., & Defee, M. (1998). Nonability-grouped, multilevel instruction: Eight years later. *The Reading Teacher, 51,* 652–663.

Derewianka, B. (1990). *Exploring how texts work. Maryborough.* Victoria, Australia: Australian Print Group.

Dickson, S. V., Collins, V. L., Simmons, D. C., & Kameenui, E. J. (1998). Metacognitive strategies: Research bases. In D. C. Simmons & E. J. Kameenui (Eds.), *What research tells us about children with diverse learning needs: Bases and basics* (pp. 295–360). Mahwah, NJ: Lawrence Erlbaum Associates.

Dole, J. A., Duffy, G. G., Roehler, L. R., & Pearson, P. D. (1991). Moving from the old to the new: Research on reading comprehension instruction. *Review of Educational Research, 61,* 239–262.

Donovan, C. A. (2001). Children's development and control of written story and informational genres: Insights from one elementary school. *Research in the Teaching of English, 35,* 394–447.

Donovan, C. A., & Smolkin, L. B. (2002). Considering genre, content, and visual features in the selection of trade books for science instruction. *The Reading Teacher, 55,* 502–520.

Dreher, M. J. (2000). Fostering reading for learning. In L. Baker, M. J. Dreher, & J. Guthrie (Eds.), *Engaging young readers: Promoting achievement and motivation* (pp. 94–118). New York: Guilford.

Dreher, M. J., & Dromsky, A. (2000, December). *Increasing the diversity of young children's independent reading.* Paper presented at the National Reading Conference, Scottsdale, AZ.

Duke, N. K. (2000a). 3.6 minutes per day: The scarcity of informational texts in first grade. *Reading Research Quarterly, 35,* 202–224.

Duke, N. K. (2000b). For the rich it's richer: Print experiences and environments offered to children in very low- and very high-SES first grade classrooms. *American Educational Research Journal, 37,* 441–478.

Duke, N. K. (2003). Reading to learn from the very beginning: Information books in early childhood. *Young Children, 58(2),* 14–20.

Duke, N. K., Bennett-Armistead, V. S., & Roberts, E. M. (2002). Incorporating informational text in the primary grades. In C. Roller (Ed.), *Comprehensive reading instruction across the grade levels* (pp. 40–54). Newark, DE: International Reading Association.

Duke, N. K., Bennett-Armistead, V. S., & Roberts, E. M. (2003). Bridging the gap between learning to read and reading to learn. In D. M. Barone & L. M. Morrow (Eds.), *Literacy and young children: Research-based practices* (pp. 226–242). New York: Guilford Press. (Please note: This is an only slightly different version of the chapter listed immediately above.)

Duke, N. K., & Kays, J. (1998). "Can I say 'Once upon a time'?": Kindergarten children developing knowledge of information book language. *Early Childhood Research Quarterly, 13,* 295–318.

Duke, N. K., Martineau, J. P., Frank, K. A., & Bennett-Armistead, V. S. (2003). *33.6 minutes per day: What happens when we include more informational text in first grade classrooms?* Unpublished manuscript, Michigan State University.

Duke, N. K., & Pearson, P. D. (2002). Effective practices for developing reading comprehension. In A. E. Farstrup & S. J. Samuels (Eds.), *What research has to say about reading instruction* (3rd ed., pp. 205–242). Newark, DE: International Reading Association.

Duke, N. K., & Purcell-Gates, V. (in press). Genres at home and at school: Bridging the new to the known. *The Reading Teacher.*

Duke, N. K., & Tower, C. (in press). Nonfiction texts for young readers. In D. Schallert & J. Hoffman (Eds.), *Read this room: Texts, tasks, and the teaching and learning of reading.* Mahwah, NJ: Lawrence Erlbaum Associates.

Duthie, C. (1996). *True stories: Nonfiction literacy in the primary classroom.* York, ME: Stenhouse.

Egan, K. (1986). *Teaching as storytelling.* Chicago: University of Chicago Press.

Egan, K. (1993). Narrative and learning: A voyage of implications. *Linguistics and Education, 5,* 119-126.

Estes, T. H., & Vaughn, J. L. (1973). Reading interest and comprehension: Implications. *The Reading Teacher, 27,* 149–153.

Feathers, K. M. (1993). *Infotext reading and learning.* Scarborough, Ontario, Canada: Pippin Publishing.

Fielding, L., & Roller, C. (1992). Making difficult books accessible and easy books acceptable. *The Reading Teacher, 45,* 678–685.

Flood, J., & Lapp, D. (1994). Teacher book clubs: Establishing literature discussion groups for teachers. *The Reading Teacher, 47,* 574–576.

Florio-Ruane, S. (1994). The future teachers' autobiography club: Preparing educators to support literacy learning in culturally diverse classrooms. *English Education, 26,* 52–66.

Florio-Ruane, S., & deTar, J. (1995). Conflict and consensus in teacher candidates' discussion of ethnic autobiography. *English Education, 27,* 11–39.

Florio-Ruane, S., & deTar, J. (2001). *Teacher education and the cultural imagination: Autobiography, conversation and narrative.* Mahwah, NJ: Lawrence Erlbaum Associates.

Florio-Ruane, S., Raphael, T. E., Glazier, J., McVee, M., & Wallace, S. (1997). Discovering culture in discussions of autobiographical literature: Transforming the education of literacy teachers. In C. K. Kinzer, K. A. Hinchman, & D. J. Leu (Eds.), *Inquiries into literacy theory and practice* (pp. 452–464). Chicago: The National Reading Conference.

Foster, M., & Peele, T. (1999). Teaching and learning in the contexts of African-American English and culture. *Education and Urban Society, 31,* 177–189.

Fountas, I., & Pinnell, G. S. (1996). *Guided reading: Good first teaching for all children.* Portsmouth, NH: Heinemann.

Fractor, J. S., Woodruff, M. C., Martinez, M. G., & Teale, W. H. (1993). Let's not miss opportunities to promote voluntary reading: Classroom libraries in the elementary school. *The Reading Teacher, 46,* 476–484.

Fredericks, A. D. (1998). Evaluating and using nonfiction literature in the science curriculum. In R. A. Bamford & J. V. Kristo (Eds.), *Making facts come alive: Choosing quality nonfiction literature K–8* (pp. 109–121). Norwood, MA: Christopher-Gordon Publishers.

Fresch, S. L. (1995). Self-selection of early literacy learners. *The Reading Teacher, 49,* 220–227.

Gambrell, L. (1996). Creating classroom cultures that foster reading motivation. *The Reading Teacher, 5,* 14–25.

Gambrell, L. B., Almasi, J. F., Xie, Q., & Heland, V. J. (1995). Helping first graders get a running start in reading. In L. M. Morrow (Ed.), *Family literacy: Connections in schools and communities* (pp. 143–154). Newark, DE: International Reading Association.

Gambrell, L., Koskinen, P., & Kapnius, B. (1991). Retelling and the reading comprehension of proficient and less-proficient readers. *Journal of Educational Research, 84,* 356–362.

Gavelek, J. R., Raphael, T. E., Biondo, S. M., & Wang, D. (2000). Integrated literacy instruction. In M. L. Kamil, P. B. Mosenthal, P. D. Pearson, & R. Barr (Eds.), *Handbook of reading research* (Vol. 3, pp. 587–607). Mahwah, NJ: Lawrence Erlbaum Associates.

Goldenberg, C. (1992/1993). Instructional conversations: Promoting reading comprehension through discussion. *The Reading Teacher, 46,* 316–326.

Green, P. (1992). *A matter of fact: Using factual texts in the classroom.* Armadale Victoria, Australia: Eleanor Curtain Publishing.

Guthrie, J. T., & McCann, A. D. (1996). Idea circles: Peer collaborations for conceptual learning. In L. B. Gambrell & J. F. Almasi (Eds.), *Lively discussions! Fostering engaged reading* (pp. 87–105). Newark, DE: International Reading Association.

Guthrie, J. T., & McCann, A. D. (1997). Characteristics of classrooms that promote motivations and strategies for learning. In J. T. Guthrie & A. Wigfield (Eds.), *Reading engagement: Motivating readers through integrated curriculum* (pp. 128–148). Newark, DE: International Reading Association.

Guthrie, J. T., Van Meter, P., McCann, A. D., Wigfield, A., Bennett, L., Poundstone, C. C., et al. (1996). Growth of literacy engagement: Changes in motivations and strategies during concept-oriented reading instruction. *Reading Research Quarterly, 31,* 306–332.

Guthrie, J. T., & Wigfield, A. (2000). Engagement and motivation in reading. In M. L. Kamil, P. B. Mosenthal, P. D. Pearson, and & R. Barr (Eds.), *Handbook of reading research* (Vol. 3, pp. 403–424). Mahwah, NJ: Erlbaum.

Guzzetti, B. J., Kowalinski, B. J., & McGowan, T. (1992). Using a literature-based approach to teaching social studies. *Journal of Reading, 36,* 114–122.

Halliday, M. A. K., & Hasan, R. (1985). *Language, context and text: A social-semiotic perspective.* Geelong, Australia: Deakin University Press.

Harrop, A., & McCann, C. (1983). Behavior modification and reading attainment in the comprehensive school. *Educational Research, 25,* 191–195.

Harste, J. C., Woodward, V. A., & Burke, C. (1984). *Language stories and literacy lessons.* Portsmouth, NH: Heinemann.

Harvey, S. (1998). *Nonfiction matters: Reading, writing, and research in Grades 3–8.* York, ME: Stenhouse.

Harvey, S. (2002). Nonfiction inquiry: Using real reading and writing to explore the world. *Language Arts, 80,* 12–22.

Harvey, S., & Goudvis, A. (2000). *Strategies that work: Teaching comprehension to enhance understanding.* Portland, ME: Stenhouse.

Heath, S. B. (1982). What no bedtime story means: Narrative skills at home and school. *Language and Society, 11,* 49–76.

Henk, W., & Melnick, S. (1998). Upper elementary-aged children's reported perceptions about good readers: A self-efficacy influenced update in transitional literacy contexts. *Reading Research and Instruction, 38,* 57–80.

Hiebert, E. H. (1999). Text matters in learning to read. *The Reading Teacher, 52,* 552–566.

Hoffman, J. V., McCarthey, S. J., Abbott, J., Christian, C., Corman, L., Curry, C., et al. (1994). So what's new in the new basals? A focus on first grade. *Journal of Reading Behavior, 26,* 47–73.

Horowitz, R., & Freeman, S. H. (1995). Robots versus spaceships: The role of discussion in kindergartners' and second graders' preferences for science text. *The Reading Teacher, 49,* 30–40.

Hoyt, L. (2002). *Make it real: Strategies for success with informational texts.* Portsmouth, NH: Heinemann.

Hoyt, L., Mooney, M., & Parkes, B. (Eds.) (2003). *Exploring informational texts: From theory to practice.* Portsmouth, NH: Heinemann.

Hubbard, R. S., & Power, B. M. (1993). *The Art of Classroom Inquiry: A Handbook for Teacher-Researchers.* Portsmouth, NH: Heinemann.

International Reading Association (IRA) & National Association for the Education of Young Children (NAEYC) (adopted, 1998). *Learning to read and write: Developmentally appropriate practices for young children* [a joint position statement]. Newark, DE and Washington, DC: Author.

Irwin, P. A., & Mitchell, J. N. (1983). A procedure for assessing the richness of retellings. *Journal of Reading, 26,* 391–395.

Jobe, R., & Dayton-Sakari, M. (2002). *Infokids: How to use nonfiction to turn reluctant readers into enthusiastic learners.* Markham, Ontario, Canada: Pembroke.

Kamberelis, G. (1998). Relations between children's literacy diets and genre development: You write what you read. *Literacy Teaching and Learning, 3,* 7–53.

Kamberelis, G. (1999). Genre development and learning: Children writing stories, science reports, and poems. *Research in the Teaching of English, 33,* 403–460.

Kamil, M. L., & Lane, D. M. (1997, March). *A classroom study of the efficacy of using information text for first-grade reading instruction.* Paper presented at the American Educational Research Association Meeting, Chicago, IL.

Kamil, M. L., & Lane, D. M. (1998). Researching the relation between technology and literacy: An agenda for the 21st century. In D. R. Reinking, L. D. Labbo, M. McKenna, & R. Kieffer (Eds.), *Literacy for the 21st century: Technological transformations in a post-typographic world* (pp. 235–251). Mahwah, NJ: Erlbaum.

Keene, E. O., & Zimmerman, S. (1997). *Mosaic of thought: Teaching comprehension in a reader's workshop.* Portsmouth, NH: Heinemann.

Kempe, A. (2001). No single meaning: Empowering students to construct socially critical readings of the text. In H. Fehring & P. Green (Eds.), *Critical literacy: A Collection of articles from the Australian Literacy Educators' Association.* Newark, DE: International Reading Association. Originally published in the *Australian Journal of Language and Literacy, 16* (November, 1993).

Klingner, J. K., & Vaughn, S. (1999). Promoting reading comprehension, content learning, and English acquisition through Collaborative Strategic Reading (CSR). *The Reading Teacher, 52,* 738–747.

Kobrin, B. (1995). *Eyeopeners II: Children's books to answer children's questions about the world around them.* New York: Scholastic.

Korkeamaki, R. L., & Dreher, M. J. (2000). What happened when kindergarten children were reading and writing information text in teacher- and peer-led groups? In T. Shanahan & F. V. Rodriguez-Brown (Eds.), *National Reading Conference Yearbook, 49,* 452–463.

Korkeamaki, R. L., Tiainen, O., & Dreher, M. J. (1998). Helping Finnish second graders make sense of their reading and writing in their science project. *National Reading Conference Yearbook, 47,* 334–344.

Koskinen, P., Blum, I., Bisson, S., Phillips, S., Creamer, T., Baker, T. (2000). Book access, shared reading, and audio models: The effects of supporting the literacy learning of linguistically diverse students in school and at home. *Journal of Educational Psychology, 92,* 23–36.

Krashen, S. (2001). More smoke and mirrors: A critique of the National Reading Panel report on fluency. *Phi Delta Kappan, 83,* 119–123.

Kucan, L., & Beck, I. L. (1997). Thinking aloud and reading comprehension research: Inquiry, instruction and social interaction. *Review of Educational Research, 67,* 271–299.

Kuhn, M., & Stahl, S. (2000). *Fluency: A review of developmental and remedial practices* (Technical Report #2-008). Ann Arbor, MI: Center for the Improvement of Early Reading Achievement. (Eric Document Reproduction Service Number ED 438 530)

Labaree, D. F. (2000). On the nature of teaching and teacher education: Difficult practices that look easy. *Journal or Teacher Education, 51,* 228–233.

Lennox, S. (1995). Sharing books with children. *Australian Journal of Early Childhood, 20,* 12–16.

Leslie, L., & Caldwell, J. (2001). *Qualitative reading inventory, 3.* Boston: Allyn and Bacon.

Levstik, L. S. (1986). The relationship between historical response and narrative in a sixth-grade classroom. *Theory and Research in Social Education, 14,* 1–15.

Lewis, M., Wray, D., & Rospigliosi, P. (1994). "…And I want it in your own words." *The Reading Teacher, 47,* 528–536.

Lieberman, A. (2000). Networks as learning communities: Shaping the future of teacher development. *Journal of Teacher Education, 51,* 221–227.

Lipson, M., & Wixson, K. (1991). *Assessment and instruction of reading disability.* New York: Harper Collins.

Lipson, M., & Wixson, K. (1997). *Assessment and instruction of reading and writing disability: An interactive approach* (2nd ed.). New York: Longman.

Lord, B. (1994). Teachers' professional development: Critical colleagueship and the role of professional communities. In N. Cobb (Ed.), *The future of education: Perspectives on national standards in education* (pp. 175–204). New York: College Entrance Exam Board.

Lytle, J. H. (2000). Teacher education at the millennium: A view from the cafeteria. *Journal of Teacher Education, 51,* 174–179.

McClure, A. A. (1998). Choosing quality nonfiction literature: Examining aspects of writing. In R. A. Bamford & J. V. Kristo (Eds.), *Making facts come alive: Choosing quality nonfiction literature K–8* (pp. 39–54). Norwood, MA: Christopher-Gordon Publishers.

McKenna, M. C., & Kear, D. (1990). Measuring attitude toward reading: A new tool for teachers. *The Reading Teacher, 43,* 626–636.

McMahon, S. I., & Raphael, T. E., with Goatley, V. J., & Pardo, L. S. (1997). *The Book Club Project: Exploring alternative contexts for literacy instruction.* New York: Teachers College Press.

McMillan, B. (1993). Accuracy in books for young readers: From first to last check. *The New Advocate, 6,* 97–104.

McQuillan, J. (1997). The effects of incentives on reading. *Reading Research and Instruction, 36,* 111–125.

Mahoney, J. W. (2002). *Introducing nonfiction writing in the early grades.* New York: Scholastic.

Mallett, M. (1999). *Young researchers: Informational reading and writing in the early and primary years.* London: Routledge.

Marten, P., Flurkey, A., Meyer, R., & Udell, R. (1999). Inventing literacy identities: Intratextual, intertextual, and intercontextual influences on emerging literacy. *National Reading Conference Yearbook, 48,* 73–85.

Martinez, M., Roser, N. L., Worthy, J., Strecker, S., & Gough, P. (1997). Classroom libraries and children's book selections: Redefining "access" in self-selected reading. In C. K. Kinzer, K. A. Hinchman, & D. J. Leu (Eds.), *Inquiries in literacy theory and practice / Forty-sixth yearbook of the National Reading Conference* (pp. 265–272). Chicago: National Reading Conference.

Martinez, M. G., & Teale, W. H. (1989). [Children's book selections in a kindergarten classroom library]. Unpublished raw data.

Mason, J. M., Peterman, C. L., Powell, B. M., & Kerr, B. M. (1989). Reading and writing attempts by kindergartners after book reading by teachers. In J. M. Mason (Ed.), *Reading and writing connections* (pp. 105–120). Boston: Allyn & Bacon.

Meyer, M., & Felton, R. (1999). Repeated reading to enhance fluency: Old approaches and new directions. *Annals of Dyslexia, 49,* 283–306.

Miller, C. R. (1984). Genre as social action. *Quarterly Journal of Speech, 70,* 151–67.

Miller, D. (2002). *Reading with meaning: Teaching comprehension in the primary grades.* Portland, ME: Stenhouse.

Moffett, J. (1968). *Teaching the universe of discourse.* Boston: Houghton Mifflin.

Moll, L. C. (1992). Funds of knowledge for teaching: using a qualitative approach to connect homes and classrooms. *Theory into Practice, 31,* 132–141.

Morrow, L. M. (1989). Designing the classroom to promote literacy development. In D. Strickland & L. M. Morrow (Eds.), *Emerging literacy: Young children learn to read and write* (pp. 121–134). Newark, DE: International Reading Association.

Morrow, L. M., Gambrell, L., Kapinus, B., Koskinen, P. S., Marshall, N., & Mitchell, J. N. (1986). Retelling: A strategy for reading instruction and assessment. In J. A. Niles and R. V. Lalik (Eds.), *Solving problems in literacy: Learners, teachers and researchers: Thirty-fifth yearbook of the National Reading Conference* (pp. 73–80). Rochester, NY: National Reading Conference.

Morrow, L. M., Pressley, L., Smith, J. K., & Smith, M. (1997). The effect of a literature-based program integrated into literacy and science instruction with children from diverse backgrounds. *Reading Research Quarterly, 32,* 54–76.

Morrow, L. M., & Weinstein, C. (1986). Encouraging voluntary reading: The impact of a literature program on children's use of library centers. *Reading Research Quarterly, 21,* 330–346.

Moss, B. (1997). A qualitative assessment of first graders' retelling of expository text. *Reading Research and Instruction, 37,* 1–13.

Moss, B. (2003). *Exploring the literature of fact: Children's nonfiction trade books in the elementary classroom.* New York: Guilford Press.

Moss, B., Leone, S., & Dipillo, M. L. (1997). Exploring the literature of fact: Linking reading and writing through information trade books. *Language Arts, 74,* 418–429.

Moss, B., & Newton, E. (1998, December). *An examination of the informational text genre in recent basal readers.* Paper presented at the National Reading Conference, Austin, TX.

Murphy, C., & Lick, D. (1998). *Whole-faculty study groups: A powerful way to change schools and enhance learning.* Thousand Oaks, CA: Corwin Press.

National Reading Panel (2000). *Teaching children to read: An evidence-based assessment of the scientific research literature on reading and its implications for reading instruction: Reports of the subgroups.* Washington, DC: National Institute of Child Health and Human Development. (NIH Publication No. 00-4754)

Neate, B. (1992). *Finding out about finding out: A practical guide to children's information books.* Winchester, UK: Infopress.

Neuman, S. B., Celano, C. C., Greco, A. N., & Shue, P. (2001). *Access for all: Closing the book gap for children in early education.* Newark, DE: International Reading Association.

Neuman, S. B., & Roskos, K. (1993). Access to print for children of poverty: Differential effects of adult mediation and literacy-enriched play settings on environmental and functional print tasks. *American Educational Research Journal, 30,* 95–122.

Newkirk, T. (1987). The non-narrative writing of young children. *Research in the Teaching of English, 21,* 121–144.

Newkirk, T. (1989). *More than stories: The range of children's writing.* Portsmouth, NH: Heinemann.

Ogle, D. (1986). K-W-L: A teaching model that develops active reading of expository text. *The Reading Teacher, 39,* 564–570.

Opitz, M. F. (1998). *Flexible grouping in reading: Practical ways to help all students become better readers.* New York: Scholastic.

Orr, L. (1986). Intertextuality and the cultural text in recent semiotics. *College English, 48,* 811–823.

O'Shea, L., Sindelar, P., & O'Shea, D. (1985). The effects of repeated reading and listening while reading skills on reading fluency and comprehension. *Journal of Reading Behavior, 17,* 129–142.

Oyler, C., & Barry, A. (1996). Intertextual connections in read-alouds of information books. *Language Arts, 73,* 324–329.

Palincsar, A. S. (1982). *Improving the reading comprehension of junior-high students through the reciprocal teaching of comprehension-monitoring strategies.* Unpublished doctoral dissertation, University of Illinois, Urbana-Champaign.

Palincsar, A. S. (1986). The role of dialogue in providing scaffolded instruction. *Educational Psychologist, 21,* 73–98.

Palincsar, A. S., & Brown, A. L. (1984). Reciprocal teaching of comprehension fostering and monitoring activities. *Cognition and Instruction, 1,* 117–175.

Palincsar, A. S., & Brown, A. L. (1986). Interactive teaching to promote independent learning from text. *The Reading Teacher, 39,* 771–777.

Palinscar, A. S., Brown, A. L., & Campione, J. C. (1993). Dialogues among communities of first-grade learners. In E. Foreman, N. Minnich, & A. Stome (Eds.), *The institutional and social context of mind: New directions in Vygotskian theory and research* (pp. 43–57). Oxford: Oxford University Press.

Palincsar, A. S., & Magnusson, S. J. (2000). *The interplay of firsthand and text-based investigations in science education.* Ann Arbor: Center for the Improvement of Early Reading Achievement, University of Michigan.

Pappas, C. C. (1986, December). *Exploring the global structure of "information books."* Paper presented at the annual meeting of the National Reading Conference, Austin, TX. (ERIC Document Reproduction Service No. ED 278 952)

Pappas, C. C. (1987, August). *Exploring the generic shape of "information books": Applying typicality notions to the process.* Paper presented at the World Conference of Applied Linguistics, Sydney, New South Wales, Australia. (ERIC Document Reproduction Service No. ED 299 834)

Pappas, C. C. (1991a). Fostering full access to literacy by including information books. *Language Arts, 68,* 449–462.

Pappas, C. C. (1991b). Young children's strategies in learning the "book language" of information books. *Discourse Processes, 14,* 203–225.

Pappas, C. C. (2002). *Identifying and describing the information book genre: The analysis of discursive features of both typical and atypical texts.* Paper presented at the National Reading Conference, Miami, FL.

Pearson, P. D., & Duke, N. K. (2002) Comprehension instruction in the primary grades. In C. C. Block & M. Pressley (Eds.), *Comprehension instruction: Research-based best practices,* (pp. 247–258). New York: Guilford.

Pearson, P. D., & Gallagher, M. C. (1983). The instruction of reading comprehension. *Contemporary Educational Psychology, 8,* 317–344.

Pearson, P. D., Roehler, L., Dole, J., & Duffy, G. (1992). Developing expertise in reading comprehension. In S. J. Samuels & A. E. Farstrup (Eds.), *What research has to say about reading instruction* (2nd ed., pp. 145–199). Newark, DE: International Reading Association.

Pellegrini, A. D., Perlmutter, J. C., Galda, L., Brody, G. H. (1990). Joint reading between black Head Start children and their mothers. *Child Development, 61,* 443–453.

Pinnell, G. S., Pikulski, J., Wixson, K., Campbell, J., Gough, P., & Beatty, A. (1995). *Listening to children read aloud: Data from NAEP's integrated reading performance record (IRPR) at grade 4.* Washington, DC: National Center for Education Statistics.

Pinnell, G. S., & Scharer, P. L. (2003). *Teaching for comprehension in reading, grades K–2: Strategies for helping children read with ease, confidence, and understanding.* New York: Scholastic.

Portalupi, J., & Fletcher, R. (2001). *Nonfiction craft lessons: Teaching information writing K–8.* Portland, ME: Stenhouse Publishers.

Pressley, M. (2000). What should comprehension instruction be the instruction of? In M. Kamil, P. Mosenthal, P. D. Pearson, & R. Barr (Eds.), *Handbook of reading research* (Vol. 3, pp. 545–561). Hillsdale, NJ: Lawrence Erlbaum Associates.

Pressley, M. (2002). Metacognition and self-regulated comprehension. In A. E. Farstrup & S. J. Samuels (Eds.), *What research has to say about reading instruction* (3rd ed., pp. 291–309). Newark, DE: International Reading Association.

Pressley, M., & Afflerbach, P. (1995). *Verbal protocols of reading: The nature of constructively responsive reading.* Hillsdale, NJ: Lawrence Erlbaum Associates.

Pressley, M., Almasi, J., Schuder, T., Bergman, J., Hite, S., El-Dinary, P. B., et al. (1994). Transactional instruction of comprehension strategies: The Montgomery County, Maryland, SAIL Program. *Reading and Writing Quarterly: Overcoming Learning Difficulties, 10,* 5–19.

Pressley, M., El-Dinary, P. B., Gaskins, I., Schuder, T., Bergman, J. L., Almasi, J., et al. (1992). Beyond direct explanation: Transactional instruction of reading comprehension strategies. *Elementary School Journal, 92,* 513–555.

Pressley, M., Wharton-McDonald, R., Allington, R., Block, C. C., Morrow, L., Tracey, D., et al. (2001). A study of effective grade-1 literacy instruction. *Scientific Studies of Reading, 5,* 35–58.

Purcell-Gates, V., & Duke, N. K. (2001, August). *Explicit explanation/teaching of informational text genres: A model for research.* Paper presented at Crossing Borders: Connecting Science and Literacy conference, sponsored by the National Science Foundation, Baltimore, MD.

Purcell-Gates, V., Duke, N. K. (2003, April). *Learning to write informational and procedural science text in second and third grade in two instructional conditions.* Paper presented at the Annual Meeting of the American Educational Research Association, Chicago, IL.

Purcell-Gates, V., & Duke, N. K. (in press). Texts in the teaching and learning of reading. In D. Schallert & J. Hoffman (Eds.), *Read this room: Texts, tasks, and the teaching and learning of reading.* Mahwah, NJ: Erlbaum.

Rasinski, T. V. (2003). *The fluent reader: Oral reading strategies for building word recognition, fluency, and comprehension.* New York: Scholastic.

Read, S. (2001). "Kid mice hunt for their selfs": First and second graders writing research. *Language Arts, 78,* 333–342.

Reischl, C. D. (1999). *Telling stories of self in multilingual contexts: Beginning and experienced teachers' conversations in an autobiography discussion group.* Unpublished doctoral dissertation, Michigan State University, East Lansing, MI.

Renninger, K. A., Hidi, S., & Krapp, A. (Eds.) (1992). *The role of interest in learning and development.* Hillsdale, NJ: Lawrence Erlbaum.

Rice, D. C. (2002). Using trade books in teaching elementary science: Facts and fallacies. *Reading Teacher, 55,* 552–565.

Roberts, E. M. (2002). *A journey of transformation: Teacher professional development at an African-centered public school.* Unpublished doctoral dissertation, Michigan State University, East Lansing, MI.

Robinson, D. H. (1998). Graphic organizers as aids to text learning. *Reading Research and Instruction, 37,* 65–105.

Rogovin, P. (2001). *The research workshop: Bringing the world into your classroom.* Portsmouth, NH: Heinemann.

Rosenshine, B., & Meister, C. (1994). Reciprocal teaching: A review of research. *Review of Educational Research, 64,* 479–530.

Rupley, W. H., Logan, J. W., & Nichols, W. D. (1999). Vocabulary instruction in a balanced reading program. *The Reading Teacher, 52,* 336–346.

Samuels, S. J. (1979). The method of repeated readings. *The Reading Teacher, 32,* 403–408.

Saul, W., & Jagusch, S. A. (1991). *Vital connections: Children, science, and books.* Portsmouth, NH: Heinemann.

Saunders, W. M., & Goldenberg, C. (1999). Effects of instructional conversations and literature logs on limited- and fluent-English-proficient students' story comprehension and thematic understanding. *The Elementary School Journal, 99,* 277–301.

Sawyer, W., & Watson, K. (1987). Questions of genre. In I. Reid (Ed.), *The place of genre in learning: current debates* (pp. 46–57). Deakin University: Centre for Studies in Literary Education.

Schiefele, U. (1991). Interest, learning, and motivation. *Educational Psychologist, 26,* 299–323.

Schiefele, U., Krapp, A., & Winteler, A. (1992). Interest as a predictor of academic achievement: A meta-analysis of research. In K. A. Renninger, S. Hidi, & A. Krapp (Eds.), *The role of interest in learning and development* (pp. 183–211). Hillsdale, NJ: Lawrence Erlbaum.

Schwartz, R. M., & Raphael, T. E. (1985). Concept of definition: A key to improving students' vocabulary. *The Reading Teacher, 39,* 198–205.

Shanahan, T. (1988). The reading-writing relationship: Seven instructional principles. *The Reading Teacher, 23,* 636–647.

Silver, H. F., Strong, R. W., & Perini, M. (2000). *Discovering nonfiction: 25 powerful teaching strategies grades 2–6.* Los Angeles, CA: Canter and Associates.

Siu-Runyan, Y. (1998). Writing nonfiction: Helping students teach others what they know. In R. A. Bamford, & J. V. Kristo (Eds.), *Making facts come alive: Choosing quality nonfiction literature K-8* (pp. 169–178). Norwood, MA: Christopher-Gordon.

Smith, J. A., Monson, J. A., & Dobson, D. (1992). A case study on integrating history and reading instruction through literature. *Social Education, 56,* 370–375.

Smith, M. C. (2000). The real-world reading practices of adults. *Journal of Literacy Research, 32,* 25–32.

Smith, M. W. (1996). Conversations about literature outside classrooms: How adults talk about books in their book clubs. *Journal of Adolescent & Adult Literacy, 40,* 180–186.

Smolkin, L. B., & Donovan, C. A. (2002). "Oh excellent, excellent question!" Developmental differences and comprehension acquisition. In C. C. Block & M. Pressley (Eds.), *Comprehension instruction: Research-based best practices* (pp. 140–157). New York: Guilford Press.

Snow, C., & Ninio, A. (1986). The contracts of literacy: What children learn from learning to read books. In W. Teale and E. Sulzby (Eds.), *Emergent literacy: Writing and reading* (pp. 116–138). Norwood, NJ: Ablex.

Stahl, S. A. (1998). Four questions about vocabulary knowledge and reading and some answers. In C. Hynd (Ed.), *Learning from text across conceptual domains* (pp. 73–94). Mahwah, NJ: Lawrence Erlbaum Associates.

Stead, T. (2002). *Is that a fact? Teaching nonfiction writing K–3.* Portland, ME: Stenhouse Publishers.

Sudol, P., & King, C. (1996). A checklist for choosing nonfiction trade books. *The Reading Teacher, 49,* 422–424.

Swan, E. A. (2003). *Concept-oriented reading instruction: Engaging classrooms, lifelong learners.* New York: Guilford.

Sweet, A. P., & Snow, C. E. (Eds.) (2003). *Rethinking reading comprehension.* New York: Guilford Press.

Taberski, S. (2000). *On solid ground.* Portsmouth, NH: Heinemann.

Taylor, B. M., Pearson, P. D., Clark, K., & Walpole, S. (2000). Effective schools and accomplished teachers: Lessons about primary-grade reading instruction in low-income schools. *Elementary School Journal, 101,* 121–165.

Taylor, B. M, Pearson, P. D., Peterson, D., & Rodriguez, M. C. (2002). *The CIERA school change project: Supporting schools as they implement home-grown reading reform.* Center for the Improvement of Early Reading Achievement, University of Michigan, Ann Arbor. (CIERA Report #2-016)

Taylor, B. M., Pressley, M. P., & Pearson, P. D. (2002a). Research-supported characteristics of teachers and schools that promote reading achievement. In B. M. Taylor & P. D. Pearson (Eds.), *Teaching reading: Effective schools, accomplished teachers* (pp. 361–374). Mahwah, NJ: Erlbaum.

Taylor, B. M., Pressley, M. P., & Pearson, P. D. (2002b). *Research-supported characteristics of teachers & schools that promote reading achievement.* Washington, DC: National Education Association.

Teale, W., & Sulzby, E. (1986). Emergent literacy as a perspective for examining how young children become writers and readers. In W. Teale and E. Sulzby (Eds.), *Emergent literacy: Writing and reading* (pp.vii–xxv). Norwood, NJ: Ablex.

Tharp, R. (1982). The effective instruction of comprehension: Results and description of the Kamehameha Early Education Program. *Reading Research Quarterly, 17,* 503–527.

Topping, K. (1989). Peer tutoring and paired reading: Combining two powerful techniques. *The Reading Teacher, 40,* 488–494.

Trussell-Cullen, A. (1999). *Starting with the real world: Strategies for developing nonfiction reading and writing, K–8.* Carlsbad, CA: Dominie Press.

Vaughn, S., & Klingner, J. K. (1999). Teaching reading comprehension through collaborative strategic reading. *Intervention in School and Clinic, 34,* 284–292.

Vaughn, S., Klingner, J. K., & Bryant, D. (2001). Collaborative strategic reading as a means to enhance peer-mediated instruction for reading comprehension and content-area learning. *Remedial and Special Education, 22,* 66–74.

Venezky, R. L. (1982). The origins of the present-day chasm between adult literacy needs and school literacy instruction. *Visible Language, 16,* 112–127.

Warren, L., & Fitzgerald, J. (1997). Helping parents to read expository literature to their children: Promoting main-idea and detail understanding. *Reading Research and Instruction, 36,* 341–360.

Watkins, M. W., & Edwards, V. A. (1992). Extracurricular reading and reading achievement: The rich stay rich and the poor don't read. *Reading Improvement, 29,* 236–242.

Wilhelm, J. D. (2001). *Improving comprehension with think-aloud strategies: Modeling what good readers do.* New York: Scholastic.

Wilson, P. T., & Anderson, R. C. (1986). What they don't know will hurt them: The role of prior knowledge in comprehension. In J. Oransano (Ed.), *Reading comprehension from research to practice* (pp. 31–48). Hillsdale, NJ: Erlbaum.

Wray, D., & Lewis, M. (1992). Primary children's use of information books. *Reading, 26,* 19–24.

Yopp, R. H., & Yopp, H. K. (2000). Sharing informational text with young children. *The Reading Teacher, 53,* 410–423.

Zarnowski, M. (1998). It's more than dates and places: How nonfiction contributes to understanding social studies. In R. A. Bamford & J. V. Kristo (Eds.), *Making facts come alive: Choosing quality nonfiction literature K-8* (pp. 93–108). Norwood, MA: Christopher-Gordon Publishers.

Zarnowski, M., Kerper, R. M., & Jensen, J. M. (Eds.) (2001). *The best in children's nonfiction: Reading, writing, and teaching Orbis Pictus Award books.* Urbana, IL: National Council of Teachers of English.

Children's Book and Magazine References Cited

Anton, W. (1998). *Corn: From farm to table.* New York: Newbridge.

Anton, W. (1999). *Day and night.* New York: Newbridge.

Barton, B. (1989). *Dinosaurs, dinosaurs.* New York: Harper Collins.

Berger, M. (1983). *Why I sneeze, shiver, hiccup, and yawn.* Illustrated by P. Meisel, copyright 2000. New York: Harper Collins.

Berger, M. (1993). *Make mine ice cream.* New York: Newbridge.

Berger, M. (1995). *The mystery of magnets.* New York: Newbridge.

Berquist, P., & Berquist, S. (1997). *Saguaro cactus.* New York: Children's Press.

Branley, F. M. (1983). *Rain and hail.* Illustrated by H. Barton. New York: Thomas Y. Crowell. Original text copyright 1963.

Broderbund. (2000). *Compton's encyclopedia 2000.* Navato, CA: Author.

Butterfield, M. (1992). *1,000 Facts about wild animals.* Cornwall, UK: Kingfisher.

Chanko, P. (1999). *Baby animals learn.* New York: Scholastic.

Cole, J. (1990). *The magic school bus lost in the solar system.* Illustrated by B. Degen. New York: Scholastic.

Conover, A. (2001, October). "Pass the chocolate." *National Geographic for Kids.* Washington, DC: National Geographic Society.

Cooper, J. (1992). *Great places to visit: Farms.* Vero Beach, FL: Rourke Corporation.

Cronin, D. (2000). *Click, clack, moo: Cows that type.* Illustrated by B. Lewin. New York: Scholastic.

Davis, G. W. (1997). *Coral reef.* New York: Children's Press.

Davis, W. (1997). *Douglas fir.* New York: Children's Press.

Delafosse, C. (1993). *Portraits.* Illustrated by T. Ross. New York: Scholastic.

Dorling Kindersley, Inc. (1992). *What's inside? Planes.* Illustrated by J. Sayer. New York: Dorling Kindersley.

Ellis, G. (1995a). *From sand to glass.* Littleton, MA: Sundance.

Ellis, G. (1995b). *From tree to paper.* Littleton, MA: Sundance.

Florian, D. (1994). *Beast feast.* San Diego: Voyager Books.

Forman, M. H. (1997). *Arctic tundra.* New York: Children's Press.

Fowler, A. (1991). *What's the weather today?* Chicago: Children's Press.

Fowler, A. (1994). *Horses, horses, horses.* New York: Children's Press.

Gelman, R. G. (1992). *Body battles.* Illustrated by E. Freem. New York: Scholastic.

Gibbons, G. (1982). *The post office book: Mail and how it moves.* New York: Harper Collins.

Gill, S. (1990). *Alaska's three bears.* Illustrated by S. Cartwright. Homer, AK: Paws Publishing.

Gill, S. (1992). *Kiana's iditarod.* Illustrated by S. Cartwright. Homer, AK: Paws Publishing.

Gill, S. (1995). *Swimmer.* Illustrated by S. Cartwright. Homer, AK: Paws Publishing.

Gill, S. (1997). *Thunderfeet: Alaska's Dinosaurs and Other Prehistoric Critters.* Illustrated by S. Cartwright. Homer, AK: Paws Publishing.

Gill, S. (2001). *The egg.* Illustrated by J. Bosson. Watertown, MA: Charlesbridge Publishing.

Glaser, L. (1992). *Wonderful worms.* Illustrated by L. Krupinski. Brookfield, CT: The Millbrook Press.

Goodall, J. (1991). *Baboon family.* Toronto: Madison Marketing Limited.

Goodall, J. (1991). *Chimpanzee family.* Toronto: Madison Marketing Limited.

Goodall, J. (1991). *Elephant family.* Toronto: Madison Marketing Limited.

Goodall, J. (1991). *Giraffe family.* Toronto: Madison Marketing Limited.

Goodall, J. (1991). *Hyena family.* Toronto: Madison Marketing Limited.

Goodall, J. (1991). *Lion family.* Toronto: Madison Marketing Limited.

Goodall, J. (1991). *Wildebeest family.* Toronto: Madison Marketing Limited.

Goodall, J. (1991). *Zebra family.* Toronto: Madison Marketing Limited.

Heller, R. (1984). *Plants that never ever bloom.* New York: Penguin Putnam.

Lanczak Williams, R. (1995a). *If a tree could talk.* Huntington Beach, CA: Creative Teaching Press.

Lorenz Books. (1996). *Let's look at shapes.* Illustrated by L. Tizard. New York: Anness Publishing.

Maass, R. (1989). *Fire fighters.* New York: Scholastic.

Maynard, C. (1997). *Why are pineapples prickly? Questions children ask about food.* London: Dorling Kindersley.

Micucci, C. (1995). *The life and times of the honeybee.* Boston: Houghton Mifflin.

Mitchell, J. (1987). *Michigan: An illustrated history for children.* Illustrated by T. Woodruff. Suttons Bay, MI: Suttons Bay Publications.

Mitchell, J. (1991). *Great lakes and great ships: An illustrated history for children.* Illustrated by T. Woodruff. Suttons Bay, MI: Suttons Bay Publications.

Mitchell, J. (2000). *Prehistoric great lakes: An illustrated history for children.* Illustrated by T. Woodruff. Suttons Bay, MI: Suttons Bay Publications.

Mora, P. (2001). *Listen to the desert/Oye al desierto.* Illustrated by F. X. Mora. New York: Clarion Books.

Morris, A. (1990). *On the go.* Photographs by K. Heyman. New York: HarperCollins.

National Geographic Society. (2000). *Tree frogs.* Washington, DC: National Geographic Society.

National Geographic Society. (2001, October). "Pumpkin powerhouses." *National Geographic for Kids.* Washington, DC: National Geographic Society.

National Geographic Society. (2002, January-February). "Put on a happy face!" *National Geographic for Kids.* Washington, DC: National Geographic Society.

Nayer, J. (1996). *How many?* New York: Newbridge.

Nayer, J. (1997a). *Fall.* New York: Newbridge.

Nayer, J. (1997b). *In spring.* New York: Newbridge.

Nelson, R. L. (1997). *Our ocean home.* Chanhasson, MN: Northwood Press.

Nystrom. (1999). *Exploring where and why.* Chicago: Herff Jones.

Pallotta, J. (1994). *The spice alphabet book: Herbs, spices, and other natural flavors.* Illustrated by L. Evans. Watertown, MA: Charlesbridge.

Parkes, B. (1997). *In summer.* New York: Newbridge.

Parkes, B. (1999). *Where are the eggs?* New York: Newbridge.

Phelan, G. (2003). *Finding the first vaccines.* Washington DC: National Geographic Society.

Polly, J. A. (2001). *Net-mom's Internet kids & family yellow pages,* fourth edition. Berkeley, CA: Osborne.

Reid, M. E. (1996). *Let's find out about ice cream.* Photographs by J. Williams. New York: Scholastic.

Rinard, J., & O'Neill, C. (1981). *Amazing animals of the sea.* Washington, DC: National Geographic.

Saksie, J. (1995). *The seed song.* Huntington Beach, CA: Creative Teaching Press.

Scillian, D. (2001). *A is for America.* Illustrated by P. Carroll. Chelsea, MI: Sleeping Bear Press.

Selsam, M. (1973). *How kittens grow.* New York: Scholastic.

Snapshot Books. (1995). *Around town.* New York: Covent Garden Books.

Soutter-Perrot, A. (1993). *Earthworm.* Mankam, MN: Creative Editions.

Steele, P. (2002). *Going to School.* Danbury, CT: Franklin Watts.

Stonehouse, B. (2000). *Fighters.* Illustrated by J. Francis. New York: Tangerine Press (Scholastic).

Trumbauer, L. (1997). *Winter.* New York: Newbridge.

Uchida, Y. (1993). *The bracelet.* Illustrated by J. Yardley. New York: The Putnam & Grosset Group.

Walsh, M. (1997). *Do monkeys tweet?* Boston: Houghton Mifflin.

Watts, B. (1988). *Potato.* Englewood Cliffs, NJ: Silver Burdett Press.

Wexler, J. (1995). *Everyday mysteries.* New York: Dutton.

White, E. B. (1952). *Charlotte's web.* Illustrated by G. Williams. New York: Harper & Row.

Index

Note: This index contains only the names of children's book authors and illustrators cited in this book. The names of researchers, theorists, and teachers are not included due to space restrictions.